EAST ANGLIAN ARCHAEOLOGY

Lincolnshire Salterns: Excavations at Helpringham, Holbeach St Johns and Bicker Haven

by Antony Bell,
David Gurney and
Hilary Healey

with contributions from
the late F.W. Anderson, N.D. Balaam,
Justine Bayley, M. Beech, R.A.G. Carson,
Peter Chowne, H.E.M. Cool, Brenda Dickinson,
Helen Gandy, the late Professor H. Godwin,
A.J. Gouldwell, B.R. Hartley, Kay Hartley,
A.K.G. Jones, D.F. Mackreth, J. Redshaw,
J.D. Robson, Brian Simmons and Penny Spencer

illustrations by
Kim Addy, Peter Chowne, John A.Davies,
Sheila Elsdon, David Gurney, Hilary Healey,
Siriol Hinchliffe, Philippa Ratcliffe, Julia Royall,
Hoste Spalding and David Taylor

photographs by
Peter Chowne, Ernest Greenfield and
Hilary Healey

East Anglian Archaeology
Report No.89 1999

Heritage Trust of Lincolnshire

EAST ANGLIAN ARCHAEOLOGY
REPORT NO.89

Published by
Heritage Trust of Lincolnshire
The Old School
Cameron Street
Heckington
Sleaford NG34 9RW

in conjunction with
The Scole Archaeological Committee

Editor: David Buckley
EAA Managing Editor: Jenny Glazebrook

Scole Editorial sub-committee:
David Buckley, County Archaeologist, Essex Planning Department
Keith Wade, County Archaeological Officer, Suffolk Planning Department
Peter Wade-Martins, County Field Archaeologist, Norfolk Museums Service
Stanley West

Set in Times by Joan Daniells using Corel Ventura ™
Printed by F. Crowe and Sons, Norwich NR6 6BJ

© Heritage Trust of Lincolnshire

ISBN 0 948639 23 7

For details of *East Anglian Archaeology,* see inside back cover

This volume is published with the aid of a grant from English Heritage

Cover illustration
Romano-British earthworks at Holbeach St Johns
(*Crown copyright reserved: Cambridge University Collection*) Ref. FN45.
Photo by J.K. St Joseph

Contents

List of Plates

List of Figures

List of Tables

Contributors

Kim Addy,
Illustrator

The late F.W. Anderson,
Formerly Petrological Consultant, Ancient Monuments Laboratory

Justine Bayley, B.Sc., M.Sc., Ph.D., F.S.A.,
Head of Technology Section, Ancient Monuments Laboratory, English Heritage

N.D. Balaam,
English Heritage

M. Beech,
Formerly Ancient Monuments Laboratory, English Heritage

Antony Bell,
Formerly with the Central Excavation Unit, English Heritage

R.A.G. Carson, F.B.A., F.S.A.,
Formerly Keeper, Department of Coins and Medals, British Museum

Peter Chowne, Ph.D., M.I.F.A.,
Formerly Director, Museum of London Archaeology Service

H.E.M. Cool, Ph.D., F.S.A., M.I.F.A.,
Formerly Research Assistant, Department of Adult and Continuing Education, University of Leeds

John A.Davies, Ph.D., F.R.N.S., M.I.F.A.,
Formerly Research Assistant, Norfolk Archaeological Unit

Brenda Dickinson, B.A.,
Romano-British Pottery Consultant

Sheila Elsdon,
Research Assistant, Nottingham University

Helen Gandy,
Formerly with the Trust for Lincolnshire Archaeology

The late Professor H. Godwin, F.R.S.,
Professor of Botany, University of Cambridge, 1960–8

Anthony Gouldwell,
School of Archaeological Studies, University of Leicester

David Gurney, B.A., M.I.F.A.,
Principal Landscape Archaeologist, Norfolk Museums
Service

B.R. Hartley, F.S.A.,
School of Classics, University of Leeds, Leeds LS2 9JT

Kay Hartley, B.A., F.S.A.,
Romano-British Pottery Consultant

Hilary Healey, N.N.D., M.Phil., F.S.A.,
Formerly Field Officer, Trust for Lincolnshire
Archaeology

A. Jones, Ph.D., M.I.F.A.,
Archaeological Resource Centre, York

D.F.Mackreth, B.A., F.S.A.,
126 London Road, Peterborough

J. Redshaw,
7 Fennell Road, Pinchbeck, Spalding

J.D. Robson,
Formerly Soil Survey and Land Research

Brian Simmons,
Formerly Director, Trust For Lincolnshire Archaeology

Hoste Spalding, Dip. Memb. S.I.A.D.,
Illustrator

Penny Spencer,
Formerly Scunthorpe Museum and Art Gallery

David Taylor,
Illustrator

Acknowledgements

Chapter 1. Helpringham
Thanks in particular are due to Mr J. Forman, and to the Committee of the former Car Dyke Research Group (in particular the Chairman, Dr Kenneth R. Fennell). The resistivity survey was carried out by the late Mr K. Wood and Andrew Wood and the excavation by members and friends of the Group and of WEA classes who also took part in fieldwalking, survey, and finds processing. A special mention should be made of Carol and John Aram and the late Sheila N. Simmons. The lively interest and encouragement of the late Mrs E.H. Rudkin was particularly welcomed. Jane Ostler provided important references.

The plans were drawn by Peter Chowne, Hilary Healey and David Taylor, the pottery and finds illustrations by Kim Addy, Sheila Elsdon and Hilary Healey. Photographs are by Peter Chowne and Hilary Healey with the exception of Plate I (RAF aerial photograph 1947) reproduced by kind permission of the Ministry of Defence. Photographs of the 1972 excavations include imperial photographic scales.

The authors are indebted to Dorian Williams of the Environmental Archaeology, University of York (at the time of writing) for his kind assistance with the environmental evidence.

Chapter 2. Holbeach St Johns
The author is indebted to Mr Philip Mayes for kindly allowing access to his records of the excavations in OS 33 with the Boston Archaeological Group in 1960. Without these it would not have been possible to report fully upon Site A or Site B East.

Thanks are also due to the specialists who have contributed to this report, and to the illustrators, John A. Davies (Figs 1–4, 6–18, 30 and 35–38) and Hoste Spalding (Figs 5, 19–23 and 31–34).

Mr Brian Simmons of the former Trust for Lincolnshire Archaeology kindly read a manuscript of this report, and provided much useful comment and information on the Lincolnshire sites.

Chapter 3. Holbeach St Johns
I would like to thank Nic Appleton for the supervision and on-site recording for site sub-divisions 2–6, Varian Denham for help in the production of the post-medieval pottery report, Rob Perrin for unpublished parallels for the Romano-British pottery, Siriol Hinchliffe for the pottery drawings, and Julia Royall and Philippa Ratcliffe for the other drawings.

Chapter 4. Bicker Haven
Thanks are due to Mr R. Bratley for allowing the excavation to take place and to Mr A. Johnson for co-operation in regard to earthmoving. The then Department of the Environment allowed a small grant left over from another site in the county to be transferred which assisted with equipment and travelling expenses, and this was available through the Lincoln Archaeological Research Committee.

It is impossible to name all the site helpers, most of whom were members of the Boston and South Lincolnshire Archaeology Group or students from Spalding High School and Grammar School. The hard core of volunteers included Brian Bayston, David and Nigel Casswell, Mr Peter Davey, Nigel Kerr, the King family, Christopher Pinder, Maxine Shutt, Mr Brian Simmons and Mr Peter Wells; also the late Miss Elisabeth Exwood, Mrs Sheila Simmons, and Mr Charles Kelk.

Help, advice and information was provided by Mr J.G. Hurst, Miss C.M. Mahany, Dr J.B. Whitwell, the late Mrs E.H. Rudkin and Mr M.J. Dean and the then Central Electricity Generating Board. Assistance with the text was given by Messrs. A. Bilham Boult, J. Cherry, P. Everson and D. Roffe. Specialist comments or reports were received from Ms M. Archibald and Ms H. Gandy, Messrs. L. Biek, P. Davey, I. Goodall, A. Jones, J. Redshaw and J.D. Robson as well as the former Central Electricity Generating Board.

The illustrations were prepared by Hilary Healey and David Taylor. The photographs were taken by Hilary Healey with the exceptions of Plates XXVII (Cambridge University Committee for Air Photography) and XXXVIII (Don Yorke). Photographs of the excavations include imperial photographic scales.

General Introduction

by B.B. Simmons

So little is known of the processes used in ancient salt-making in Britain that any new information is to be welcomed. It is only in comparatively recent years that, for example, a new Iron Age and Roman salt landscape has been recognised on the western fen-edge of Lincolnshire (Simmons 1980a, fig. 29). With the advent of more fieldwork our knowledge of the salt industry in Lincolnshire is enhanced, as is evidenced through the Fenland Survey Project (Hayes and Lane 1992). The finding and identifying of the many salterns in the silt fens of the county has been one of the achievements of the Survey. Equally, the predecessors of the Survey had already recorded the discovery of a large number of salt-making sites generally in Lincolnshire. These sites have been summarised to some extent in de Brisay and Evans (1975), Baker (1975, 31–33), Simmons (1980a, 33–36), Healey (1975, 36–37), Rudkin (1975, 37–41) and Kirkham (1975, 41–42).

The four reports contained in this present volume cover a time scale of 1500 years or more and deal with three cultural periods: Iron Age, Romano-British and medieval. Of these, the Iron Age site in Helpringham is on the western fen edge almost exactly on the boundary between the silty clays and the gravels skirting the limestone further to the west. This group of salterns is one of two such groups in Helpringham and contains an unknown number of hearths with associated mounds, now almost ploughed away. Today, the Helpringham salt complexes are situated c. 24km from the coast; in the middle Iron Age the influence of the sea reached this low lying area. In the intervening centuries human activity and nature have combined to create a new landscape.

Some four or five centuries after the Helpringham salt industry had ceased operating, Romano-British salters extended and moved the location of their industry eastwards. There is a large body of evidence for the considerable activity in salt-making in this period. This has been summarised in Simmons (1980a, 61–63), and now extensively broadened through the work of the Fenland Survey Project (Hayes and Lane 1992). Two reports contained here (Gurney and Bell) deal with a microcosm of the Romano-British salt producers at Holbeach St John's.

The final report of the four published here, Bicker Haven, takes the process forward through a millennium into the middle ages. In this temporal leap the landscape altered yet again (see Fig. 58, Bicker Haven report for location), as did salt-making methods. It has left a large gap in our rudimentary understanding of salt-making, as the Saxon period is ignored, not through design, but through a lack of physical evidence. At the time when the Bicker Haven site was excavated (1968–9) there was not a Saxon salt-making site known on the ground in Britain. Now, two decades later, possibly the first of these Saxon salterns has been located and, curiously, within a few miles of the Bicker Haven excavation (Healey 1988, 44).

Much has been written previously of salt-making. Two authors, Nenquin (1961) and Brown (1980) have attempted to summarise in various ways what was already known in Europe, North America and elsewhere. A salt conference in Colchester in 1974 also brought together workers and commentators on salt, both in the early and modern industries. Other, ancient authors have had much to say, too. Pliny the Elder gives hints to the uses of salt in the Roman period, as does Columella. Our present day usage of salt has changed considerably since Pliny's day, as well as its relative cheapness now with then. For instance, nowhere in Pliny is there the recommendation of a wholesale application of salt on the roads of the Roman Empire in icy weather, in contrast to a major need for our present day system.

We tend to forget that salt was not only used for flavouring foods, one of the least requirements in total weight, but also for more mundane purposes: tanning, at a time when leather was more widely used than now, (and certainly in the Roman period the quantity of leather required by the Roman army for tents, armour and shoes must have been prodigious) or for preserving foodstuffs — meat, fish and vegetables amongst them — before the days when refrigeration took away this necessity; for medicinal purposes — Pliny the Elder has some exotic and eyebrow-raising remarks to say on this subject (an eye treatment made from a concoction of salt and copper could have been, indeed, eyebrow-raising (Pliny XXXIV. XXIII, 106)); or for a money allowance given to Roman soldiers for the purchase of salt. The word 'salary' after all, comes from the Latin for salt, *sal* (O.E.D. 1971, 2624). Columella tells us that salt can be used as part of the training of oxen (VI, II, 7) and, elsewhere in the ancient world, salt had been used as a contraceptive medium. These are minor irrelevances to test our imaginations, but at the same time indicate the range of purposes for which salt has been manufactured.

Apart from the flavouring of food, human need for salt is a more basic physiological necessity. If salt is not readily and regularly available the body organs can desiccate and death eventually occurs (Bloch 1963, 89). All animals, especially herbivores and omnivores, have the same common requirement. If animals, including humans, become more dependent upon an agriculturally based economy, as happened from the Neolithic period onwards, the requirements for the bodily intake of salt increase. When a person eats, primarily, freshly killed meat the amount of free salt, crucial for the proper working of the body's chemistry, decreases correspondingly. Thus, in Britain, from about the fourth millennium BC and following the introduction of arable farming practices, there arose an escalating priority to produce, from one source or another, more salt for physiological needs. As dietary habits oscillated between the extremes of vegetarianism and meat eating, so salt requirements varied. In a culture which eats more meat than another the production of salt will, perhaps, diminish. Equally, when more leather, or more food preservation is demanded than in another era, so more salt is demanded. To an extent these observations may account for the apparent imbalance between the known industries of the Iron Age and Roman periods, and that of the unknown industry of the Saxon period where very few, if any, salterns are archaeologically visible. The exceptions to this statement are those mentioned in the *Domesday Book*, and these may relate to the very end of the Saxon period when cultural habits could have changed. The actuality remains that only one probable Saxon site (Bicker Bends) has so far been located. It may well be that early and middle Saxons had very little use for salt because they ate predominantly meat and were carpenters rather than leather workers, whilst the preservation of meat could have been achieved by a different method such as drying.

This hypothesis requires proof and negative evidence is peculiarly difficult to prove. In the Saxon period in Europe there is only slender information for the use of salt. However, at the other end of the time scale, the Neolithic period provides better opportunity for study in that same continent. The evidence for Polish salt-making in the Neolithic period has been established; the sites have survived in a good state of preservation (Jodlowski 1975, 85–87). Yet, in Britain, the earliest known salterns are found in the Bronze Age and late in that epoch (Bond 1988, 39; Gurney 1980, 1–11). It is surprising, therefore, that nothing has been discovered for the period from the beginning of the Neolithic to 1000 BC. The sad truth is that archaeology has only produced evidence for salt-making for short spaces in that time scale when it could be anticipated that salt could have been a necessity throughout the five millennia in question. Of those 5,000 years British archaeology has gathered information for only a quarter of that time. It is difficult to understand why the archaeological account which should be available for the remaining 3,800 years or so, still awaits discovery.

Our lack of knowledge of large parts of our history and immediate prehistory is only equalled by our ignorance of how salt was actually produced. From studies around the world (for example in Brown 1980 or in de Brisay and Evans 1975) it would appear that non-industrial communities preferred either lagoons for the solar evaporation of brine solutions, or pottery vessels for simmering over hearths. Ceramic dishes have been used worldwide from the earliest times. What is superficially surprising is the similarity between these techniques and the pots required in the various stages of salt-making, together with the hearth apparatus often found in association on those disparate salterns. From Japan in 800 AD to Lake Chad in 1970 AD, from Austria in 1000 BC to USA in 1600 AD there is a curious analogy between completely different cultures, not only of space but also of time. There can be no sociological links between these cultures; no exchange of ideas or inventions, no bridging of gaps of period or distance. Ian W. Brown considered that 'The peoples of America, Europe, Africa and Asia apparently learned the appropriate techniques independently' (Brown 1980, 88). Whilst it is possible to argue that this generalisation and the one contained in the previous sentence are not strictly true — the Celtic people of Hallstatt, for instance, could have passed on their experience directly or indirectly to those of Helpringham — the principle in Brown's comment is, nonetheless, sound. The fulfilment of fundamental processes, including that of salt-making, is gained separately, if the raw materials are at hand together with some basic skills, not least that of producing pottery.

It has been mentioned above that after the Roman occupation of Britain ceased and before the Norman conquest became reality, there is a conspicuous hiatus in our awareness of salt-making. What is known of Saxon salt producing is minimal and almost entirely learned from the *Domesday Book*. During the later medieval period, however, a change took place. Pottery was no longer required for the purpose of salt water evaporation. When Columbus, coincidentally commissioned by the wealthy salt producers of Spain, was setting sail to discover a land where the true indigenes were using ceramic utensils, Britain was employing lead containers for the same purpose and with little regard to health and safety. Healey's report on Bicker Haven (this volume, Chapter 4) is, importantly, specific on this point. The question of when the change from pots to lead vessels took place in Britain is an intriguing one. A related question of why it happened is also unresolved. What occurred in the eight hundred years between Roman Britain and the high middle ages is difficult to explain. A further factor to be learned from the Bicker Haven report is that the relatively large mounds, built up from the waste of salt production, indicate an industry where the salt water is brought into the site over a long period, rather than the salters moving their *loci* in order to keep up with changes in sea level and concomitant alterations in the courses of the salt water bearing creeks. In other words, these medieval salters controlled their basic raw material, salt water, and its flow to the salt floors.

What is not known from the excavation reports published in this volume, or, indeed, from anywhere else in Britain, is exactly how the salt was made. Hilary Healey's account of Bicker Haven goes some of the way in answering the questions for the middle ages. This excavation is to be applauded for it was executed with limited resources of finance and equipment, typical of the 'shoestring' archaeology of a time when so little money was available. Nevertheless, the information from Bronze Age, Iron Age and Roman salterns is scant. There have been several, if not many, excavations nationally from these three periods, but the answers to the questions of how salt was produced remain elusive. Many theories and hypotheses have been put forward; some are more convincing than others. It could be argued that the emphasis on where the excavations are sited has been wrongly applied. Instead of retrieving the evidence from the obvious, that is the remains of slight mounds and hearths and the features immediately associated with these, a more expansive view should be taken of the subject. The problems of salt-making might be better studied through anthropology rather than archaeology. The International Conference held at the University of Essex in 1974 pointed the way towards that goal. Other conferences have also been held world wide, not least of which have been those in the USA. The experience gained from all these conferences could be applied to Britain. In particular, Gouletquer's report (1975) of contemporary salt-making in Manga is illuminating. It is suggested that more work of this nature, using the evidence from modern primitive peoples, might give the salt researchers fresh ideas.

Of course there are dangers in using one set of criteria to establish another. It goes without saying that caution should be exercised in making the evidence fit the theory. Nonetheless, the inescapable truth is that there is so much commonality between the processes of salt-making throughout the world that analogies could be tested more liberally than they have been so far. Excavators of salterns, no matter how well intentioned are their research designs and strategies, to use the modern jargon, seem to be groping in the dark. Having uncovered their hearths and gullies, post-holes and briquetage, most excavators have difficulty in attempting even the vaguest interpretation of what has been found. Salt as an ancient and expensive commodity is significant enough to demand more of its researchers than it is, at present, receiving. For these reasons and others alluded to in this Introduction, a different approach could be made.

There are, first of all, the elements common to many salt-making processes at different times and in different places. Pairs of hearths are evident in Bicker Haven in the thirteenth century AD (p. 101). The same is true of Ingoldmells in the Iron Age (Baker 1960, fig. 71) and elsewhere. Furthermore, this coincidence, if coincidence it is, is heightened by the fact that often the hearths are of similar dimensions, length and breadth. To add to this apparent concurrence of events is the similarity of hearth apparatus on the earlier sites (that is, excluding the medieval process of using lead) from firebars, as in the Red Hills, Essex, to Middlewich in Cheshire, and many sites in Lincolnshire, to containers, distance pieces and other clay artifacts. And yet in all these places, in all these processes, there is no indication from where the raw material was taken, how it was stored and how it was eventually used. Were there channels dug from the creeks to claylined storage pits? Were there special filters of wicker-work or peat or twigs? Were there lagoons or storage pits covered to protect the brine from dilution by rain water? The questions are endless, the answers imponderable on present knowledge received from the Iron Age and Roman sites in Lincolnshire; neither Helpringham nor the two excavations in Holbeach give many hints for the clarification of the puzzle.

Do we need to look further afield for the clues? Are some of the solutions to be sought in other places? It is tempting to suggest that the report on Bicker Haven may give an insight into the method of trapping the salt water. The so-called floors, the large, shallow artifical settling ponds could be the key to this important aspect of producing common salt. A failing in archaeological research is that the archaeologist is tempted and yields to the obvious, whether the obvious is a mark on an aerial photograph, or a pronounced hump in a field, or a concentration of pottery on the surface of the same field. Has the excavator of the Iron Age and Romano-British (and maybe the Bronze Age) saltern site been guilty of ignoring the archaeologically unattractive land around the hearths believing it to be devoid of features? Lagoons, or settling ponds, or narrow leats leading from creeks to salterns could have been missed in this way. Much more work requires to be done on these sites in order that we can understand the industry better, and particularly for those periods before the middle ages.

A further point to be made on this theme, and one which has been made elsewhere (Brown 1980, 6) is that many of the world's ancient trade routes were based on salt roads. In Lincolnshire the Salters Way, stretching from Donington to Saltersford and beyond may be one such route. Another, linking the Iron Age salt trade along the western fen edge, could have been Mareham Lane. Other information is beginning to suggest that Mareham Lane, a possible prehistoric trackway, brought together the products from the many salterns close to its alignment (Simmons and Oetgen, Old Place, Sleaford: archive). If this is true of the Iron Age, were there comparable means of transporting the commodity which had been won with so much difficulty in time and effort from the sea in the Roman, Saxon and medieval periods, and even in the Bronze Age and Neolithic?

The four papers published in this monograph have a common topic, salt in Lincolnshire. Each of the papers faithfully records the results of excavations. These excavations, as well as those that have been made and published elsewhere, should be seen as the beginning of the understanding of salt production, not its definitive conclusion. Today's common salt was yesterday's difficult and costly process, imperfectly understood by modern archaeologists.

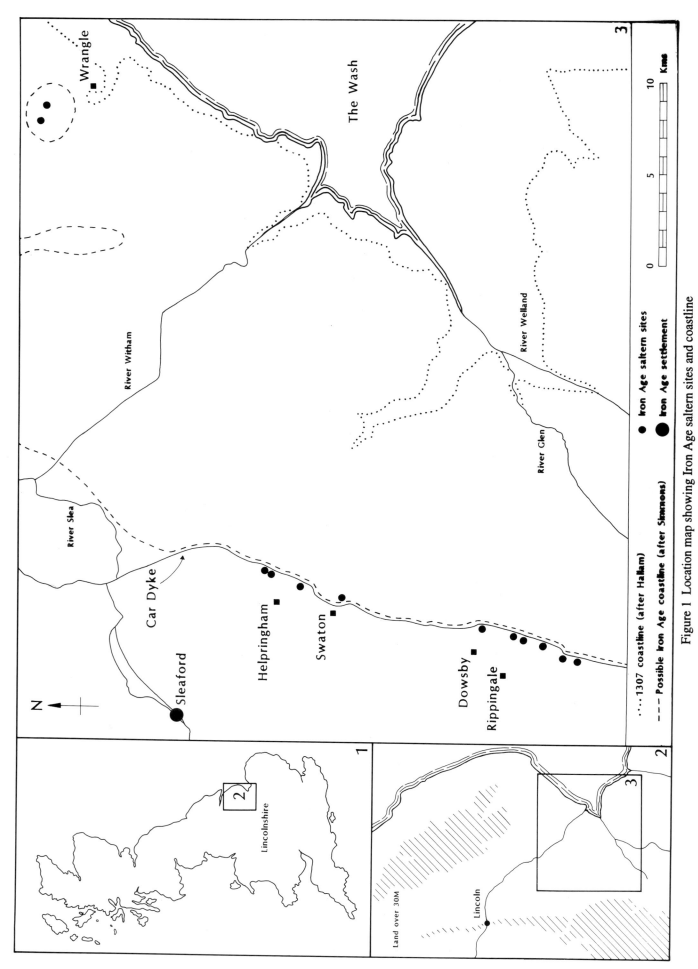

Figure 1 Location map showing Iron Age saltern sites and coastline

Chapter 1. An Iron Age Salt-making Site at Helpringham Fen, Lincolnshire: Excavations by the Car Dyke Research Group, 1972–7

compiled by Hilary Healey

I. Summary

Field survey by the Car Dyke Research group in 1971 revealed evidence of salt-making in Helpringham Fen, Lincolnshire. The site, on the west bank of the Car Dyke, appeared to pre-date the Roman watercourse, which is thought to have been principally a catchwater drain. Excavations in 1972 and 1974–5 exposed the fragmentary remains of a series of hearths set on low mounds and associated with Iron Age pottery dating from the third century BC to the end of the first century BC. A C14 determination of 379–116 cal BC was recorded for timber from one of the later hearths, and a less reliable date of 487–370 cal BC for a smaller charcoal sample (see Appendix). Plant remains suggested that the site was situated on the coastal margins, although adjacent to a tidal watercourse. The following report is based on the notes of Peter Chowne, Anthony Gouldwell and Brian Simmons.

II. Introduction

The salt-making site itself lies near the fen margin east of Helpringham village, one of a string of villages situated along the spring line where limestone uplands and fen edge gravels meet (Fig. 1). Early Saxon pottery has been found in or near most of these villages between Heckington and Bourne, and one can therefore suggest that they have a Saxon origin. Each has a length of fen extending some four miles east of the village centre, and much of the area remained common land until enclosed in the late eighteenth and early nineteenth centuries.

The saltern sites occur at the junction of chalky till and marine alluvium (Hodge 1984), which also happens to be more or less on the line of the Roman Car Dyke. The Geological Survey map shows the underlying boulder clay cut by alluvium on an east-west alignment as for a watercourse, a route still followed by the Helpringham Eau (Fig. 2). The strong clayey soil is evident to anyone walking on field OS 387 as is the contrast provided by the low saltern mounds. These appear as faint pale patches on some aerial photographs taken by the RAF in 1947 (Pl. I). The presence of ash, burnt earth and fragments of fired clay changes the nature as well as the appearance of the soil making it more friable and encouraging earlier germination of cereals (Pl. II).

Iron Age salt-making sites have been recognised both on the Lincolnshire coast and the fen edge since the mid nineteenth century (Maudson Grant 1890; Hallam S.J. 1970, 270). Many more examples in the fens and along the fen edge were recorded by the Car Dyke Research Group (Simmons 1980a). In the 1980s the work of the Fenland Survey Project has again added considerably to our information about the character and distribution of these sites. Much of this work has yet to be published at the time of writing, and is not referred to in detail here.

Over the last twenty-five years there has been a considerable advance in our knowledge of Iron Age settlement in South Lincolnshire, both on the limestone uplands (May 1976; 1984), the Fen margins (Simmons 1980a) and, most recently, in the Fens themselves (Lane 1986). The last summary of recent work was published in the early 1980s (May 1984), but this dealt with major sites in the region. A map of the reconstructed coastline and salt-making sites of the period, based on Simmons (1980a) appears as Figure 1. Results of Fenland research have modified our thoughts about the pre-Roman and Roman coastline.

Discovery of the Site

During the fieldwalking programme initiated by the Car Dyke Research Group in the 1960s (Simmons 1979) a number of mounds were recorded, centred on TF 155 405, in Helpringham North Fen to the west of the Roman Car Dyke. These produced a scatter of fired clay debris and a few sherds of Iron Age pottery. A total of twelve mounds was observed running in a line more or less parallel to and immediately south of the Helpringham Eau. This group of features extends westwards 1.2km from the west bank of the Car Dyke (Pl. III) (Simmons 1975b). As mentioned above, the saltern sites are easily identified both as soil and crop marks.

In addition to the artefacts referred to at the above grid reference there is a light scatter of Romano-British pottery over the whole field, together with worked and waste flints and a few sherds of medieval fabrics. The latter is consistent with the manuring of the medieval arable fields, and the ridge and furrow which formerly existed here can be seen on the 1946–7 RAF air photographs. There are a number of Romano-British sites close by; one extensive pottery scatter lies almost immediately to the south-west, and is of particular interest in that a Coritanian half stater, the first recorded from this part of Lincolnshire, was found here in 1971 (Trust for Lincolnshire Archaeology (TLA) records), although Iron Age pottery has not been recovered from that site. The mound at TF 155 405 is remembered locally as having been quite a substantial 'hill' and rabbit warren when the field was still under grass before World War II. This is the part of the site chosen for excavation, since in 1971 the subsoiling plough had brought up very large fragments of fired clay artefacts of the kind associated with Romano-British and earlier salt-making (Baker 1960; Hallam, S.J. 1960).

Plate I Aerial view of Helpringham Fen and Car Dyke, 1947. North is at top of picture, arrow indicates area of excavation. *Photo: RAF*

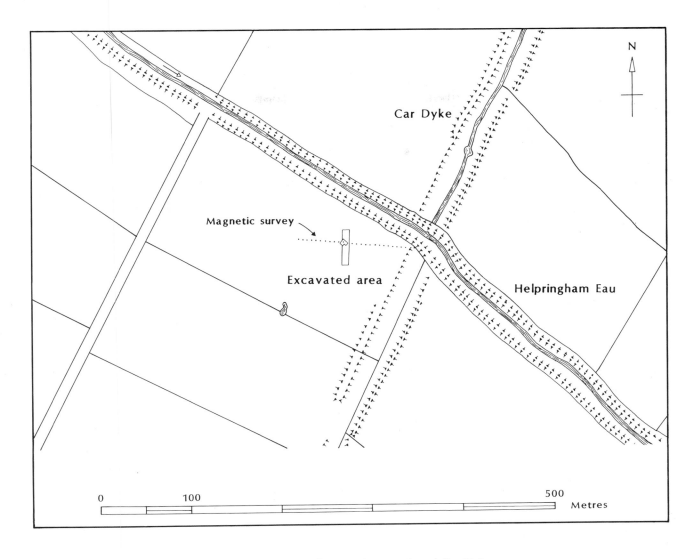

Figure 2 Location of excavation trench and Car Dyke

Plate II View of mounds in 1972 from Helpringham Eau bank, looking south

Plate III Car Dyke in 1972 from Helpringham Eau bank, looking south

3

Plate IV General view of site in 1975, looking south

Plate VI Hearth complex I (1975)

III. The Excavations 1972 and 1975

1972 Excavation
(Figs 2–5)

Method

Before the excavation a detailed proton gradiometer survey was made between the mound and the Car Dyke. This survey indicated a particular anomaly consistent with the presence of a hearth or area of intense burning. A cutting 4m by 7m was opened above this feature 73.2m west of the Car Dyke (Fig. 2) 'in order to determine the exact nature of the disturbance causing the anomaly and to see how much of it had survived the subsoiling. Removal of topsoil revealed a series of re-cut gullies outlining the shape of a mound (Figs 3, 4). The mound itself consisted of layers of ash, fragments of fired clay *etc*. The base of a rectangular hearth, 1m by 0.5m, lay immediately below the ploughsoil at the highest part of the mound, and the height of the mound top above natural blue clay was 0.5m (Fig. 5).

Results

Although only part of the mound surface was uncovered, it appeared to have been sub-circular, with a diameter of approximately 7m. It had been surrounded by a shallow flat-bottomed gully 0.4m wide cut into the natural clay (Pl. VIII). In the bottom of this gully stake-holes were seen (Fig. 4) which followed its exact course suggesting a palisade trench. Other gullies on other alignments were also noted at this level, but within the limited area opened it was not possible to discover the extent and relationship of these features (Fig. 4). A black ashy depression associated with the hearth was interpreted as the area of the stoke-hole (Simmons 1975c, 35, fig. 19), but there was no indication of a furnace throat between hearth and stoke-hole. The south end of the hearth had been destroyed by later activity. As a consequence of the very soft soil the site had clearly been favoured by rabbits for many years, and the damage caused not only by their burrowing but by that of smaller mammals was considerable (Pl. V). Removal of the fill of these numerous runs and tunnels left extremely fragmentary remains in position, and the resulting gaps, often in critical relationships, were a major hindrance to establishing relationships and stratigraphy.

Plate VII Post-holes (1972)

Plate VIII Gully around base of mound (1972)

Plate V Remains of hearth (1972). Note damage by rodents

5

1975 Excavation
(Figs 5, 6)

Method

In 1975, following the employment of a full-time archaeologist for the Car Dyke Research Group, grant aid was obtained from the then Department of the Environment to continue excavation on the same site. An extended area of 68m by 7m was laid out to the south of and including part of the 1972 excavation (Fig. 3, Pl. IV). Ultimately excavation of the area opened was not completed and only the ditch sections were taken down to the underlying boulder clay (Figs 5, 6).

Results

The major parts of two additional mounds with hearth complexes were exposed to the south of the 1972 discovery. At the north end of the excavated area the clay subsoil sloped downwards as if towards a watercourse, presumably the original Helpringham Eau. The proximity of the present flood bank of the river prevented further examination of this feature.

The series of mounds lay more or less north/south within the area opened, at right angles to the Helpringham Eau. None of the mounds was completely excavated but they appeared to be approximately circular, an interpretation supported by the position of various other features and the tip-lines of the debris of which the mounds were made. Possible parallels are the Iron Age salt-making mounds in Essex which are described as being generally of circular or oval form (Reader 1910; de Brisay 1978). Damage by rodents was as severe as in the 1972 excavation. In addition two modern field drains crossed the site and modern subsoiling had removed or displaced large pieces from several features (Pls VI, X).

On each mound were remains of hearths within clay-built enclosure walls, but little height remained either of walls or of hearths, even where the latter had been rebuilt. Hearth complex II for example, had been rebuilt at least twice on different alignments. The clay walls may represent the remains of boiling houses erected to provide some shelter for the hearths or the salt-makers, as was apparently done in medieval times (Hallam H.E. 1960, 98). Deep plough damage prevented any recognition of original openings in these walls. The mounds themselves, as noted in 1972, were composed entirely of made-up ground but appeared to have ditches around them and possibly causewayed entrances (Fig. 3). The causeway entrance to mound B was 3.25m wide; the end of one of its ditches was excavated (Pl. XIII).

Hearths

Three main hearth complexes were uncovered, but there was considerable evidence of rebuilding and relocation of these structures. For example, the hearth found in 1972 had itself been cut through in order to make a new mound, probably for hearth complex I. Evidence of superimposed ditches reinforces this suggestion, but the lack of stratification in the upper levels made it uncertain as to which of the latest hearths were contemporary. There is no conclusive evidence of the use to which the hearths had been put, and the possibility of their being kilns (Rodwell 1982, 19–20) cannot be ruled out.

The most complete hearths surviving were single hearths cut into earlier ones and often on different alignments from them. There was no evidence of any of them having been operated as one of a pair, as at Goldhanger, Canewdon (Reader 1910, 73, fig. 4) Ingoldmells area, Lincolnshire (Swinnerton 1932, 242, fig. 1) and on Ingoldmells beach (Baker 1960, 30, fig. 5). A pair of hearths which may be of a slightly earlier date were found at Billingborough (Chowne *et al.*, forthcoming). At most only some 5cm of 'wall' at the sides of the hearth survived, and no reconstruction has been attempted. No stoke-hole areas were obvious in the 1975 excavation.

Ditches
(Figs 5, 6)

A number of the ditches were sectioned (Fig. 5 Section 2 and Fig. 6 Sections 3–5). Those that appeared to surround mounds were approximately flat bottomed (Fig. 5 Section 1 and Fig. 6, Section 3). The ditch *F102* around Complex II was flat bottomed on the south side of the mound whereas on the north side it was broader and shallower affair with only a single fill. It cannot be proved that these ditches are contemporary, although it seems likely, but it can be conjectured that the shallow north side of *F102* (Fig. 6, Section 4) is equivalent to the upper fill of the south side of *F102*. This would explain the homogeneous nature of the fill.

In only one of the ditches, *F84*, was anything resembling primary silting seen, comprising a layer of ash and burnt material with briquetage fragments. For the remainder, the usual fill was a series of deposits of a similar nature, varying only in the differing proportions of sand, broken briquetage, ash or fired clay than each other. The impression given is that the ground on which the saltmakers worked was an entirely artificial surface, where mounds were constantly accumulating and the material tipped or dumped into ditches, with fresh ditches being regularly re-cut and hearths rebuilt. The section of part of the mound uncovered in 1972 reinforced this view (Fig. 5, Section 1).

6

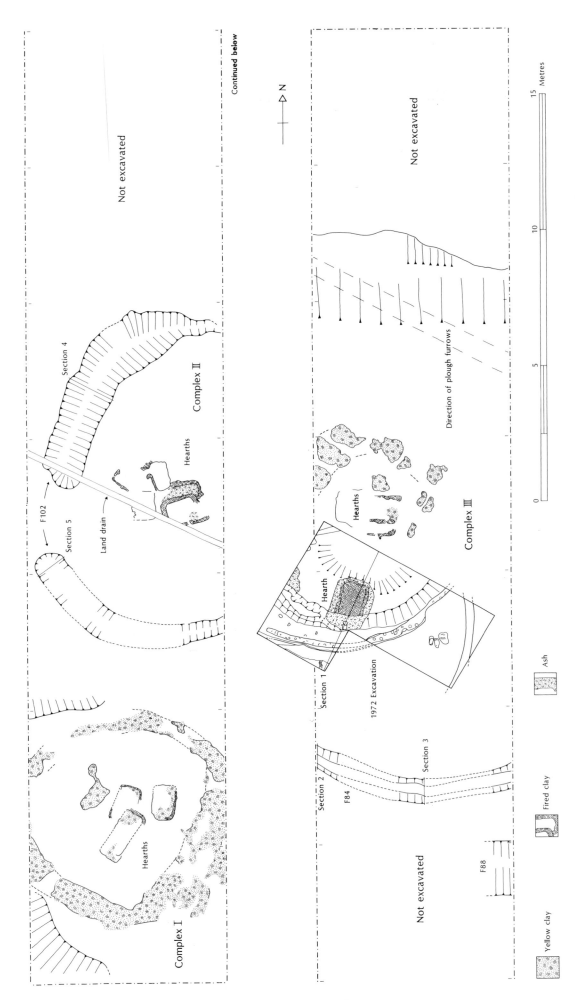

Figure 3 Site Plan

7

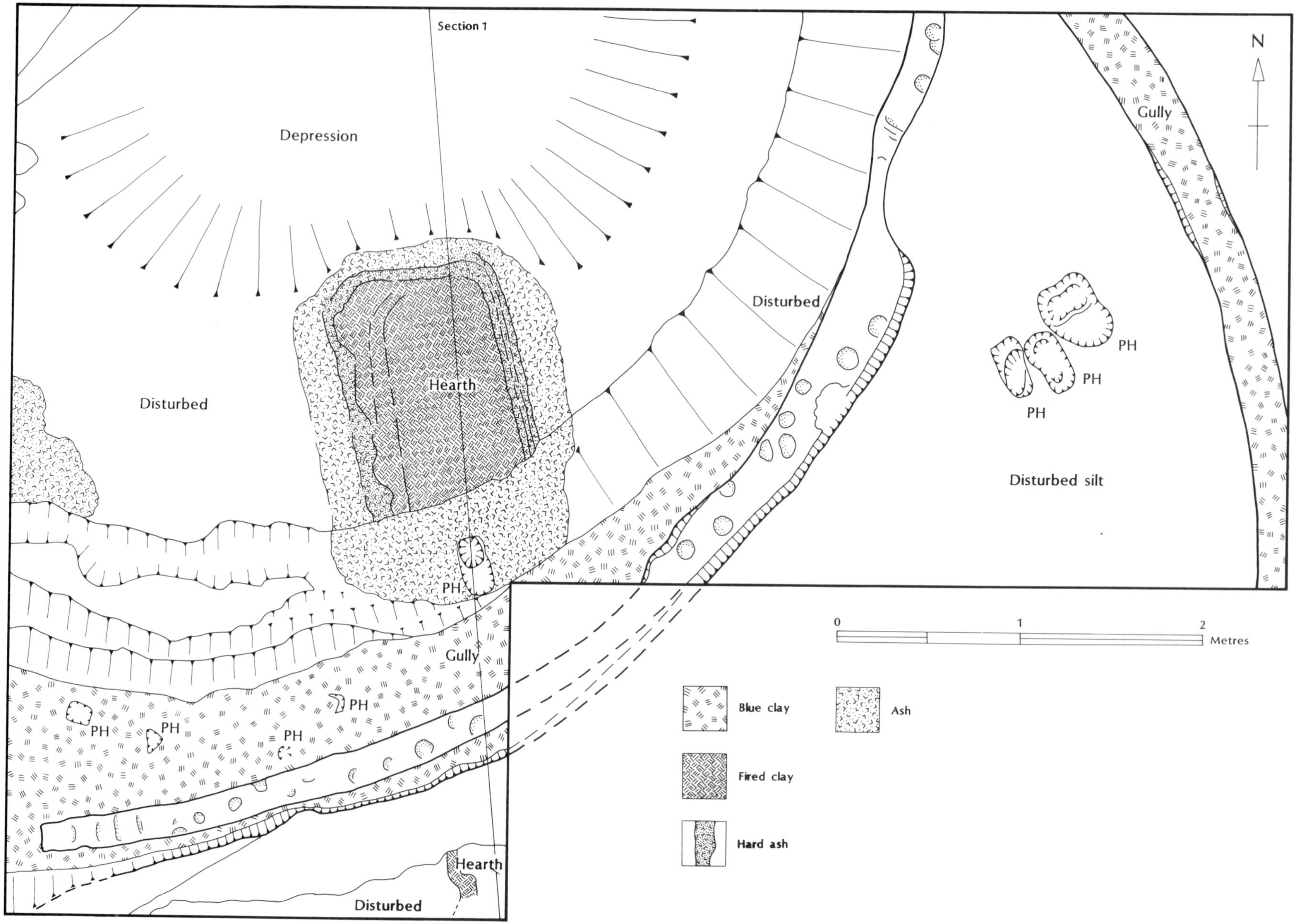

Figure 4 Plan of 1972 excavation

8

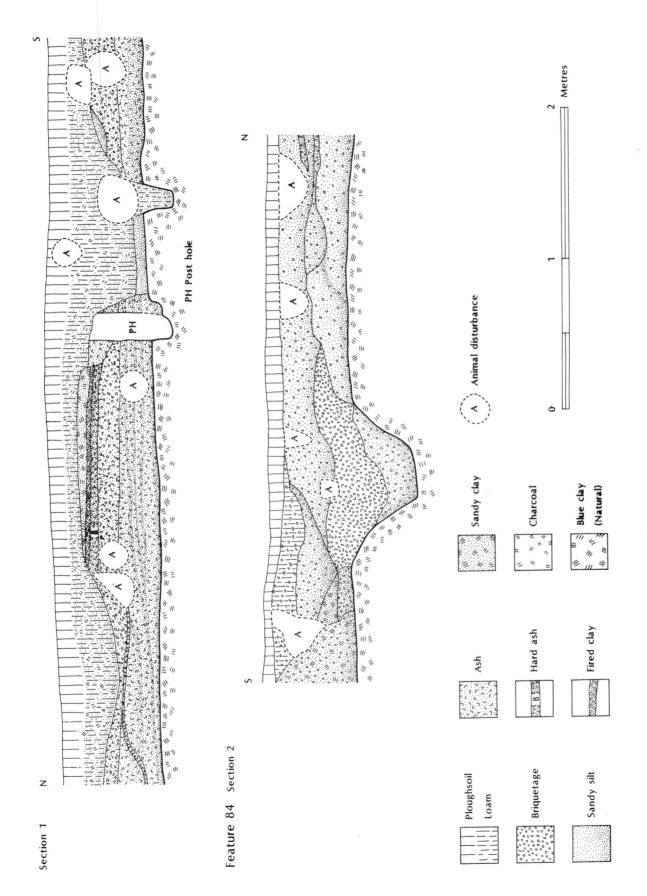

Section 1

Feature 84   Section 2

PH Post hole

Ploughsoil
Loam

Briquetage

Sandy silt

Ash

Hard ash

Fired clay

Sandy clay

Charcoal

Blue clay
(Natural)

Animal disturbance

Metres
0   1   2

Figure 5 Ditch sections 1 and 2

9

Feature 84 Section 3

N   S

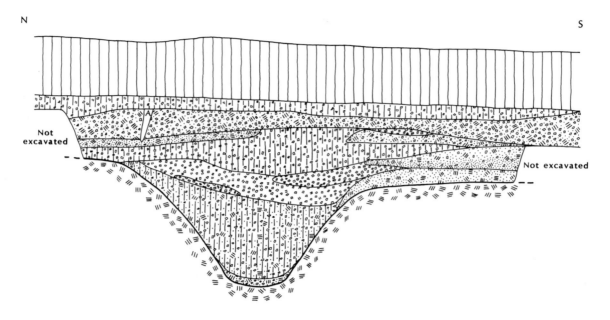

Not excavated   Not excavated

Feature 102 Section 4

Topsoil removed

S   W

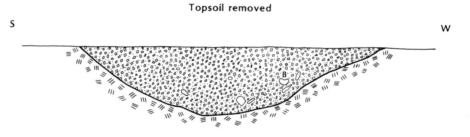

Feature 102 Section 5

E   W

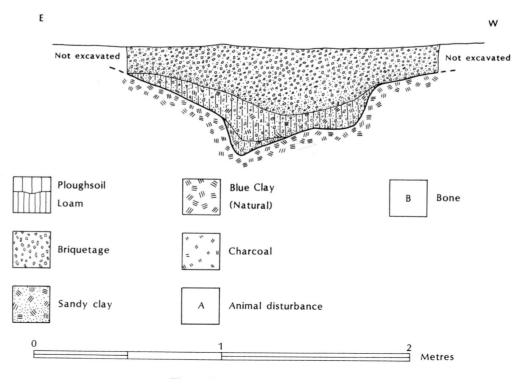

Not excavated   Not excavated

Ploughsoil
Loam

Briquetage

Sandy clay

Blue Clay
(Natural)

Charcoal

A   Animal disturbance

B   Bone

0   1   2
                                                                            Metres

Figure 6 Ditch sections 3, 4 and 5

Plate IX Hearth complex II

Plate XII Section 3, across ditch *F15*, complex III

Plate X Hearth complex III

Plate XIII Section 5, across ditch *F102*, near causeway
entrance, complex II

Plate XI Section 1, across ditch *F15*, complex III

Plate XIV Section 4, across ditch *F102*, complex II

IV. The Artefacts

Introduction

The principal type of artefact recovered was briquetage, the shaped fired clay pieces associated with prehistoric and Romano-British sites. This was widely distributed over the site as it had been on the surface of the field. Pottery, also widely distributed over the site, formed the next largest group, although there is no record that either of these artefact collections have been counted or weighed. Objects of other materials are few in number, comprising two quern fragments, one worked flint and three waste flints. A piece of antler tine, sawn at both ends, was found on the surface of the site in 1971. This was perhaps a knife handle. The pottery, quern fragments and flints indicate settlement in the vicinity, but no metalwork was found. Perhaps none survived.

The Pottery

by Peter Chowne and Hilary Healey
(Fig. 7)

The pottery assemblage illustrated here consists of thirty rims, thirty-four decorated pieces and six bases, comprising a total of seventy-nine drawings. Some of the sherds were unstratified, and the limited nature of the excavation precludes the production of a more detailed study. Nevertheless certain aspects of the material deserve comment since results from fieldwalking by the Car Dyke Research Group and later fieldwork in this area as well as in the limestone uplands to the west of Helpringham suggest that Iron Age sites in this region leave little if any ceramic evidence on the surface (Chowne 1980, 303). The pottery can be placed in four general groups:

1. Coarse ware in the Ancaster/Breedon tradition.
2. Coarse ware not in the Ancaster/Breedon tradition.
3. Fine wares.
4. Wheel-made wares.

Group 1
(Fig. 7 Nos 1–47)

This is the largest group, comprising forty-seven sherds in all. The fabric is low fired and soft to the touch. It is generally dark grey in colour and some sherds appear to have internal sooting. External surfaces are occasionally oxidised to a buff or pale reddish brown. The well sorted calcite inclusions appear to consist chiefly of fossil shell, probably from local limestone. The shell has a very hard texture and the particles vary in size from 1mm to 5mm long. In a few instances the shell has leached out, but even where it is present the sherds are very light in weight for their size. Quartzite is also present.

Three classes of vessel have been identified:

A. Large jars with scored decoration on the exterior. The scoring occurs on the vessel walls extending in a zone from about 2cm below the rim down to within 2cm of the base. Sherds are approximately 1cm thick.

B. Smaller thin walled jars or bowls with flattened rims. The scoring is more shallow than on group A and it has been suggested that it was made using a coarse-grained pebble, although many types of tool could have produced this effect.

C. Undecorated jars. There appears to be only a single vessel in this category, represented by two non-joining sherds (Fig. 7.3).

Group 2
(Fig. 7 Nos 48–64)

The fabric of this group, of which seventeen sherds are illustrated, is similar to that of Group 1, except that the shell inclusions are more variable in size (some are as large as 5mm across) and less well sorted. Colours are similar to those in Group 1, but the surface of the clay has been smoothed over and the pots were apparently fired at a higher temperature, as they are hard to the touch. One tiny rim sherd, Fig. 7.55, has been decorated with finger-nail impressions. Similar sherds have been found within the Billingborough Phase IIIA material (Chowne 1979, 246). These vessels are thin walled small jars or bowls with plain or slightly beaded rims. One or two have flat, knife-trimmed rims. The colours are similar to those described for Group 1. Little decoration is evident other than the occasional incised line.

Group 3
(Fig. 7 Nos 65–71)

Four rims and three body sherds make up this group of sandy wares. The fabric is close-textured and firm, fully oxidised to red or a dull orange. Additional sand and shell inclusions are visible, the latter tending to be less than 1cm across and well sorted. In some instances the shell has leached out. The thickness of the sherds, averaging between 14 and 16mm, indicates large storage type vessels, and it has been suggested that rim diameters might be as much as 45cm across. This expanded rim, described as a heavy bead, does not occur with the Ancaster/Breedon style. Body sherds have fine scored decoration which may have been made using a comb; similar pieces have been recovered from Aldwinckle, Northamptonshire (Jackson 1977, 40 no. 71).

Group 4
(Fig. 7 Nos 72–79)

4a: Dark grey/brown fabric, occasionally reddish-buff, with fine well sorted shell inclusions. The core is grey. Stamped and rouletted decoration, as well as grooves and cordons formed during wheel-throwing, are characteristic. One sherd, Fig. 7.77, has been included in this group because of its decoration, even though the fabric is closer to that of group 1. Stamp and roulette decorated wares have been recovered from various parts of eastern England as well as from Sussex and the Upper Thames areas. Vessels in this fabric with cordons are also known locally from Sapperton (Simmons pers. comm) and from Old Place, Sleaford (Simmons pers. comm).

4b: Two sherds are present in a dark grey to grey/brown fabric with buff to light grey surfaces. The exterior is burnished. Figure 7 no. 73 has two horizontal tooled grooves 3cm apart, whilst no. 74 has the more usual wheel-made cordons and grooves.

4c: A single sherd (Fig. 7.76) of a jar with a pronounced carination, has been included in the illustrated material, although the fabric is more closely paralleled amongst local Romano-British wares. It has sparse shell inclusions and is very hard.

Dating

Group 1 as a whole is typical of what was formerly regarded as within the Ancaster/Breedon style zone covering a large part of the East Midlands (Cunliffe 1974, 40). Noticeably absent, however, are the finger-impressed rims which occur at both Ancaster, Lincolnshire (May 1976, 139) and Breedon on the Hill (Kenyon 1950, 17–82). The reason for this may be chronological, since the finger-impressed rims are common in Phase III at Billingborough (Chowne 1978, 15–21 and forthcoming) and have also been found in a surface collection from an Iron Age site some 10km to the south in Rippingale Fen (Hardon 1973) as well as from Fengate, Peterborough (Pryor 1974, 28, fig. 21, 1–3).

The decoration on No. 78 can be paralleled in historic Lincolnshire at Ancaster, Dragonby and Kirmington (Elsdon 1975). This type of pattern has yet to be closely dated, but examples from Dragonby occur in a first century AD context (May 1970, 241 no. 30). The sherd 72, classified as fabric 4c, is similar to a jar from Dragonby for which a date in the opening years of the first century has again been suggested (May 1970, 241 no. 30).

Stylistically the majority of the pottery from Helpringham appears to date from the middle part of the Iron Age. This is not inconsistent with the C14 date of 379–116 cal BC (HAR-2280) taken from a wood sample. However, with such a small amount of material (only thirty-eight of the seventy-nine drawn sherds are stratified) any conclusions must be treated with caution. Unstratified Romano-British pottery lay around and on the site, and finds from fieldwalking in the vicinity and along the Car Dyke indicate activity in the area in the first and second centuries AD. From the largest of these sites, with surface material predominantly Roman, came a Coritanian base silver stater.

Catalogue of illustrated pottery
(Fig. 7)

In the pottery catalogue the fabric colours are not described separately for each sherd in groups 1 and 2, since they are more or less uniform, and the variations seen do not appear to be significant. Group 4 is categorised by manufacturing technique rather than by fabric.

Most sherds are drawn in front view and left hand cross-section, with the sections in solid black. Only a few rims were of sufficient size to calculate the diameter; No. 33, which appears to be exceptionally broad, may well be exaggerated due to distortion. No Romano-British pottery, which was all unstratified, has been included in the report or illustrations.

Group 1 Shell-filled fabric
1. HF75 SUS/B Upper part of jar with finger impressions externally below rim and deep criss-crossed scoring on body. Diam. 15cm
2. HF75 US Two joining sherds of jar with slightly flattened rim and beginnings of shallow vertical scoring on body. Diam. 18cm
3. HF75 SU Thick walled jar with flattened, inward sloping rim. Two- non joining sherds. Exterior shallow, horizontal scoring.
4. HF75 LI US Jar with tapered rim. Shallow diagonal scoring on body.
5. HF75 US D Slightly everted rim. One deeply scored groove diagonally across sherd.
6. HF75 LI US Rim and part of body with deep scoring.
7. HF75 US Rim and part of body with one shallow scored groove.
8. HF75 F15 US Rim, inward turning.
9. HF72 6 Flattened rim.
10. HF75 SUS/A Sherd with deep vertical scoring.
11. HF75 US Sherd with deep scoring.
12. HF75 SUN/A Sherd with criss-cross scoring.
13. HF75 US Two joining sherds with close scoring. This is drawn as if vertical but may not be so.
14. HF72 17 Sherd with scoring in two directions.
15. HF75 SU/A Sherd with deep scoring within two parallel scored lines.
16. HF75 US Sherd with criss-cross scoring.
17. HF75 US Sherd with close scoring, not necessarily vertical.
18. HF75 SU/A Sherd with deep criss-cross scoring.
19. HF75 SUS/A Sherd with shallow scoring.
20. HF75 SU/A Sherd with scoring.
21. HF75 US Sherd with close scoring.
22. HF75 LI Sherd with scoring.
23. HF72 17 Sherd with very shallow scoring.
24. HF75 US Sherd with groove and shallow scoring.
25. HF75 US Angle of flat base.
26. HF75 US Flat base. Diam. 12cm
27. HF72 11 Thick rounded rim, damaged.
28. HF72 11 Sherd with slight scoring.
29. HF72 11 Flat base sherd with slight finger impressions.
30. HF75 US Slightly everted rim.
31. HF75 F17 Flat base, slight scoring on upper part of sherd.
32. HF75 L28 Tapered rim.
33. HF75 L28 Large jar with pronounced shoulder angle. Sparse approximately horizontal scoring. Diam. suggested 29.5cm
34. HF75 L82 Flat base, slight pedestal effect, but handmade. Diam. 9cm
35. HF75 L82 Sherd with slight scoring.
36. HF75 L82 Sherd with scoring at different angles.
37. HF75 L82 Sherd with scoring.
38. HF75 F84 Three joining sherds. Jar with slightly inturned rim. Diagonal close scoring on body. Diam. 13cm
39. HF75 F84 Sherd with close scoring.
40. HF75 F84 Sherd with close scoring.
41. HF75 F84 Sherd with diagonal scoring.
42. HF75 F84 Sherd with diagonal scoring.
43. HF75 F84 Sherd with scoring. Sherds. 38, 40, 41, 42 and 43. May all be from the same vessel.
44. HF75 F105 Tapered rim and part of body with diagonal scoring.
45. HF75 112 Sherd with scoring.
46. HF75 112 Sherd with scoring.
47. HF75 L169 Flattened rim and part of body with close vertical scoring.

Group 2 Shell-filled fabric
48. HF75 SU/A Slightly flattened rim.

49. HF72 US Rounded rim.
50. HF75 SUS/A Flattened rim.
51. HF75 US Flattened rim
52. HF75 SU/A Flattened rim.
53. HF72 2 Body sherd. External scored lines at different angles.
54. HF75 US 3 Base.
55. HF75 US Flattened rim. Decoration of indented lines (?finger nail impressions).
56. HF75 US Body sherd. External scored lines at different angles.
57. HF72 114 Body sherd. External scored lines in two directions.
58. HF72 12 [also marked 1 10] Flattened rim. Two more or less horizontal lines scored externally below rim.
59. HF72 12 Flattened rim.
60. HF72 12 Flattened and expanded rim.
61. HF72 17 Flat base. Diam. 8cm
62. HF75 F80 Slightly flattened rim.
63. HF75 L82 Slightly flattened rim going into shoulder.
64. HF75 F103 Slightly flattened rim.

Group 3 Sandy fabrics, various
65. HF75 L3a US Large jar, slightly beaded everted rim, bevelled on external edge. Possibly part made on wheel, but also knife trimmed internally where jar begins to broaden out to main body. Light red, sandy fabric, slightly browner core with well sorted inclusions 1–2mm.
66. HF72 14 Heavy bead rim, possibly wheel made. Light red fabric similar to 3(1) but shell on exposed surfaces leached out.
67. HF72 US Body sherd, deep straight combed scoring (illustrated as if vertical but not necessarily so). Coarse sandy fabric with very little shell and with quartzite grains up to 4mm. Light red surface, medium grey core and interior. Shallow scoring.
68. HF72 10 Body sherd, deep straight combed scoring as No. 33, Similar fabric but hardly any shell visible. Buff exterior surface, medium grey core and interior. Shallow scoring.
69. HF72 14 Body sherd, shallow external scoring in two directions at acute angles to each other. Fine sandy fabric with fine well-sorted shell, some leached out. Interior surface very smooth, light brown. Buff exterior light red and grey core. Deep scoring in two directions.
70. HF75 US Large jar rim, similar to 31. Shell filled sandy fabric but texture and colour disguised by having apparently been in a fire, or in ashy material, so pale buff, grey in colour with shell leached out.
71. HF72 15 Large jar rim, heavy bead. Possibly wheel made? Smooth sandy fabric with some shell. Light red surface with grey-red core.

Group 4 Wheel-made pottery, various fabrics
72. HF75 US Fabric 4c Body sherd, grey/brown fabric. Carinated vessel with horizontal groove above the carination.
73. HF75 LI US Fabric 4b Three joining body sherds of round bodied jar. Soft fabric, buff exterior burnished, grey interior. Two horizontal grooves mm apart and signs of a third.
74. HF75 SU Fabric 4b Shoulder sherd of large cordoned jar. Diameter at this point *c*.13cm. Wheel thrown but hand finished internally. Exterior dark brown, burnished, core reddish brown and exterior brown.
75. HF75 US Fabric 4b Body shed of large jar very weathered but appears to be wheel made. Light buff-orange to light red. Horizontal ?combed scoring externally and shallow cordon.
76. HF75 LI Fabric 4b Shoulder sherd of fine cordoned jar, pale buff surfaces with medium grey core.
77. HF75 F76 Fabric 4a Body sherd, probably from a shouldered large rounded vessel. Pale brown with pale grey/brown exterior. Deeply impressed circular stamp with horizontal line of double impressed circular stamp. S. Elsdon suggests whitish material in roulette holes in inlay, but it may only be white ash from the site. Slight indication of diagonal rouletting as with a chevron pattern.
78. HF75 F103 Fabric 4 Body sherd, probably shoulder of large vessel. Exterior abraded, dark brown, interior light brown, dark grey core. Double square notched rouletted decoration in triangular zones above horizontal grooves.
79. HF75 F103 Fabric 4 Reddish brown to grey shoulder sherd, possibly same vessel as 7 but less abraded. Slight burnishing.

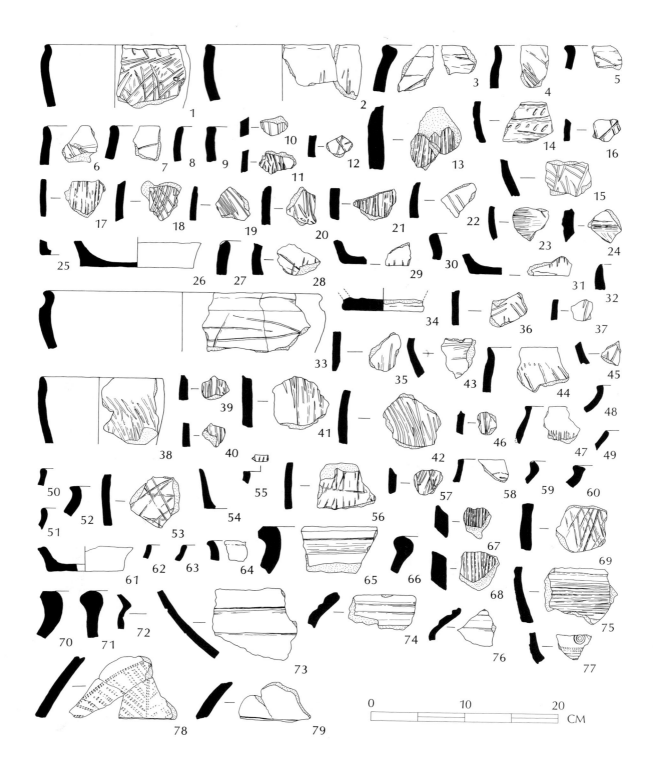

Figure 7 Pottery. Scale 1:4

14

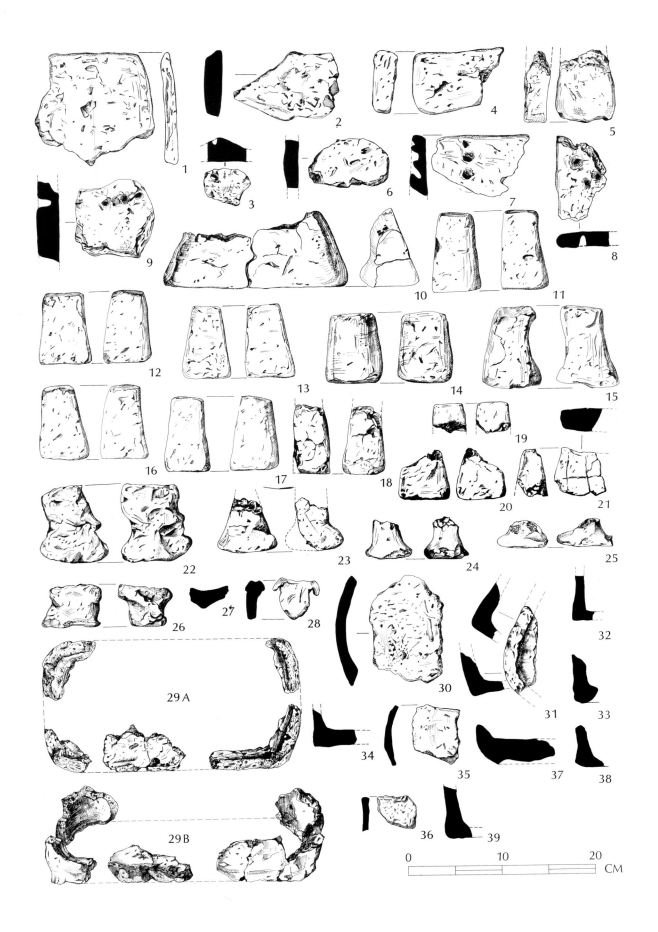

Figure 8 Briquetage. Scale 1:4

15

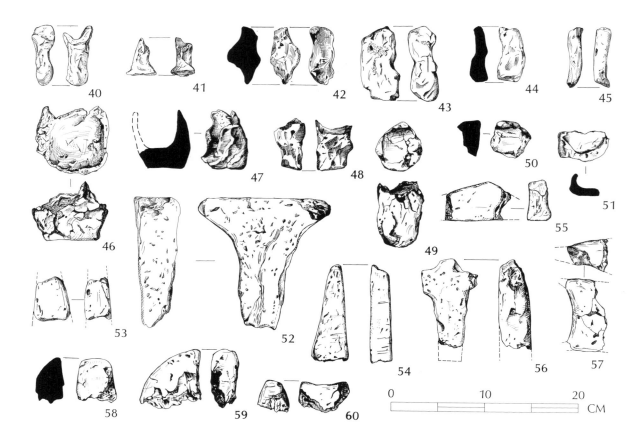

Figure 9 Briquetage. Scale 1:4

The Briquetage

by Peter Chowne and Hilary Healey

(Figs 8, 9)

Most of the artefacts recovered from the excavation were pieces of fired clay commonly known as 'briquetage' and usually associated with Roman and pre-Roman salt-making sites. Many of these pieces were in a very fragmentary state, often reduced to mere crumbs, for the clay is fired at very low temperatures and is soft and easily damaged by frost and plough. A selection of the larger and more complete pieces has been made to illustrate the various categories of briquetage represented. A classification based on a combination of the work of Swinnerton (1932, 246–251), Bestwick, de Brisay and Farrar (de Brisay and Evans 1975) was first considered, but the more simplified system used by Gurney for Holbeach St Johns (this volume) has now been adopted.

The briquetage fabric mixture includes a filler of hay or chaff, presumably added in order to lessen the plasticity of the clay and perhaps to make it go further. The need to avoid shrinkage or distortion, two other reasons for adding a tempering agent or grog, do not seem relevant in this type of material, except perhaps in the case of actual vessels. Disappointingly, few fragments of these were identified.

The classification of the types follows Gurney (p.56) with minor additions. Colours are not described in detail for each piece since the material is of a relatively uniform red or orange-red appearance, with occasional paler or purplish colouring, generally on parts of the object which are slightly harder fired.

The illustrations give the elevation and a section shown in black. It has been found that external views are more informative than sections. In one or two instances dashed lines indicate suggested reconstruction based on recorded parallels from elsewhere. One other interesting discovery was a cloth impression on a piece of briquetage. This was examined by Dr J.P. Wild and a note on it and a similar Lincolnshire find has already been published (Kirkham 1985).

Bricks and Plates

(Fig. 8, Nos 1–10)

Several pieces of brick or plate (Gurney's 'flat slabs') were recovered, not dissimilar to some found in a Romano-British salt-making context at Middlewich (Bestwick 1975). Three of these pieces have rows of stick impressions the purpose of which is unclear. Had they been sticks used in some way in the manufacture of these slabs they would probably have been fixed right through the clay. 10 is thicker than the other pieces and may be a brick or part of a loom weight.

Truncated Pyramids

(Fig. 8 Nos 11–21)

Gurney notes Greenfield's references to 'truncated pyramidical stilts' and the 'accessory' pieces conforming to this description recorded by Swinnerton (Gurney, this volume). Good examples were found at Helpringham. 21 bears part of a scratched pattern.

Props

(Fig. 8, Nos 22–26; Fig. 9, Nos 40–45)

This title covers a range of roughly cylindrical shapes, embracing various 'handbricks' or 'squeezes' which are characteristic of Romano-British and Iron Age saltern sites.

Plate XV Human skull fragment (1972). *Copyright English Heritage.* Scale 1:1

Bridges
(Fig. 8, Nos 27–28)
These are another common type overall, although there were very few complete or near complete examples recorded from this site.

Vessels
(Fig. 8, Nos 29–39)
The thicker sherds 29 to 34 and 37–9 have been identified as trough fragments. Sherds 35 and 36 are apparently rims of smaller, more upright vessels.

Seats
(Fig. 9, Nos 46–51)
These are a squat type of prop with a very clear impression of another prop on one or both ends. Similar examples are illustrated in Gurney, although 49 is a somewhat taller variation.

Bars
(Fig. 9, Nos 52–60)
This is another group covering a wide variety of shapes. The large T-shape 52 is paralleled by one from the Essex Red Hills (Reader 1910) and Dorset (Farrar 1975, 17, fig. 8b, 18); 57 and 61 are not quite props but seem to have been pressed against the side of a ?vessel.

V. Zoological and Botanical Evidence

Human Skull Fragment
by Justine Bayley
(A.M. Lab. No. 791624)
The fragment is the anterior portion of the frontal bone, cut off about 15mm behind the orbits; only the right-hand two-thirds survives. The skull was that of an adult individual of indeterminate sex. Despite some erosion the cut surface is sufficiently well preserved that the original 'sawmarks' can be seen. There is also some evidence that the cut was realigned after it had been started.

The cutting of the skull must have been carried out at or after the death of the individual as there is no sign of the bone healing (Pl. XV). Two virtually identical pieces have been found among the human bone fragments from Billingborough (Chowne *et al.*, forthcoming).

Animal Bones
identified by Helen Gandy
Of the animal bones found ninety pieces were identifiable but of these only three, all of cattle, showed butchering cuts. Two in context twelve (1972) appeared water-worn. No horse bones were found other than six molars. Pigs were represented by two bones and fowl by one. There were eighteen pieces of cattle bone. However, the largest group was of sheep, totalling twenty-four pieces altogether with the addition of a near complete skeleton in *F77*, about 50% of the bones of which had been burnt. Those groups contaminated by rabbits or where identification was not positive have been disregarded. A complete list of animal bone recovered is given in the microfiche.

Molluscs
by Penny Spencer
Samples taken from six deposits during the 1975 excavation were examined for molluscan remains. The techniques of snail analysis employed were those described by Evans (1972). Unfortunately, it was not possible to use samples of a standard size or weight, as all had previously been washed down and examined for seeds; the sample weights given in Table 1 are those of the samples prior to washing down. It is not therefore possible to compare the absolute abundance of snails in the various samples.

Sample code	L138	F84	L7	F8/L6	L4	F8
Sample weight (kg)	0.5	1.75	2.25	2.25	0.75	2.25
BW *Assiminea grayana* Flem	4	-	-	-	-	-
BW *Hydrobia ulvae* (Penn)	24	135	11	120	162	65
BW *H. ventrosa* (Mont)	17	18	486	92	106	59
Hydrobia spp.	2	-	638	174	4	61
BW *Potamopyyrgus jenkinsi* (Smith)	-	-	10	-	1	-
BW *Pseudamnicola confusa* (Frau)	2	13	-	3	5	-
BW *Phytia myosotis* (Drap)	-	3	-	-	-	-
M *Carychium minumum* Mull	-	-	-	-	1	-
FWc *Lymnaea peregra (Mull)*	-	-	34	-	-	-
FWs *Planorbis leucostoma* (Millet)	-	-	23	-	-	1
FWc *P. laevis* Alder	-	-	1	-	-	-
FWc *P. crista* (L) -	-	5	-	-	-	-
Vertigo Pygmaea (Drap) L	-	-	1	-	2	-
Truncatellina cylindrica (ferussac) L	-	-	1	1	3	6
Pupilla muscorum (L) L	-	-	5	2	7	13
Vallonia pulchella (Mull) M	-	-	8	8	-	5
Ostracod valves	-	-	1	1	-	-

Note:
BW = Brackish-water species; FW = Freshwater species; FWc = Catholic species; FWs = Slum species; M = Marsh species; L = Land species

Table 1 Helpringham Fen: Mollusca

Samples

L128	Saltern mound accumulation layer. Sandy. Probably briquetage residue in origin. Sandy.
F84	From the bottom of a ditch cutting or surrounding one of the salt mounds. Containing much charcoal and tiny briquetage fragments.
F8	From F8; a shallow depression on the north side of the mound in complex I.
L7	Gleyed clay; rich in shells. Thought to be flood deposit. From a depression on the south side of the mound in complex I.
F8/L6	Gleyed clay; overlying and filling F8.
L4	Gleyed clay; in the depression to the north of the Northern mound
L7, F8/L6, L4	All similar gleyed clay, later than F8, and all sealed by a brown, ungleyed, clay. This is in turn covered by the modern plough-soil, and was not sampled.

Results

L128 and *F84* together contained snails of only five different species, and all of these are of brackish water habitat. The dominant species in each case is *Hydrobia ulvae*, a snail that is common in estuaries and salt-marshes (Ellis 1969; Macan 1969). *H. ventrosa* occurs in somewhat fewer numbers in both samples, and is also typical of estuaries, ditches and lagoons. *Phytia myosotis* and *Assiminea grayana* are inhabitants of mud-flats in estuaries and *Pseudamnicola confusa* likes brackish water.

The other four samples contained a wider variety of species, including land snails and some freshwater species. The molluscan fauna of *F8* is comprised mainly of the brackish water dwelling Hydrobidae, with a few land snails in addition. *Vallonia pulchella* is a land snail that occurs most frequently in marsh habitats, while *Pupilla muscorum* and *Truncatellina cylindrica* are open-country species that prefer drier conditions (Evans 1972).

Sample *L7* was extremely rich in shells. Most of these are again the Hydrobidae, plus a few *Potamopyrgus jenkinsi*. This particular species lives inland, in freshwater, at the present day, but before c.1893 was known only from a brackish water (Macan 1969). There are, however, a number of freshwater species in this sample, including several of catholic habitat requirements, and one slum species. This latter species, *Planorbis leucostoma*, is a snail that can withstand poor water conditions and occasional drought (Macan 1969). *Mallonia pulchella* is again present, and is joined by *Vertigo pygmaea*, which, although more typically terrestrial than *V. pulchella*, often occurs in marshes. Again there are the two open-country species present in small numbers.

F8/L6 and *L4* contained very similar faunas to that in *L7*, except that they had no freshwater species. Both contained an additional brackish water species, *Pseudamnicola confusa*, and *L4* had one individual of *Gary-*

chium minimum, which is like *Vallonie pulchella* in its frequent occurrence in marsh habitats.

The overall picture given by these faunas is one of an area of marsh or mud-flats with freshwater and brackish areas. If, however, the deposits that these faunas occurred in are due to flooding, then the snails will have come from a wide area, and may represent a variety of habitats: terrestrial, freshwater and brackish water and marsh, rather than one *in situ* habitat.

Plant Analysis
by A.J. Gouldwell

The deposits

The upper levels of the 1975 excavation consisted of clays and clay loam, flood deposits which would have surrounded the saltern mounds. These deposits yielded no artefact dating evidence, but were sealed by modern plough soil. *L2* was used to describe three deposits running across the site, roughly 0 to 15m north, and 25 to 41m north and 60 to 65m north occupying the lower lying areas on the archaeological mound-debris surface. These *L2* deposits were brown clays, overlying grey gleyed clays with brown mottling, indicating periodic waterlogging at these lower depths, which comprised contexts *L3 L4* (less gleyed than *L3* or *L7*). Below *L3*, occupying the western part of the excavated ditch *F8*, the clay changed to a more evenly grey deposit with smaller mottles and noticeable shell, *L6*. These lower flood layers were sampled, namely *L4*, *L6* and *L7*. The bottom 20cm, *i.e.* L150, of ditch *F84* bordering the southern side of mound IV was seen in section 5 to be dark and rich in carbonised organic remains, possibly derived from a hearth. This was sampled in the hope of obtaining evidence of local vegetation at the time of burning. A sample of sandy infill (*L138*) was taken from the eastern part of the excavated ditch *F8*.

Sample	L4	L7	L150
Species			
Chenopodium sp.	-	-	3
Chenopodium album L.	-	-	11
Chenopodium sp. cf. C. album L.			
Atriplex cf. hastata/patula L.	-	1	-
Polygonum convolvulus L	-	2	0
Polygonum lapathifolium L.	1	-	-
Juncus sp.	-	-	1
Carex sp.	-	-	1
Isolepis setacea (L) R.Br.	-	-	1
Cladium mariscus (L) Pohl	-	-	1
L6 and 139 were unproductive of botanical remains			

Table 2 Helpringham Fen: Plant Analysis

Results

Plant remains were very scarce and must be evaluated with reserve. Species identified are given in Table 2 indicating observed numbers of seeds and fruits. Samples *F8/L6* and *L138* were barren of seed remains.

The *Chenopodium*, *Atriplex* and *Polygonum* species are ubiquitous weeds and ruderals, occurring in open habitats, such as waste ground, arable farm land and by the sea, generally preferring nitrogen rich soil conditions. Their presence is to be expected in sites of human occupation. Furthermore, the relative abundance of these seeds and fruits in ancient deposits owes much to their robustness and consequent selective preservation.

L150 yielded single fruits of *Juncus* (rush) and *Carex* (sedge) species which may indicate wet conditions. Unfortunately the charred condition of these remains rendered identification to species level impossible. *Isolepis setacea*, also from this group, is found on damp, often sandy or gravelly ground, including land inundated in winter. *Cladium mariscus* is characteristically a fen plant of neutral alkaline soil; it has a submerged root structure, occurring where the water table is normally not less than about 15cm below soil level (Conway 1942). Also in *L150*, fine carbonised fragments of oak twigs were found, perhaps representing the principal fuel used in the evaporation hearths.

VI. Discussion

The site is envisaged as having been used for the manufacture of salt, and as being a predominantly industrial area. However, the presence of a quern and a considerable amount of pottery appear to indicate repeated, if not permanent, occupation of the site. The industry was operational in an open landscape close to the sea, such as an estuary with large tidal creeks, where both saltmarsh and mudflat were present; this would be consistent with the plant remains which show the presence of fresh and brackish as well as salt water. Conditions of freshwater fen nearby are confirmed by the presence of the sedge, *Cladium mariscus* and of alder, *Alnus*. Cladium has historically been an important species in the fenland economy, and as late as the nineteenth century was widely used for thatching. Alder was evidently used for fuel, but it is of course also an important species in this type of environment, since the wood can withstand waterlogging. It is ideal for such purposes as the manufacture of posts and stakes which are required in use on marshy or flooded ground. Oak was also present.

The evidence available from this relatively small excavation is limited but important for future Fen edge studies. The site appears to have been part of an industrial complex with which it is likely that other activities were associated at not too great a distance. These might have included other works necessary for salt production and animal husbandry as well as domestic buildings. The suggested date of activity on the excavated part of the site is in the middle of the third century BC. The presence of later Iron Age and Roman material in the upper levels implies some continuity of use of the area, but this cannot be proven. Carbon 14 samples from two contexts were submitted to Harwell via the Ancient Monuments Laboratory. The first, charcoal described by Harwell as 'from fairly large timbers' was collected from the makeup of mound C. It gave a reading of 379–116 cal BC. The other sample, from charcoal in mound A, was identified as alder and Rosaceae family (*e.g.* hawthorn) from mature timbers. It was a somewhat small sample resulting in a larger than normal error and this came out as 487–370 cal BC. The bulk of the pottery found cannot be dated more closely than the third to first century BC, although examples of first century wheel-made forms are in the minority, only four sherds being stratified.

Plate XVI Holbeach St Johns, OS 33; aerial photograph of OS 33, looking south.
The positions of Sites A and B are marked.

Chapter 2. A Romano-British Salt-making Site at Shell Bridge, Holbeach St Johns: Excavations by Ernest Greenfield, 1961

by David Gurney

I. Summary

Excavations in field OS 33, Holbeach St Johns, Lincs. were carried out by Philip Mayes in 1960 and Ernest Greenfield (for the Ministry of Works) in 1961. The main features of the Romano-British landscape survived as earthworks in this field, and two areas were temporarily reserved from ploughing to allow excavation.

The two areas, Site A and Site B, were first surveyed by grids of small test-pits. The subsequent excavation focused on features within the surviving earthworks rather than the earthworks themselves, although a Roman droveway and an enclosure were sectioned. On Site B, the main area, linear features and irregular hollows were excavated. Pottery of mid-second to early-third-century date was recovered and briquetage supports were found *in situ*. A single coin was recovered, dated AD180–192, and the pottery assemblage is typical for a fenland site. Seven types of briquetage artefacts can be recognised, and these can be paralleled at other saltern sites in Lincolnshire. The precise ways in which the features and briquetage types were utilised for salt-production remain unclear, and the mechanics of the industry will only be clarified by further research and excavation.

II. Introduction
(Figs 10–14; cover plate and Pl. XVI)

'In this county upon the sea shore they made salt formerly in great abundance' (Stukeley, *Itinerarium Curiosum* (1725), I, 5)

The site
(Fig. 10)
The area with which this report is concerned is Ordnance Survey Parcel No. 33, Holbeach St Johns, a field of *c.* 35 acres (14ha) to the north-west of Shell Bridge (also known as Lamming's Bridge) on the B1168 road from Holbeach St Johns to Holbeach Drove where it crosses the South Holland Main Drain (Fig. 10). The site is approximately 2km south-south-west of the village of Holbeach St Johns, 11km south-east of Spalding and 14km north-west of Wisbech, Cambs. It is centred on grid reference TF 341 163, and in the gazetteer in *The Fenland in Roman Times* (Phillips 1970) is Site 3416N.

In this area, the Romano-British landscape survived largely as earthworks until the early 1960s, and the site was frequently photographed from the air (Fowler 1950, pl. III; Godwin 1978, pl. 24; Frere and St Joseph 1983, pl. 132). Two photographs published by Wilson (1982, pls 20–21) show the site before ploughing (21 April 1960), and after (14 March 1961).

The finds and site records have been deposited in the City and County Museum, Broadgate, Lincoln (Accession no. 12/86).

History of the excavations
In 1960, the owner of the field, Mr G.H. Robinson, made known his intention to level the earthworks. In response to this, two local archaeologists, Philip Mayes (with the Boston Archaeological Group) and J.C. Mossop started work on the site in October of that year. Mossop opened a single trench in the centre of the field, while Mayes explored two areas, one in the north-west corner of the field (Site A) and another to the east of Mossop's trench (Site B East).

Shortly after this preliminary work, levelling of the earthworks was started, but after negotiations between the owner and the Ministry of Works, two areas (around the excavations by Mayes and Mossop) were reserved for excavation. Under the agreement with the landowner, this work had to be completed by August 1961. Ernest Greenfield conducted excavations for the Ministry of Works from 23 May to 30 June 1961, assisted by S.J. Hallam and V. Russell.

The main intention of this report has been to publish the excavations by Greenfield, although where possible the earlier work by Mayes and Mossop has been integrated.

The earthworks
(Figs 11–12; cover plate and Pl. XVI)
Until 1961, the principal (linear) features of the Romano-British landscape survived as earthworks, a landscape disturbed only by the insertion of modern drains in the northern part of the field (Fig. 12). The earthworks/cropmarks in the area of Shell Bridge were first plotted by the Royal Geographical Society and published in *The Fenland in Roman Times* (Phillips 1970, map 7), and a more detailed plan of OS 33 was prepared at the time of the excavation (Fig. 11). These allow a discussion of the Romano-British landscape in the area.

Firstly, there are three major droveways which appear to converge on Dowse Farm (formerly Somerset House), approximately 500m south of Shell Bridge, one from the east, one from the north-east and one from the north (Fig. 11). The last of these crosses OS 46 to the south of the South Holland Main Drain, and continues north through OS 33, following the raised bed of a roddon. Excavations by the Central Excavation Unit in OS 46 (Bell, this volume) concluded from the distribution of surface finds that there was a settlement focus to the south, and work by J.C. Mossop over many years has accumulated a vast quantity of pottery in this area, mostly of second and third-century date (*J.Roman Stud.* 26 (1936), 248–9; Hallam S.J. 1960, 59–60; Phillips 1970, 309–10, Site 3416S).

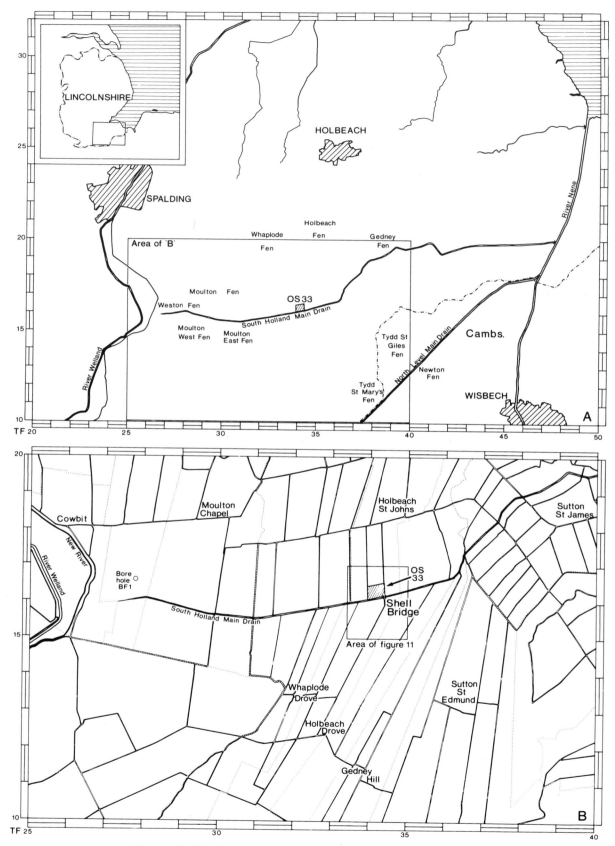

Figure 10 Site location. A; Scale 1:200,000. B; Scale 1:100,000

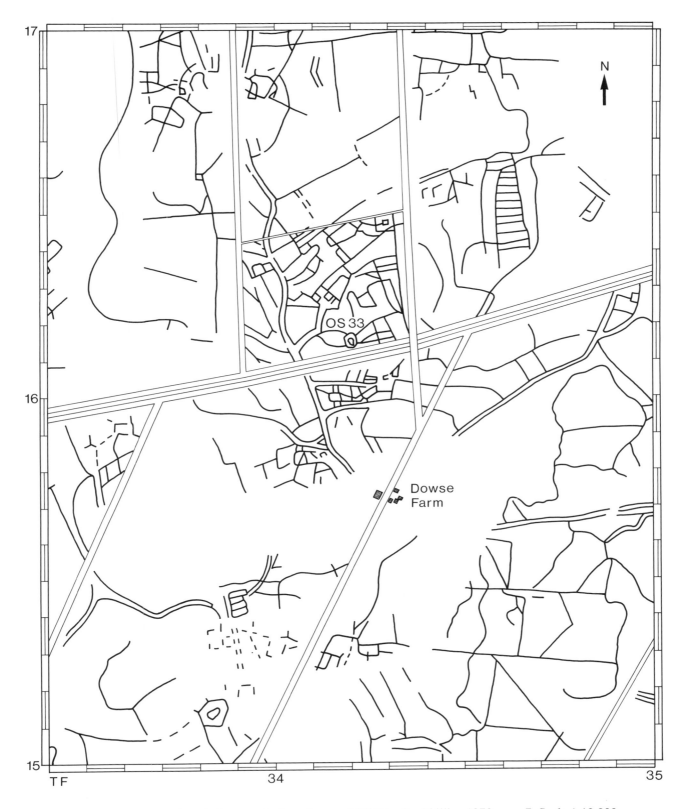

Figure 11 Earthworks/cropmarks in and around OS 33, after Phillips 1970, map 7. Scale 1:10,000

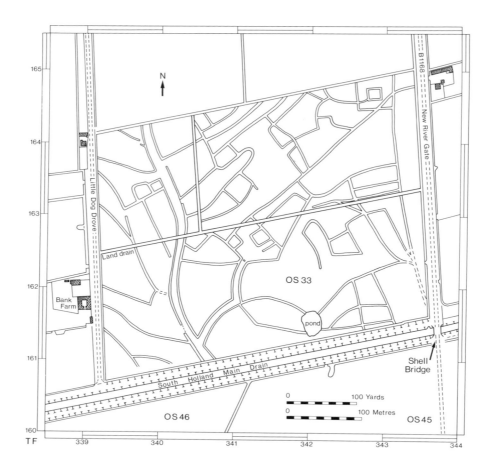

Figure 12 The earthworks in OS 33. Scale 1:5000

Secondly, there are shorter side-droves linked to the main droveways. In OS 33, one of these leads to a pentagonal enclosure, the south-western part of which contains two small square enclosures, an area in which there were industrial activities, and almost certainly occupation of a domestic character as well (see Section III, Site B West).

Thirdly, the rest of OS 33 is covered by a network of ditched enclosures or fields. There is little, if any, regularity in the layout of these, and there are small squarish and subrectangular enclosures, a few longer narrower enclosures, and larger irregular areas. In the north-east corner of the field, a ?square enclosure with a smaller square enclosure apparently central within it cuts, or is cut by, a curving ditch on its west side, and by a second ditch on both its south and east sides. The second ditch is long and straight, running for some 330m from the north-east corner of the field to the centre, where it forms the north side of a large pentagonal enclosure, part of which was excavated (see Section III, Site B West). The relationship between the square enclosure and this ditch is, however, unknown.

With the exceptions of the Enclosure ditch on Site B West and the droveway (Site A), none of the features which survived as earthworks or show as cropmarks (Fig. 13) were excavated. No overall site plan showing the excavated areas within the earthworks was prepared, but it has been possible to position the excavated plans within the earthworks plan with sufficient accuracy for unexcavated linear features to be added to plans where

they would not otherwise have appeared. On Figure 17 and subsequent plans, the unexcavated linear features around the excavated areas are shown with solid edges and stipple.

Geology, topography and soils
(Fig. 13)

The site is situated in an area of reclaimed marine alluvium, level except for ridges marking the courses of former creeks. The soils belong to the Wallasea 2 soil association, and are deep stoneless clayey soils, calcareous in places, with some deep calcareous silty soils (Hodge *et al.* 1984, 338–341).

During the excavations, some attempt was made to examine the soils of the area; five test pits were excavated to provide soil profiles to a depth of approximately one metre below the field surface, soil descriptions were made for seven areas of the field, presumably where there were distinctive variations in soil texture or colour, and an auger hole was sunk to a depth of nearly five metres. The details of these are as follows:-

Soil profiles
(Fig. 13)

1. 0–30cm   very highly organic silty loam
    30–76cm   less organic, brick rubble at 61cm
    76–91cm   heavy sandy loam
    91cm+   sandy clay loam
2. 0–30cm   crumbly organic clay loam
    30–61cm   organic clay
    61–91cm   compact clay, rusty at 91cm
3. 0–30cm   crumbly organic clay; 15–30cm more compact
    30–76cm   silty clay loam

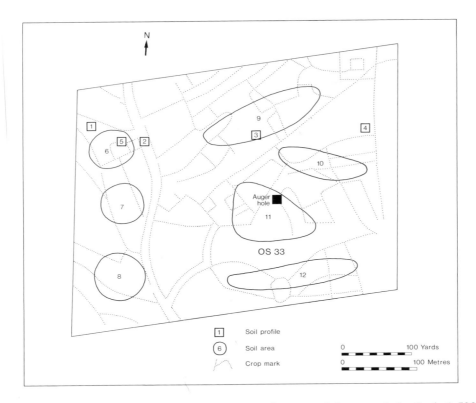

Figure 13 The positions of the soil profiles, the soil areas and the auger hole. Scale 1:5000

	76–91cm	silt loam changing to sandy loam
4.	0–20cm	very light, very fine sandy loam
	20–91cm	loamy very fine sand
5.	0–46cm	very highly organic silty loam with 'drummy' particles
	46–91cm	silty clay loam
	91–137cm	heavy clay, rusty

Soil areas
(Fig. 13)

6.	silty clay loam
7.	very fine sandy loam
8.	silty loam
9.	very fine sandy loam
10.	silty loam
11.	silt loam; highly organic
12.	silty clay loam; organic

Auger hole
(Fig. 13)

0–91cm	(layer 1)	topsoil
91–213cm	(layer 2)	yellow silt
213–442cm	(layer 3)	clean grey silt
442–447cm	(layer 4)	peat
447–488cm	(layer 5)	fine grey smooth silt

The interpretation of this data is not without its problems, although some tentative deductions may be suggested. Firstly, the depth of topsoil varies considerably, from 20cm in Profile 4 to 91cm in the Auger Hole; the Auger Hole was in an area of highly organic silt loam (Soil Area 11), so perhaps this was a peaty hollow. Secondly, Profile 2 was in the centre of the droveway, and an organic clay was reached at 30cm. The droveway follows the raised bed of a roddon (see Droveway 31, OS 46, this volume), and perhaps significantly, the soil areas which were planned do not infringe upon the droveway as it crosses the field. Thirdly, the fact that apparently discrete soil areas were defined suggests both changes in relief across the field, and also changes in soils, with roddon silts giving place laterally to other soils and peaty hollows.

Fourthly, there are the deposits in the Auger Hole to be considered. Below the ploughsoil (layer *1*), three layers of silt were found (layers *2*, *3* and *5*), the lower two of which were separated by a peat deposit *c*. 5cm thick (layer *4*). This peat layer contained abundant *Juncus* seeds and *Foraminifera*, suggesting brackish conditions, although no pollen were recorded (see report by the late Professor Godwin, Section V below).

This peat layer is likely to be the equivalent of the Lower Peat, that is, the peat deposit which began forming before 6000bp and the growth of which terminated about 4500bp (Evans and Mostyn 1979, 23). A second possibility, although less likely, is that this peat layer is part of the Upper Peat which divides the Barroway Drove Beds from Iron Age and Romano-British deposits (Terrington Beds). Both the Upper and Lower Peat band show considerable variation in height OD, the Upper Peat ranging from about +2m OD to -1m OD. The Lower Peat exhibits a similar amplitude. However, the present ground level of OS 33, probably between 1.8 and 2.4m OD (6–8ft) suggests that layer *4* is at least -2m OD, and this is too low for it to be the Upper Peat. The Upper Peat is also generally a thicker deposit than that recorded here. Seaward, the thin peat band of the Lower Peat is often discontinuous, either thinning out or absent, probably due to erosion (Evans and Mostyn 1979, 16 and figs 9–10).

Layer *4* in the Auger Hole is therefore likely to be part of the Lower Peat, formed contemporaneously with similar deposits at Wiggenhall and between Murrow and Leverington (Evans and Mostyn 1979, fig. 6).

A borehole at Weston Fen (BF1; Fig. 10B) *c*. 6.5km due west of Shell Bridge should also be noted. Three peat layers were recorded here, the uppermost of which was at -2.66 to -2.76m OD; the pollen were predominantly of aquatic plants suggesting freshwater conditions (see for full details Smith 1970, 153–4 and 160).

25

Plate XVII Holbeach St Johns; spade-marks on the surface of the subsoil, suggesting a former peat cover

It is possible too that this area once had a surface peat cover. After the removal of the topsoil, Greenfield apparently found spade-marks on the surface of the clay subsoil (Pl. XVII). This is mentioned by Hallam S.J. (1970, 26), but was not recorded in the site notebooks. Hallam goes on to suggest that there was post-Roman peat formation in the area, filling the ditches and channels of the Romano-British landscape (see for example the section across the Enclosure ditch; Fig. 24) and also lower-lying hollows. In OS 46 (Bell, this volume), the peaty upper fill of a Roman ditch gave a radiocarbon date of 397–562 cal AD (Appendix; HAR 6364). It seems probable that this was largely removed during the medieval period for fuel, the remnants being dispersed by dessication and oxidation after reclamation (Hallam S.J. 1970, 27).

III. The Excavations
(Figs 14–27; Pls XVIII–XXIV)

Introduction
(Figs 14, 15)
Given the complexities of the site, the surviving records provide a relatively clear picture of the excavations. It is however obvious from the site notes that in 1961, features like those excavated at Shell Bridge, with industrial debris or briquetage, were little understood, and it remained uncertain throughout the excavations whether the briquetage was being manufactured on the site, or if it was being used to process some other substance. Inevitably, this has led to problems in post-excavation analysis, and important questions which might have been answered by problem-orientated excavation or more comprehensive recording or sampling, have been left unresolved.

The basic records of the excavations consist of the site notebooks, and a series of plans and sections. The notebooks contain little detailed information, and details of features and their fills have had to be extrapolated from the drawings. The plans of different areas of the site, drawn at various scales and on different alignments were measured in from a fixed grid, but it has not been possible to reconstruct this grid; it was however possible to position the test-pits accurately within the excavated areas, and from this, to position the excavated trench plans, as these also showed the positions of a number of test-pits. The plans of the trenches additionally fail to show the positions of the larger features (not excavated) around them which must have survived as earthworks at the time of the excavation, and these too have had to be added by positioning the excavated trenches within the larger plan of the earthworks over the whole field. This seems to have been reasonably successful; while precise accuracy is not claimed, it is estimated that the excavated trenches have been positioned to an accuracy of ± 5 metres, with an error in orientation of ± 10°.

In the following description of the excavated areas, features and layers are described as fully as possible. Basic soil descriptions of the layers and feature fills were noted on the drawn sections, and the conventions used on the published sections for layers and features are shown on Figure 14.

The excavated areas within OS 33 consist of Site A and Site B (Fig. 15). Site A lies in the north-west corner of the field. Site B in the centre of the field is divided into Site B West and Site B East. The former area continued a small trench by Mossop, while the latter continued the excavation of a feature which had been partly excavated by Mayes. The positions of Site A and Site B within OS 33 are shown on Figure 15, and the division of Site B into Site B West and Site B East on Figure 19.

Site A
(Figs 13–18)

Introduction
(Figs 13, 15)
Site A in the north-west corner of the field was partly excavated by Mayes in 1960, this area being completed by Greenfield in 1961. The farmer, Mr Robinson, had ploughed a strip of land in this part of the field to lay a drain, and in doing so ploughed up a large quantity of pottery. Test pits were dug over this area, and on the basis of the findings, three trenches were excavated, two over features exposed in the test pits and a third across the adjacent droveway.

This corner of the field was the highest area of the field, just west of the main north to south droveway which follows the raised bed of a roddon across the western part of the field. The soil here appears to have been a silty clay loam (Soil Area 6; Fig. 13).

The area of Site A includes part of the main droveway, and there was an entrance from the droveway to the west into a tapering side-drove or perhaps a triangular enclosure. On the southern side of this side-drove or enclosure there were two small adjacent square ditched enclosures, similar to those on Site B West (see below). To the east of Site A, an entrance opposite that into the side-drove or enclosure to the west of the droveway appears to have led into a large square ditched enclosure or field.

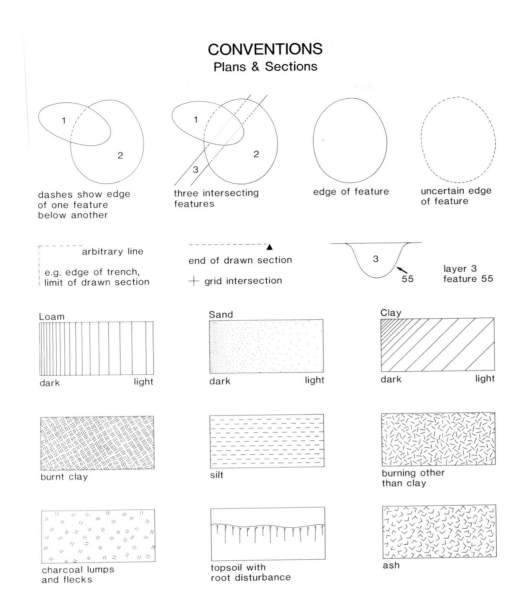

CONVENTIONS
Plans & Sections

dashes show edge
of one feature
below another

three intersecting
features

edge of feature

uncertain edge
of feature

arbitrary line

e.g. edge of trench,
limit of drawn section

end of drawn section

+ grid intersection

layer 3
feature 55

Loam

dark   light

Sand

dark   light

Clay

dark   light

burnt clay

silt

burning other
than clay

charcoal lumps
and flecks

topsoil with
root disturbance

ash

Figure 14 OS 33: plan and section conventions

The test-pit survey
(Figs 15, 16)

Seventy-five test-pits were excavated in various parts of the side-drove or enclosure to the west of the droveway, and two lines of test-pits were excavated along the droveway itself. The latter produced few finds, in only a single test-pit, the rest being devoid of finds. The test-pits to the west, in the area of the two small enclosures, suggested a concentration of occupation debris in a discrete area in the narrow gap between the north sides of the two small enclosures and the north side of the larger side-drove or enclosure. Surface finds suggest a second area of occupation debris just north of this (Fig. 15).

The main concentration of finds seems to have been coincident with a dark soil mark. One of the test-pits (No. 269; Fig. 16) seemed to be above a feature, and this was subsequently expanded into a larger trench (see The 'Hut', below). The finds from the test-pit survey on Site A are not extant, and there are no detailed records of this survey.

The 'Hut'
(Figs 16, 17)

This was the feature exposed in the base of test-pit 269 (Fig. 16). Removal of the ploughsoil (c. 30cm deep at this point) exposed the west side of an oval or subrectangular hollow dug into compact silt loam to a depth of c. 45cm in the centre. The feature does not seem to have had a clearly defined edge, the base of the feature sloping gradually up from the deepest point to the base of the ploughsoil on all sides. The fill included a layer of ash, c. 12–15cm thick in the centre of the feature, thinning towards the edges. Around the perimeter of the hollow, shallow post-holes (c. 5–7cm deep) were noted, but not planned. On the west side of the feature, a cluster of brick and stone was found, and this was described as a 'hearth'. Finds included wood and bark of grey poplar, black poplar or aspen, ash, slag, pottery, a quern fragment and fragments of brick and stone.

The main trench over the 'Hut' was extended to the south, and a section was dug through the north ditch of the

Figure 15 The positions of Site A and Site B within OS 33. Also shown are other areas of 'occupation' suggested by field survey (after Greenfield). Scale 1:5000

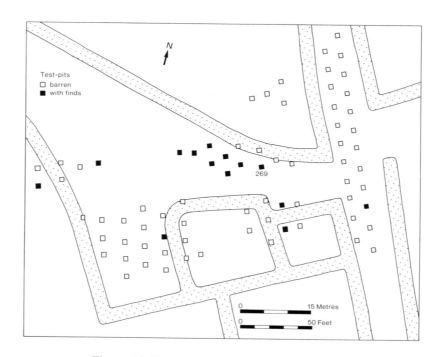

Figure 16 Site A; the test-pit survey. Scale 1:800

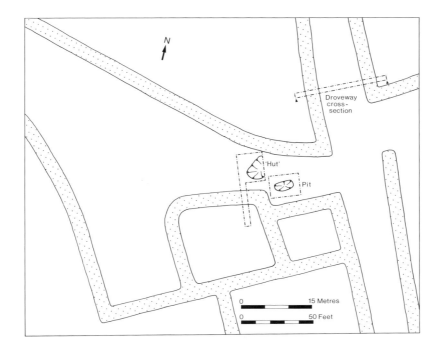

Figure 17 Site A; the positions of the 'hut', the pit and the droveway cross-section. Scale 1:800.

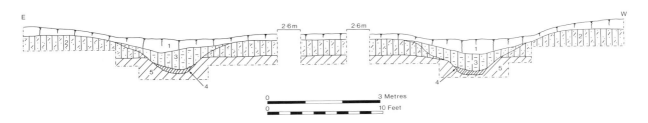

Figure 18 Site A; the droveway cross-section. Scale 1:100

western enclosure. No details are given of this, but it was shown to be of Roman date.

The Pit
(Fig. 17)
A large pit to the south-east of the hut was totally excavated, this being started by Mayes and completed by Greenfield. In shape it was roughly oval, with dimensions of *c*. 3.80m east to west by *c*. 2.13m north to south. The sides of the feature sloped gently to a roughly pointed base in the centre of the feature, its depth at this point being *c*. 61cm below the level of the compact silt loam subsoil. No details of its fill or finds were recorded.

The Droveway
(Figs 17, 18)
A trench *c*. 60cm wide and *c*. 20m long was dug across the droveway just north of the opposed entrances into the enclosures on either side of the droveway (Fig. 17). The section (Fig. 18) shows that the droveway ditches were *c*. 3m wide and *c*. 90cm deep, being dug through a layer of organic clay loam (layer *2*) overlying rusty blue clay (layer *5*) (see also Soil Profile 2, above). The width of the

droveway between the ditches was *c*. 14m. The fills of the droveway ditches on each side were identical, with a basal fill of brown clay with rusty particles (layer *4*) probably similar to the lower gleyed silt fill of Droveway 58 in OS 46 (Bell, this volume). The upper fill of the ditches was a grey silt loam (layer *3*).

It is also possible that part, if not all, of the droveway was fenced as well as ditched. On an aerial photograph of the site after ploughing (Wilson 1982, pl. 21), narrow dark lines fringe the ditches on either side of the droveway in the southern part of the field, and the most probable explanation of these is that they represent fence-lines.

Site B West
(Figs 19–24; Pls XVIII–XXIII)

Introduction
(Figs 15, 19, 23)
Site B West was the main focus of the excavations by Greenfield in 1961, this being an area in the centre of the field which had not been ploughed. This area was occupied by a large pentagonal enclosure, its long axis aligned north-east to south-west, and this was linked to the main

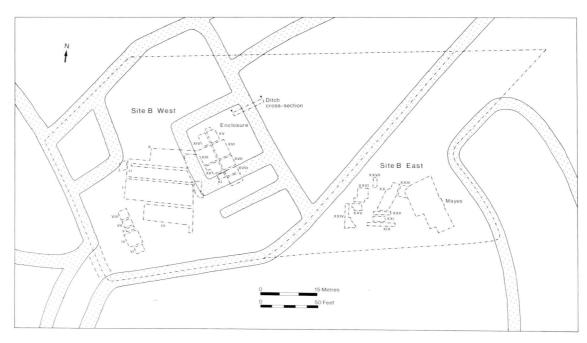

Figure 19 Site B; the excavated areas within Site B West and Site B East. The trenches excavated by Greenfield have Roman numerals; the area excavated by Mayes is also shown. Scale 1:1000

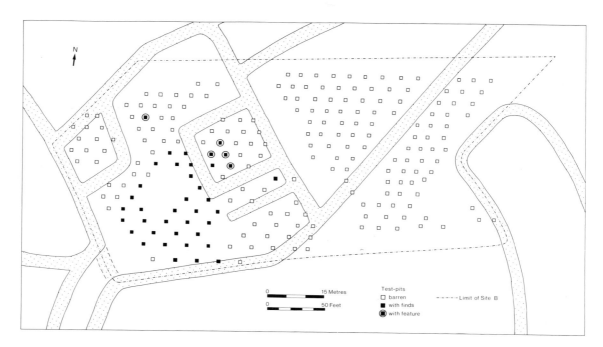

Figure 20 Site B; the test-pit survey. Scale 1:1000

north to south droveway by a side-drove (Fig. 15). The pentagonal enclosure had a number of subdivisions. Firstly, it was divided into two by a north-west to south-east ditch, and this was sectioned (see the 'Ditch cross-section'; Figs 19, 23). Secondly, the area to the north of this ditch, partly within the area of Site B (Fig. 15) was divided into a subrectangular and an L-shaped area by an L-shaped ditch. Thirdly, the area to the south of the ditch which bisects the enclosure, virtually all within the limits of Site B (Figs 15–19) contained two small square enclosures. That to the west had as its north-west and south-west sides parts of the ditches of the larger pentagonal enclosure, while its north-east and south-east sides were formed by an L-shaped ditch. These ditches enclosed an area roughly square in shape, and measuring *c.* 13m by 13m. That to the east had as its north-east side part of the ditch which bisected the large pentagonal enclosure, with its other sides formed by a U-shaped ditch enclosing an area measuring *c.* 15m by 17.5m. This second, eastern square enclosure was partly excavated, and throughout the report it is referred to as the Enclosure, and labelled thus on all appropriate plans (Fig. 21 and following figures).

The site was first surveyed by a series of test-pits (Fig. 20). In the area between the two small square enclosures, two groups of trenches were excavated, IV to VIII and I, II, III and X (Fig. 19). The ditch of the Enclosure was sectioned at three places, and part of the interior of the Enclosure was excavated (Trenches XII to XVII; Fig. 20). These will be described in turn.

The Test-Pit Survey
(Fig. 20)
Two hundred and twenty-seven test-pits were excavated on Site B. Of these, 188 were blank, thirty-four produced finds, and five produced evidence of underlying features.

All of the test-pits with finds were in the western part of the site, either within the Enclosure, or in the area between the Enclosure and the entrance into the side-drove leading off to the south-west. This side-drove joins the main north to south droveway. The test-pits in the eastern part of the site produced neither finds nor evidence of features.

Five test-pits produced evidence of features. Four of these were within the Enclosure, on its western side, and excavation later showed that there was a large irregular hollow in this area (see Trenches XII to XVII, Feature 8, below). The eastern half of the Enclosure produced no evidence of finds or features, and this area was not excavated.

Trenches IV to VIII
(Figs 21, 22; Pl. XVIII)
The main feature in these trenches was a north-west to south-east ditch, *F1*, *c.* 1.90m wide, *c.* 60cm deep with a U-shaped profile (Fig. 22, Section 4). The base of the feature was cut by a large number of stake-holes.

Three other linear features ran at right angles to, and probably cut, *F1* (Pl. XVIII). *F2* was *c.* 1.0m wide and *c.* 60cm deep, and it had a steep U-shaped profile and a flat base. It was filled with a clay loam with some briquetage. *F2* probably continued to the north-east, and may well be the linear feature which crossed Trenches III and I, and which ran through a small unnumbered trench at the south-west corner of the Enclosure.

Plate XVIII Holbeach St Johns, OS 33; Site B West, Trenches IV–VIII, looking north-west along *F1*

Virtually all of the finds from *F1* came from layer *4*. These included animal bones, shells, slag and pottery of late second to early third century date (catalogue Nos 116, 146, 149, 151 and 159). Briquetage from the feature includes vessel fragments (catalogue Nos 2, 4, 9 and 13), seats (15–18), a bridge (26), props or supports (31–36, 38) and a tapered bar or handle (40). The amount of briquetage recovered from this area (69% of the total site assemblage by weight) suggests that it was used either in, or in close proximity to *F1*.

Trenches I, II, III and X
(Fig. 21; Fig. 22, Section 7; Pl. XIX)
This was the area where an earlier trench had been excavated by Mossop (Pl. XIX). Apart from the position of this trench (Fig. 22) no details are known.

The main feature in this area was *F32*, an irregular hollow filled with layers of ashy loam and briquetage. To the south-east of *F32*, *F2* (previously described in Trench IV) ran from the south edge of Trench III to the south-west corner of the Enclosure. The relationship between these features is not recorded, although in plan the Enclosure ditch appears to cut *F2*. In an extension at the south-east corner of Trench III, a short length of ditch *F3* may have been part of a feature running parallel to *F2*.

The irregular hollow *F32* appeared to be cut by an east to west ditch *F31*, and this was also shown as cutting the Enclosure ditch. The fills of *F31* appear obliquely at the east end of Section 7 (Fig. 22). Above *F32*, ditch *F31* narrowed and it seemed to butt at the western edge of *F32*. To the east of *F32* there were two small pits, *F39* and *F40*, and also small patches of fired clay or briquetage. To the north of *F32*, two east to west ditches were exposed, *F12* and *F34*. Running into *F32* from the west was *F33*, and to

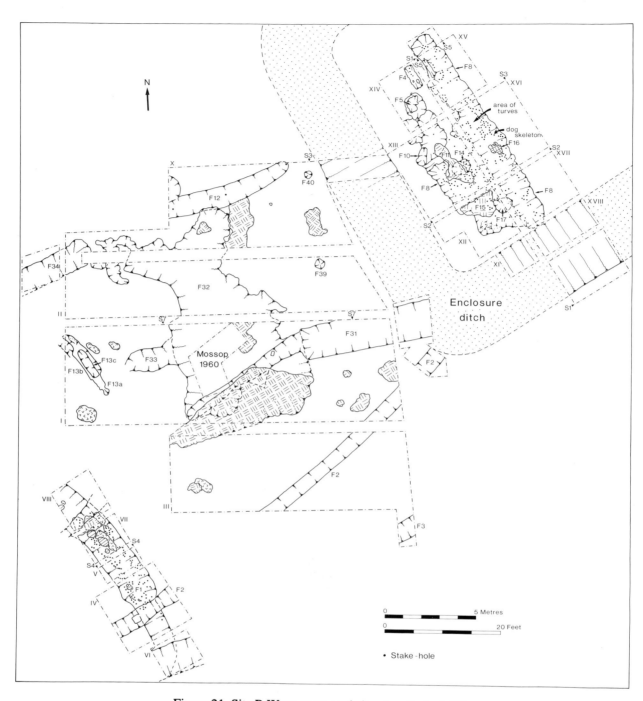

Figure 21 Site B West; excavated site plan. Scale 1:200

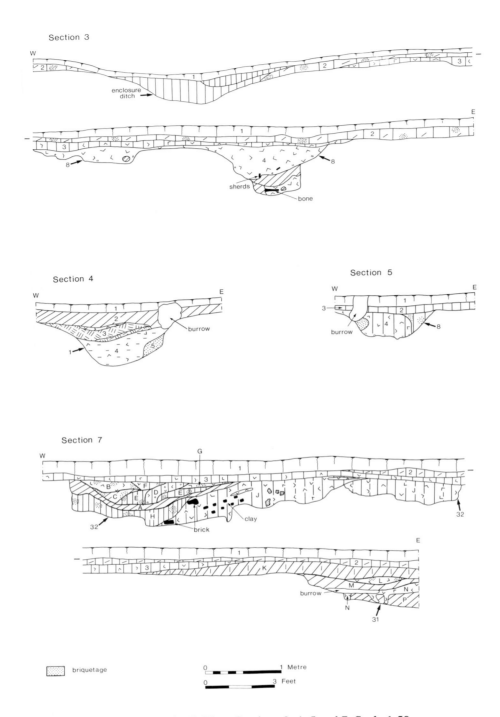

Section 3

Section 4

Section 5

Section 7

briquetage

0   1 Metre

0   3 Feet

Figure 22 Site B West; Sections 3, 4, 5 and 7. Scale 1:50

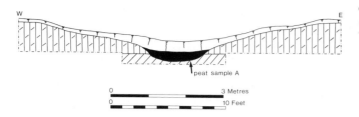

peat sample A

| 0 | | | 3 Metres |
| 0 | | | 10 Feet |

Figure 23 Site B West; the ditch cross-section.
Scale 1:100

the west of this there was a possible hearth-like feature (*F13*). The section across *F32* (Fig. 22, Section 7) shows that most of the feature was filled with a layer of ashy loam, with briquetage fragments and lumps of raw clay (layer *J*). On the west side of the feature (at the west end of Section 7) there is a possible recut, filled with layers *A-H*, mostly ashy loams with briquetage. Layer *A*, clay, may have been redeposited upcast from another feature. At the east end of Section 7, there is also an oblique section through part of *F31*. The fills of *F31* (layers *L, M, N* and *P*) were overlain by a thick clay layer (layer *K*), and this too might be upcast, possibly from *F32* to the west.

The plan by Greenfield (Fig. 21) appears to show *F31* cutting both *F32* and the Enclosure ditch. Details of these relationships are lacking, but it is possible to argue that *F31* was unlikely to have cut the Enclosure ditch; Layer *K* which sealed the upper fills of *F31* was overlain in part by layer *3*, an ashy loam, and this layer (which also overlay the upper fills of both *F8* and *F32*) appears to have been removed by the Enclosure ditch (Fig. 22, Section 3; Fig. 24, Section 1). This suggests that when the Enclosure ditch was excavated, not only were Features *8* and *32* totally filled in, but layer *3* had also formed over much of this area of the site, overlying the uppermost fills of the features, and masking even subtle undulations of the site surface where upcast from features stood slightly proud (Fig. 22, Section 7; Fig. 24, Section 2). It seems unlikely that *F31* could have cut the Enclosure ditch as shown on the plan, and if layer *K* (Fig. 22, Section 7) was also upcast, then this perhaps came from *F32* which might therefore have been the later of the two. In summary, the evidence suggests that the Enclosure ditch was excavated at a time when Features *8, 31* and *32* were totally filled in, and therefore belongs to a second phase of occupation.

The finds from this area of the site include a high percentage of the samian sherds recovered (catalogue Nos 28–34 and 36–42), the only sherd of mortarium to be found (No. 51), and the single coin of AD 180–192. The distribution of the samian sherds is concentrated in Trench I, and there are joining sherds across this area, and joining sherds from outside and inside the Enclosure. In contrast, more than 80% by weight of the other pottery recovered came from within the Enclosure.

Little briquetage seems to have been recovered from this area of the site; there are vessel fragments from Trenches I and X, and 'truncated pyramidical stilts' were noted in Trenches I and III. In general there seems to have been much less briquetage in this area than in Trenches IV to VIII to the south-west.

Other finds from this area include: a Colchester derivative brooch (catalogue No. 3) AD 75–150/175 (*F2*); a large deep vertical-sided bowl (No. 115) and a

cheese-press lid (No. 127) from *F13*; Antonine samian (catalogue No. 34) and jar No. 154 from *F31;* Trajanic/Hadrianic samian (No. 42) and Antonine samian (Nos 31, 36, 37), lead-glazed bowl (No. 109; found on Mossop's spoil heap, but almost certainly from this feature) and two bone pin fragments (Nos 51–52), all from *F32*.

The Enclosure Ditch
(Fig. 21; Fig. 22, Section 3; Fig. 23; Fig. 24, Section 1; Pl. XX)
The Enclosure measured internally *c.* 17.5m north-east to south-west and *c.* 15.0m north-west to south-east. In shape it was subrectangular, and its north-east side was part of a longer ditch, aligned north-west to south-east, which bisected a larger pentagonal enclosure.

The Enclosure ditch was sectioned in three places:-
1. Between Trenches X and XIII (Fig. 22, Section 3; Pl. XX). This section across the ditch linked Trench X outside the Enclosure to Trench XIII inside, and was a slightly oblique cutting through the south-west side of the Enclosure. The ditch here seems to have been *c.* 2.0m wide and *c.* 50cm deep. The fill of the ditch was probably a loam.
2. Trenches XI and XVIII, and an unnumbered trench to the south of XVIII. This was a cutting through the south-east side of the Enclosure, and this appears at the south end of Section 1 (Fig. 24). The Enclosure ditch here was *c.* 4.0m wide and *c.* 65cm deep, with gently sloping sides and a rounded base. The main fill was a loam. The presence of the Enclosure ditch is here indicated by a depression on the surface of the site; the ground surface above the centre of the ditch was *c.* 30cm lower than that on either side of the ditch.
3. The 'ditch cross-section'. This was a cutting through the north-east side of the Enclosure. The section here (Fig. 23) shows a very wide ditch, *c.* 7m across and *c.* 1m deep, with very gently sloping sides and a U-shaped central depression filled with peat. Peat Sample A from this layer contained pollen suggesting freshwater conditions, the presence of some woodland (by no means continuous or widespread) and local arable cultivation. There are also indications of local swamp or Fen development, and perhaps also of heathland in the neighbourhood (see report by the late Professor Godwin, Section V, below).

The sections across the Enclosure ditch (Fig. 22, Section 3; Fig. 24, Section 1) show that a widespread layer of ashy loam (layer *3*) which overlay the uppermost fills of several other features (*e.g. F8, F32*; Sections 1 and 7) did not overlie the Enclosure ditch. It seems likely that the excavation of the ditch removed this layer, and consequently the Enclosure ditch probably belonged to a later phase of occupation than the other features which were exposed. The only feature which in plan (Fig. 21) appears to cut the Enclosure ditch is *F31*, but it has previously been suggested that this apparent relationship may be incorrect. Greenfield was certainly of the opinion that the droveways and enclosures which covered the area were later in date than the phase of industrial activity, represented by features and hollows with numerous stake-holes and with briquetage and large quantities of occupation debris in their fills, although no detailed supporting evidence for this was given.

Plate XIX Holbeach St Johns, OS 33; Site B West, Trenches I, II and XX, looking north-west across *F32*.
The straight edges on the right-hand side of the feature are the edges of Mossop's trench

Plate XX Holbeach St Johns, OS 33; Site B West, *F8* looking north-west.
Note also the section across the enclosure ditch on the left

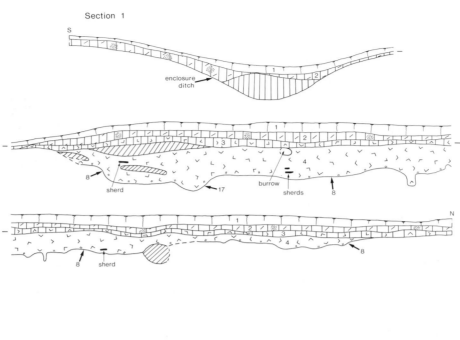

Section 1

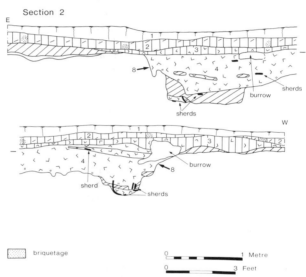

Section 2

briquetage

0   1 Metre

0   3 Feet

Figure 24 Site B West; Sections 1 and 2. Scale 1:50

No finds were recovered from the Enclosure ditch. If this feature had been open contemporaneously with *F8* for example, which was full of pottery, some finds would surely have found their way into the Enclosure ditch. It seems likely however that the Enclosure ditch was excavated when *F8* and other features were not only totally filled in, but when they were also sealed by layer *3*, the widespread layer of ashy loam. It is, however, still surprising that no residual material found its way into the Enclosure ditch.

Trenches XII to XVII
(Figs 21, 24; Sections 1–2; Pls XX–XXIII)
The main feature in this area, inside, but probably earlier than, the Enclosure, was *F8*, an irregular hollow running

parallel to the south-west side of the Enclosure for most of its length.

The base of *F8* was cut by a large number of stake-holes (Pls XX–XXII), similar to those in *F1* (Trenches IV to VIII, above). There were also a number of features either cutting the base of *F8* or its fills. *F5* was a pit (Pl. XXIII), *F10* was described as a post-hole cutting the natural clay in the base of *F8*, while *F11* was a layer of briquetage among the upper fills of *F8*. *F14* was a hollow in the base of *F8*, *F15* was a briquetage deposit at the same level as *F11*, *F16* was described as a hearth, perhaps associated with the briquetage deposits, and *F17* was a hollow in the base of the feature (Fig. 24, Section 1). *F4*, the only feature outside *F8*, was a pit to the west of and parallel to the northernmost part of *F8* (Trench XIV) (Pl. XXIII).

Plate XXI Holbeach St Johns, OS 33; Site B West, Trench XIII. Part of *F8,* looking north-east

Plate XXII Holbeach St Johns, OS 33; Site B West,
Trench XVII. Close-up of stake-holes in *F8*

Plate XXIII Holbeach St Johns, OS 33; Site B West,
Trench XI, looking south-east. *F4* is in the left
foreground and *F5* in the right background

Finds

Little samian ware was recovered from this area, only five sherds representing three vessels (catalogue Nos 35, 42, 43), of Trajanic-Hadrianic to Antonine date. More than 80 per cent by weight of the other pottery came from within the Enclosure. This includes the mica-dusted platter (catalogue No. 108) and a large group of vessels dating to the period mid-second to early third century (catalogue Nos 111, 113, 115, 117, 119–123, 125–6, 128–131, 133–8, 140, 142–5, 147–8, 150, 155–7, 160 and 161). Compared to *F1* in Trenches IV to VIII and *F55* on Site B East, very little briquetage was recovered from this area.

Other finds include: an Aesica brooch (catalogue No. 4) AD 60–75; four copper alloy needles (Nos 5–8) and four bone pins (Nos 47–50) from *F8*; the skeleton of a dog from the base of this feature on the east side of Trench XVI (Fig. 21); and pottery (Nos 131 and 134) from *F17*.

Site B East
(Figs 25–27; Pls XXIV–XXV)

Introduction

Excavation by Philip Mayes and the Boston Archaeological Group in 1960 on Site B East centred on an area where there was a pronounced concentration of brick (or ?briquetage) on the field surface. Three features were exposed, referred to as Salterns I, II and III. Work on Saltern I was continued by Greenfield in 1961 (*F55*). A number of other non-linear features were also excavated.

The limits of Site B East and the excavated areas are shown on Figure 20. The excavations fell within an area where the soil was described as a highly organic silt loam (Soil Area 11; Fig. 13).

Saltern I
(Figs 25–26; Fig. 27, Section 8)

This was a broad shallow linear feature, orientated south-east to north-west. The feature was traced from an irregular butt in the south-east corner of the trench for a distance of *c.* 13m to the north-west edge of the excavation. Later work by Greenfield showed that this feature continued beyond Mayes' trench, and that it formed part of a large U-shaped feature (see *F55* below and Fig. 25).

The area between the butt and Section 8 will be described first. Here the feature was *c.* 3m wide and it had a maximum depth of *c.* 24cm, with very shallow sloping sides at the edges, and a slightly deeper central depression (Fig. 27, Section 8). This had been dug into compact silt loam, and the hollow was lined with a thick layer of blue clay. The fill was dominated by brick debris (?briquetage) and ash, the latter particularly at the butt. The butt was described by Mayes as a 'stoke-hole'.

The site notes suggest that three lines of briquetage supports ran along Saltern I, a line on each side of the slightly deeper central depression, and a line in the centre of the feature. Three of these supports appear on the plan (Fig. 26) and on the section (Fig. 27, Section 8). In plan the outer supports seem to be *c.* 89cm apart, although the section suggests a distance of *c.* 110cm between them; this inconsistency cannot be reconciled. It was also noted that the central support stood upon a ridge of baked clay, but this is not on the drawn section.

The central support appears to have been a simple cylindrical pedestal, while the outer supports were

carefully shaped, with a concave surface at the base (which was pressed into the blue clay lining) and a right-angled notch at the top, facing towards the centre of the feature. These supports were not among the material available for study, but a possible drawing of a shaped support, based on a description of the objects in the site notes, is illustrated (Fig. 43A). Mayes considered that these were supports for a large trough-like container, and if this was the case, then it seems probable that the shaped supports were designed to fit the ends or sides of the container (for further discussion of these, see Classification of the Briquetage, below).

North-west of Section 8, the base of the feature appears to divide into two shallow gullies, with perhaps a low ridge between them. The northern gully seems to be cut by two shallow rectangular hollows. The gullies fade out towards the edge of the area excavated by Mayes, to be replaced by a single hollow in the base of the feature in the last three metres of Saltern I before the section. On the south side there appears to be a slight ledge *c.* 50cm wide, on which was a U-shaped group of five stake-holes. These were oval in shape, measuring *c.* 7cm by 11cm. It is recorded that these were dug into the blue clay lining of the feature.

According to the site notes, no pottery was found in Saltern I, finds being animal bones (mostly cattle and horse) and briquetage. The detailed plan of Saltern I (Fig. 26) shows many fragments of flat slabs or bricks. It was also noted that the supports and vessel fragments were coated with a 'glaze', presumably the distinctive surface vitrification frequently encountered on objects splashed with brine and subjected to heat. It is possible that the Colchester brooch (Fig. 28, No. 2), dated no later than AD 55/60, came from this feature.

Mayes interpreted Saltern I as a kiln- or hearth-like feature with a stoke-hole in the butt. On one plan, the central hollow to the south of Section 8 was marked as a 'flue'. Apart from the ashy fill, the only clear evidence of burning seems to have been the ridge of baked clay in the centre on which rested the central line of supports, although flecks of red burnt clay were noted 'on the surface of the working area', presumably the area around Saltern I. It is not recorded if the blue clay lining showed evidence of firing, or if it had been burnt or oxidised in the area of the butt or 'stoke-hole'. Information from Greenfield in *The Fenland in Roman Times* does include reference to 'trenches whose clay linings had been baked hard by heat' (Phillips 1970, 309; Site 3416N).

Feature 55
(Fig. 25; Fig. 27, Section 6; Pls XXIV–XXV)

This feature was a continuation of Saltern I (see above). Greenfield started excavation of this feature where Mayes had left off, placing Trench XXIII at the north-west limit of Mayes' trench. At this point, the two plans of the feature do not quite match up; where the two areas meet, the plan by Mayes shows the feature as *c.* 75cm wider than the feature shown by Greenfield.

In Trench XXIII, the drawn section across *F55* (Fig. 27, Section 6) has the following layers; layer *1*, topsoil; layer *2*, ?clay loam with briquetage fragments; layer *3* (the feature fill), ash and briquetage. At Section 6, *F55* was *c.* 1.80m wide and *c.* 20cm deep, with a wide flat base. The only finds were briquetage. Cut into the base of *F55* in Trench XXIII was *F56* (see below) and eleven stake-holes (Pl. XXIV).

Plate XXIV Holbeach St Johns, OS 33; Site B East, Trench XXIII looking north-west across *F55*.
F56 is visible in the base of *F55*, and much briquetage can be seen *in situ*

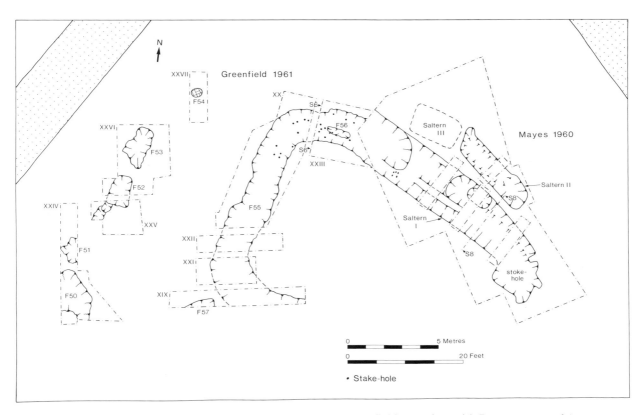

Figure 25 Site B East; plan of features exposed by Greenfield (trenches with Roman numerals)
and Salterns I, II and II by Mayes. Scale 1:200

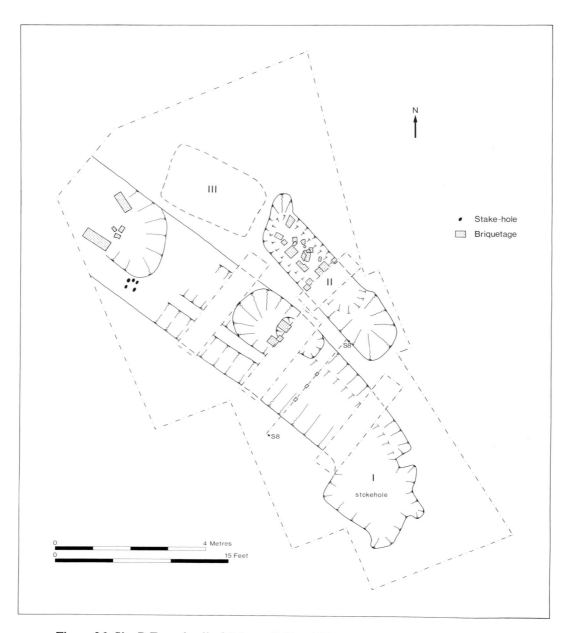

III

N

Stake-hole
Briquetage

II

S8

S8

I

stokehole

0   4 Metres
0   15 Feet

Figure 26 Site B East; detail of Salterns I, II and III excavated by Mayes. Scale 1:100

Plate XXV Holbeach St Jones, OS 33; Site B East, Trench XX, looking south along *F55*. The north-west corner of *F55* can be seen in the foreground

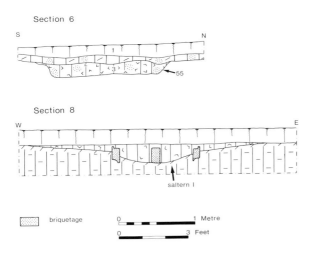

Figure 27 Site B East; Sections 6 and 8. Scale 1:50

In Trench XX, *F55* turned through a right angle, *c.* 15m from the butt and in this trench the feature was aligned north-west to south-east (Pl. XXV). This side of the feature was *c.* 10m long. At the north end of Trench XX, the base of *F55* was cut by ten stake-holes (Pl. XXV) like those in Trench XXIII.

In Trenches XXI and XIX, the feature turned through a second right angle, and while the feature was not traced beyond Trench XIX, it seems likely that this side of the feature ran parallel to the length of ditch exposed by Mayes. Greenfield described the feature as being U-shaped in plan, and there may have been a second butt opposite that in Mayes' trench. If this was the case, then the area enclosed by the feature would have been in the region of 12m (north-west to south-east) by 8m (north-east to south-west), with an entrance into this area from the south-east, between the two butts. The area enclosed by Saltern I/*F55* was not excavated, the excavated trenches following the line of the feature.

Saltern II
(Fig. 26)
Saltern II was a subrectangular feature, the southern edge of which was *c.* 50cm north of the north edge of Saltern I. Saltern II was approximately 1.40m wide and 5.0m long. The south-east end of the feature was the widest point, with a deeper slightly narrower section in the middle. At the north-west end, the butt had an irregular projection on one side. No section was drawn, but the plan suggests that the fill contained many pieces of briquetage, probably flat slabs or bricks (Pl. XXVI).

Saltern III
(Fig. 26)
Saltern III was a smaller subrectangular feature close to the north-west edge of Saltern II and the north-east edge of Saltern I. Its long axis was roughly parallel to Saltern I. It measured *c.* 2.60m long by *c.* 1.80m wide. This feature does not seem to have been excavated.

Other features
Feature 56 (Fig. 25): This feature was dug into the base of *F55* in Trench XXIII. It was *c.* 1.37m long, with an average width of *c.* 35cm, and a depth of *c.* 18cm. The sides of the feature sloped to a flattish base. The fill of the feature was a dark ashy soil with many fragments of briquetage.

Feature 54 (Fig. 25): The subsoil in Trench XXVII was covered by a scatter of briquetage, and within this, *F54* was a shallow saucer-shaped depression cut into the subsoil, with a diameter of *c.* 64cm, and a depth of *c.* 13cm. This was filled with briquetage and soil, with a layer of soot and charcoal at the base. The charcoal was from oak, hazel and poplar.

Features 50, 51, 52, 53 and 57; The 'clay pits'. (Fig. 25): These five features to the west of ditch *F55* were described by Greenfield as 'clay pits'. After the removal of the topsoil, these all showed up as irregular patches of soft buff-brown-red silt and ash with pieces of briquetage interspersed. They were all quite shallow (the maximum depth of the deepest feature (*F50*) was *c.* 23cm) and all had uneven bases. The fill of *F50* included briquetage, and charcoal from hazel and poplar.

IV. The Artefacts
(Figs 28–43; Pl. XXVI)

Introduction
In the following catalogues, the artefacts are primarily those recovered by Greenfield from Site B. The pottery from Site A excavated by Mayes is also included (samian Nos 1–27, mortaria Nos 44–50 and other pottery Nos 52–107). There are no records of finds other than pottery from Site A.

For the artefacts from Site B, endnotes give details of provenance when known in the following format: trench, layer, feature, finds no., small finds no., lab. no. where allocated, *e.g. XII, 4, F8 (HO 127), Bz 2, AML 610134* that is, Trench XII, *layer 4, Feature 8*, Finds No. 127 (preceded by the site finds code HO), small finds coding and number (Bronze (Copper Alloy) 2) and Ancient Monuments Laboratory Number (when allocated). All dates are AD unless otherwise indicated.

The coin
(not illustrated)
by R.A.G. Carson
1.　　As of Commodus. Illegible. 180–92. *III, 1 (HO 199), C1, AML 610289.*

Objects of copper alloy
(Fig. 28)

Brooches
by D.F. Mackreth
2.　　Colchester. Very little survives of this corroded brooch. The start of both the hook and the spring mark the type, otherwise only the smallest stubs of the wings are present and the lower bow, with the catch-plate, is missing. There is no trace of ornament and the corrosion has removed any evidence for faceting on the bow. *'Mayes' feature' (?Saltern I), (HO 128), Bz 3, AML 610371.*

Not enough is present to determine the sub-group this item should belong to, nor any feature which helps, specifically, to place it early or late in the general sequence of the type. Only the overall date-range for the Colchester can be offered: from the first decade to the fourth of the first century for its manufacture, and hardly more than ten to fifteen years beyond that as a survival-in-use, say, up to 55/60.

3.　　Colchester Derivative. Very badly corroded, only the details of one wing are clear. The pin was hinged, its axis bar mounted in wings of roughly circular section. At the end of the surviving wing are two sunken mouldings. The top of the bow is broad and has a median ridge which may have run to the foot. There is a shallow cut-out on each side a third or quarter of the way down and what appears to be a bordering ridge on each edge above that. The foot is hidden in accretions and, other than some of the median ridge, no decorative details can be seen below the cut-outs. *III, F2 (HO 126), Bz 1, AML 610165.*

This brooch does not belong, apparently, to any well-established sub-group. Possible parallels are few and a dated one from Camerton only has the broadest range: *c.* 90–200 (Wedlake 1958, 225, fig. 52, 22). The likely date-range is *c.* 75–150/175, but further specimens may help to narrow this down.

4.　　Aesica. Although heavily corroded, in addition to corrosion accretions and also partly split, the form is secure. The spring was once held in the Polden Hill manner: an axis bar passed through the coils and through pierced plates at the ends of the wings; the chord was held in a hole in the crest down the centre of the upper bow. The right hand wing appears to be plain. The bow tapers outwards towards the bottom and narrows suddenly to a constriction from which the fantail-shaped lower bow depends. The crest is carried down to the waist and has a deep

notch near the top, the rest may have had a beaded surface. On each side was a sunken moulding with another down the edge. There are faint traces of mouldings across the waist and the fantail is too badly damaged to reveal more than parts of a groove around its periphery. *XII, F8, 4 (HO 127), Bz 2, AML 610166.*

The full form can be restored so that the upper bow swept out to either side at the bottom to end in bosses. Mouldings across the centre can be paralleled on others of the type which remain largely unpublished (Alcester, excavations, C.M. Mahany; Chichester, excavations, A. Down). All seem to have ring-and-dot ornament on the fantail and one from *Durobrivae*, Cambs., (Peterborough Museum) is divided by grooves into three triangles each of which has the same circular motif. The state of the present specimen is such that, instead of mouldings, there may have been a 'beak' curling upwards (*e.g., Oxoniensia* 14 (1949) 10, fig. 2, 9). Either version is similar overall to the present piece, although the first is closer. The origins and initial date of the type have recently been discussed (Mackreth 1982) and the point is made there that dating of individual sub-groups is not well-established. No new information is available and it seems that the best estimate for this item should be before 75, but not necessarily before 60.

Other objects of copper alloy
5.　　Needle, with a groove above and below the eye on each side. The point is missing. Circular section. ?Third or fourth century. *XII, F8, 4 (HO 340), Bz 7, AML 610375.*
6.　　Needle, probably with a groove above and below the eye as No. 5. The eye and the point are missing. *XII, F8, 4 (HO 129), Bz 4, AML 610372.*
7.　　Lower part of needle. Circular section. *XII, F8, 4 (HO 130), Bz 5, AML 610373.*
8.　　Needle. Shaft fragment. Circular section. Corroded at each end. *XVI, F8, 5 (HO 326), Bz 6, AML 610374.*

Objects of iron
(not illustrated)
9–11.　　Three corroded nails were recovered.

Objects of stone
(Figs 28–29)
with petrological identifications by the late F.W. Anderson

Hone
(Fig. 28)
12.　　Two joining fragments. Very fine-grained micaceous sandstone. *XII, 1 (HO 198), St 16, AML 611314.*

Rubber
(Fig. 28)
13.　　Micaceous sandstone. *I, 1 (HO 103), St 5, AML 611303.*

Querns
(Fig. 29)
14.　　Not illustrated. Coarse sandstone. Sample of larger fragment. *I, 1 (HO 105), St 7, AML 611305.*
15.　　Not illustrated. Lava. Sample of larger fragment. *XII, 4 (HO 218), St 19, AML 611317.*
16.　　Not illustrated. Lava. Sample of larger fragment. *X, 2 (HO 378), St 32, AML 611330.*
17.　　Upper-stone fragment. Shelly limestone. *XV/XVI, 3 (HO 293), St 25, AML 611323.*
18.　　Upper-stone fragment. Shelly limestone. *I, 2 (HO 379), St 33, AML 611299.*
19.　　Upper-stone fragment. Shelly limestone. *VIII, 3 (HO 32), St 1, AML 611299.*
20.　　Upper-stone fragment with handle-slot. Millstone Grit. *XIII/XVI, 4 (HO 315), St 28, AML 611326.*

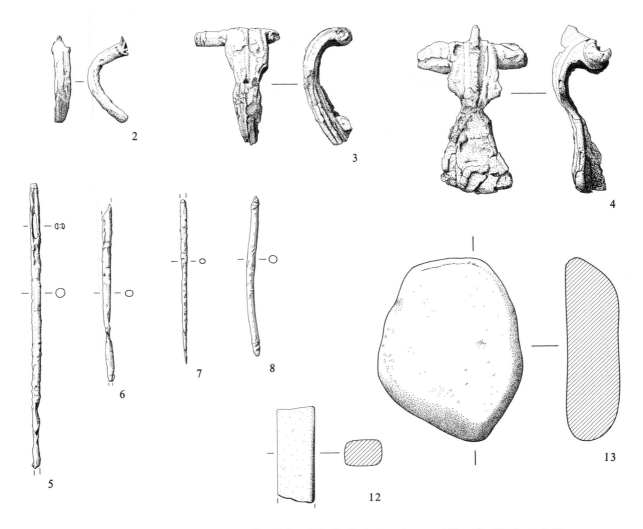

Figure 28 Objects of copper alloy (Nos 2–8; Scale 1:1) and stone (Nos 12–13; Scale 1:2)

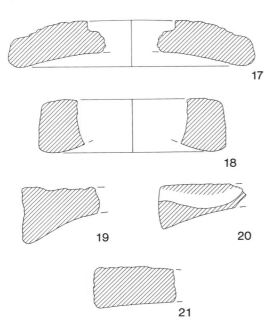

Figure 29 Objects of stone; querns. Scale 1:4

21. Upper-stone fragment. Millstone Grit. *III, 2 (HO 145), St 13, AML 611311.*

22. Not illustrated. Upper-stone fragment. Millstone Grit. *Test-hole 77, 3/4 (HO 310), St 27, AML 611325.*

23–42. Not illustrated. All fragments of Millstone Grit, and samples retained from larger quern fragments (for details, see archive).

The rotary querns collected during the excavation are without exception, either small fragments, or samples of larger fragments found. They provide insufficient data for a meaningful discussion of size and type. Lava querns in Roman Britain are generally believed to come from the Mayen quarries of the Eifel Hills of Germany (Hörter *et al.* 1951; Crawford and Röder 1955; Röder 1972), and are found throughout East Anglia (Buckley and Major 1983). Querns of Millstone Grit probably originate from Derbyshire or South Wales, if not from erratics.

The distribution of the quern fragments (not illustrated) is confined to Site B West, and within this area, they are found both in and around *F8* (Trenches XII to XVII; 13 fragments) and in the area to the west (Trenches I to X; 16 fragments).

Objects of glass
(Fig. 30)
by H.E.M. Cool

43. Not illustrated. Rim fragment of beaker. Colourless; some small bubbles; iridescent surfaces; strain crack. Outbent rim, edge broken. One horizontal wheel-cut line below rim edge, one on upper body. Dimensions 17 × 16mm, wall thickness 1mm. *III, 2 (HO 114), G1.*

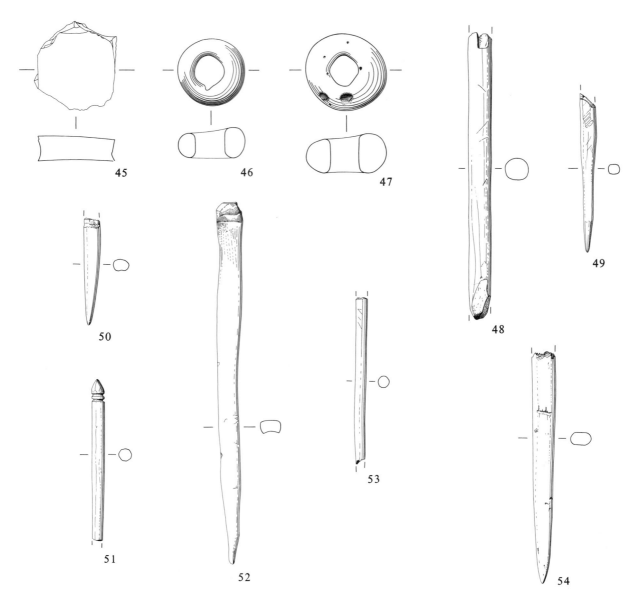

Figure 30 Objects of glass (Nos 45–47) and bone (Nos 48–54). Scale 1:1

44. Not illustrated. Body fragment of bottle. Blue/green with patchy green impurity. Vertical scratch marks. Dimensions 46 × 34mm. *XII, 1 (HO 338), G3.*

45. Body fragment of prismatic bottle. Blue/green. Grozed to sub-circular shape. *Unstratified.*

46. Annular bead. Translucent blue. 'D'-sectioned. Sub-square perforation. Two voids on surface due to bubbles bursting. *Test-hole 228, 1 (HO 332), G2.*

47. Annular bead. Very bubbly yellow/green with yellow/brown streaky impurities spiralling around the perforation. Sub-square perforation. Several large voids on surfaces due to bubbles bursting. *Unstratified.*

No. 43 is a rim fragment of a colourless wheel-cut beaker of a type that is common on Romano-British sites of the second century. These beakers have outbent rims with knocked off and ground edges and upper bodies that are either cylindrical or slope out. The lower bodies slope in to pushed-in or separately blown and applied base rings. Typical examples include one from *Verulamium* found in a context dated 150–155/160 (Charlesworth 1972, fig. 77/44) and one from a rubbish pit dated 155–165 (Price 1980, fig. 14/4). No. 43 is too small for the precise form of the beaker it came from to be identified.

No. 44 is probably a body fragment from a cylindrical bottle of Isings' (1957) Form 51, though it may be a slightly distorted fragment from a prismatic bottle of Isings Form 50. No. 45 is a fragment of the latter type which has been grozed to an approximately circular shape possibly for use as a counter. Both types were in use during the second half of the first century. Cylindrical bottles went out of use in the early second century whereas prismatic bottles continued to be used during the second century and possibly into the third.

The two undecorated annular beads, Nos 46 and 47, fall into the medium size range of Guido's (1978) Group 6. The blue No. 46 is an example of variant 6(iva) and the yellow/green No. 47 of variant 6(iiia) (1978, 66); neither can be closely dated. Blue annular beads such as No. 46 were in use for a very long period with examples being found in contexts ranging from the sixth century BC to the eighth century AD. Yellow/green examples had a shorter lifespan with the majority dating to the first centuries BC and AD.

Objects of bone
(Fig. 30)

48. Pin shaft. Broken at both ends. *VIII, 2, F1 (HO 33), CB1.*

49. Pin point. *XVI, 4, F8 (HO 255), CB2.*

50. Pin point. *XVI, 4, F8 (HO 256), CB3.*

51. Pin with two grooves beneath a conical head. First or second century. *XVI, 4, F8 (HO 259), CB4.*

52. Pin. Complete. Roughly worked. *XVII, 4, F8 (HO 276), CB5.*

53. Pin shaft. Broken at both ends. *I, F32 (HO 341), CB6.*

54. Pin point. *I, F32 (HO 342), CB7.*

The Romano-British pottery
(Figs 31–39)

with contributions by B.R. Hartley, Brenda Dickinson and Kay Hartley

Introduction

The following report includes the pottery from both Site A and Site B, and the catalogue is divided as follows:-

1–27	samian from Site A (missing)
28–45	samian from Site B
44–50	mortaria from Site A (missing)
51	mortarium from Site B
52–107	other pottery from Site A (missing)
108–162	other pottery from Site B

While the pottery from Site A is all missing, it has been possible to prepare reports on the samian from notes made in the mid-1960s, and on the mortaria and other pottery from drawings of the pottery in the site archive. It has not been possible to assign the pottery from Site A to specific contexts or features on that site.

The pottery from Site B is treated in more detail. Details of context are given as endnotes, in the following format: *e.g. XVI, 4, F8 (HO 267 (2))*; that is, Trench XVI, *layer 4, Feature 8*, finds no. HO 267 (two sherds). References to the report on the pottery from the recent excavations by the Central Excavation Unit in the area (Bell, this volume) are preceded by 'OS 46'.

Approximately 44kg of pottery were recovered from Site B. The sherds are generally large and unabraded (though occasionally water-stained), and there is an unusually large number of virtually complete vessels. The pottery assemblage as a whole gives the impression of being primary refuse. The date of the pottery ranges from the late first century to the early third century, the bulk of the material probably belonging to the mid-second to early third century, and therefore probably contemporary with the pottery from OS 46 (Bell, this volume). There is little evidence for occupation after the early third century, and very little fourth century material was recovered.

The samian

Site A
(not illustrated)
by B.R. Hartley

1. Form 31, Central Gaulish. Antonine.

2. Form 33, Central Gaulish. Two joining fragments. Hadrianic or early-Antonine.

3. Flake, possibly from Form 33, with the stamp [E]LVILLI. The potter Elvillus of Lezoux seems to have used only one die, and stamps from it occur on Forms 31, 31R, 33, 38, 46, 79 and 80. Twenty-six of his dishes were found in the gutter of the Wroxeter forum (Atkinson 1942, 140). *c.* 160–190.

4. Form 35/36 probably. The fabric appears to be South Gaulish, so the piece is probably first-century.

5. Form 33, apparently stamped SANT..N..OFC. This is almost certainly from a die giving SANTIANIO·Г·C· used by Santianus at Lezoux. Its use on Forms 31R and 80 suggest mid- to late-Antonine date. *c.* 160–190.

6. Form Curle 11, South Gaulish. Flavian-Trajanic.

7. Form 31, probably East Gaulish. Antonine.

8. Form 31, Central Gaulish. Antonine.

9. Form 18, South Gaulish. Two sherds (one burnt). Flavian.

10. Form 18, probably South Gaulish. Flavian.

11. Form 33, Central Gaulish. Antonine.

12. Form 15/17 or 18, South Gaulish. Probably Flavian.

13. Form 18/31(?R), origin uncertain. On form this could be either Flavian or second-century. On the whole, the fabric suggests the former.

14. Form 31, Central Gaulish. Antonine.

15. Form 31, Central Gaulish. Hadrianic or early-Antonine.

16. Form 31, Central Gaulish. Antonine, probably after *c.* 160.

17. Form 15/17. Although this form lost popularity after *c.* 80, a few examples were made down to the end of South Gaulish manufacture, and these seem to have been copied by some of the early Central Gaulish potters. This piece is particularly interesting, because its fabric can be matched precisely with certain products of the Central Gaulish factory at Les Martres-de-Veyre. It is likely to be Trajanic.

18. Form ?31, heavily burnt. Probably Central Gaulish and Antonine.

19. Form 35/36, Central Gaulish. Second-century.

20. Form 31, probably Central Gaulish. Antonine.

21. Form 31, burnt. Probably Central Gaulish and early-Antonine.

22. Form 18, South Gaulish. Flavian-Trajanic.

23. Form 33, burnt, Central Gaulish. Hadrianic or Antonine.

24. Form 36, Central Gaulish. A late variant of the form, with the flange curled over at the tip. It was current in the late second and early third century. Here probably late-Antonine.

25. Form 29, South Gaulish. Rather blurred decoration, with an upper zone recalling some of the work stamped by Felix i (Knorr 1952, Taf. 23A). The bird is Hermet 1934, pl. 28, 34. This is undoubtedly the earliest piece in the collection and was made *c.* 55–75.

26. Form Curle 11, South Gaulish. Flavian-Trajanic.

27. Form 15/17, South Gaulish, with stamp]ASCLIN, from a die used by Masclinus of La Graufesenque. Some of his output is pre-Flavian, but stamps from Chester and Corbridge indicate Flavian activity also, and the rather thick fabric of this piece would agree well with the later date.

Site B
(Fig. 31, No. 31 only)
by Brenda Dickinson

28. Form 33, slightly burnt, stamped [CINTV]SM. A stamp of Cintusmus i of Lezoux, where the die (5a) is known to have been used. There are many examples from the Pudding Pan Rock wreck (unpublished), and the stamp was used on Forms 31R and 79. *c.* 160–190. *I, 1 (HO 92).*

29. Form 31, stamped [MΛ]RCIMΛ. A stamp of Marcus v of Lezoux, where the die (4a) is known to have been used. Marcus v's range includes the later Antonine forms such as 79, 79R and 31R, and his stamps are common on Hadrian's Wall and at Pennine forts reoccupied *c.* 160. This particular stamp occurs at Catterick and Ilkley (unpublished). *c.* 160–200. *I, 1 (HO 93, 98).*

30. Form 31, with rivet-hole and stamp]Λ or V[, Central Gaulish. Antonine. *I, 1 (HO 94).*

31. Five fragments, three burnt, from a bowl of Form 37 in the style of Paternus v of Lezoux. The ovolo (Rogers E18), astragalus, rosette (Rogers C123) and trifid motif (Rogers G153) are all known for him, but the arrangement of the decoration seems to be rather unusual. The panel adjacent to the medallion panel and containing the trifid motif appears to contain a double festoon, which he did not normally use (though see Karnitsch 1959, Taf. 46, 1). If this festoon is repeated on the other sherd showing the medallion, it does not depend from an astragalus, which is also unusual for Paternus. However, the combination of beaded horizontal and roped vertical borders makes this almost certainly his work, rather than that of Iustus ii, who used some

45

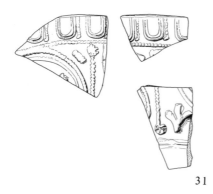

31

Figure 31 Samian, No. 31. Scale 1:2

of the motifs. *c.* 160–195. *I, F32 (HO 383); I, 1 (HO 98); III, 1 (HO 62); VI, 2 (HO 142).*

32. Form 31, Central Gaulish. Mid- to late-Antonine. Perhaps from the same vessel as No. 29. *I, 2 (HO 184).*

33. Form 33, with rivet-holes, Central Gaulish. Antonine. *I, F31 (HO 158).*

34. Form 31, Central Gaulish. Antonine. *I, F31 (HO 160).*

35. Form 36, Central Gaulish. Hadrianic-Antonine. *XVI, 4 (HO 311).*

36. Form 31, Central Gaulish. Antonine. *I, F32 (HO 383).*

37. Form 31, Central Gaulish. Antonine. *I, F32 (HO 383).*

38. Form 18/31R, Central Gaulish. Early- to mid-Antonine. *III, 1 (HO 61).*

39. Form 18/31R, Central Gaulish. Some joining sherds, one riveted and some with rivet holes. Early- to mid-Antonine. *I, 1 (HO 95, 97, 98, 99, 157, 159); III, 1 (HO 61, 74).*

40. Form 18/31R, Central Gaulish. Two sherds. Hadrianic-Antonine. *I, 1 (HO 99); III, 2 (HO 83).*

41. Form 36, Central Gaulish. Five sherds, two joining. Antonine. *I, 1 (HO 91, 96, 99).*

42. Form 35, worn inside, from Les Martres-de-Veyre. Some sherds joining. Trajanic or Hadrianic. *I, F32 (HO 383); III, 2 (HO 152); XVI, 4 (HO 253, 258); Test-hole 77 (HO 308).*

43. Form 36, Central Gaulish. Two joining sherds. Antonine. *XIV, 3 (HO 203, 204).*

This is typical samian assemblage for a Fenland site, and one which almost certainly reflects its lack of prosperity. It is small, with very little decorated ware, and a high proportion of mended vessels.

The bulk of the material is Antonine, probably mostly from the middle of the second century, though certainly extending beyond *c.* 160, or more probably, 170. There are a few earlier pieces, perhaps ranging from the Trajanic period. All the samian comes from Lezoux, with the exception of one vessel from Les Martres-de-Veyre.

The Mortaria
(Fig. 32)
by Kay Hartley

The mortaria from Site A have not been located, and the drawings and report are based upon sketches and notes by the excavator; for this reason, it has not been possible to show the trituration on Nos 44–50, while on No. 51, no trituration survived.

Site A
(Fig. 32)

44. Cream fabric. Black grits. Mancetter-Hartshill or lower Nene valley.

45. Cream fabric. Black and red grits. Mancetter-Hartshill.

46. ?Orange colour-coat. Black grits. ?Lower Nene valley, third or fourth century, but Mancetter, Antonine not impossible.

47. Cream fabric. Red grits. Mancetter-Hartshill, second century.

48. Creamy white fabric. No trituration survives. Mancetter-Hartshill.

49. Cream fabric. Red grits. Probably Mancetter-Hartshill, 130–170.

50. Grey grits. Origin uncertain, third or fourth century.

Site B
(Fig. 32)

51. Two joining fragments from the rim of a mortarium with reeded flange, and spout formed by the bead being cut and turned out over the flange. Hard, fine-textured off-white fabric with some fine quartz and ill-sorted red-brown inclusions. Undoubtedly made in Castor-Stibbington area of the lower Nene valley, probably in the third century. *II, 1 (HO 71).*

The other pottery
(Figs 33–38)

Fabric coding and description of the other pottery is consistent with that used for the pottery from OS 46 (Bell, this volume), with some additions. Nine fabrics were distinguished:

Mica-dusted ware	Hard, slightly granular fabric with moderate quartz inclusions. Inner core grey, outer core red (2.5YR 5/8), and surfaces slipped brown (7.5YR 5/4) and with golden mica (all over). For this ware see Marsh 1978, 122–3, and Type 24, 154–158. A single vessel is represented, a simple platter (Fig. 35, No. 108).
Lead-glazed ware	Fine, hard fabric with sparse quartz and mica inclusions. Grey (10YR 6/1) with reddish-brown margins. The overall glaze is medium-green with brownish patches, appearing yellow where it covers barbotine decoration. Probably made in the Staines area. A single vessel is represented, an imitation of samian Form 37 (Fig. 35, No. 109).
Nene Valley Colour-Coated Ware (OS 46, Fabric F1)	Hard smooth fabric, with core colour from white, buff or pink to pale orange or grey. Inclusions of moderate quartz, sparse very fine mica and sparse fine black and red iron ore.
Fabric R1	Hard reduced fabric, generally grey in colour throughout. Inclusions of moderate quartz and sparse magnetite.
Fabric R2	Nene Valley Grey Ware (NVGW). Hard, slightly granular or smooth fabric with moderate fine and very fine quartz, with a scatter of medium grains and sparse fine black iron ore. Core colour off-white to light grey, surfaces steel-grey and smoothed or burnished.
Fabric R3	A variant of Fabric R2. Inclusions as for R2. Hard smooth light grey fabric with a darker greyish core and dark grey surfaces.
Fabric R4	Calcite-gritted wares. Generally reduced and black in colour, with abundant very coarse or coarse calcite inclusions and medium quartz.
Fabric O1	Hard oxidised fabric with a slightly rough feel. Inclusions of moderate medium quartz. Buff in colour with a darker slip.
Fabric O4	Hard oxidised fabric, with inclusions of sparse to moderate fine quartz and fine to medium haematite.

The catalogue is divided into two parts. Firstly, there is the pottery from Site A (Mayes) which has not been located and which is known only from drawings (catalogue Nos 52 to 107). For the Site A pottery, detailed sherd descriptions cannot be given, and only the broadest subdivision into fabric categories is possible, namely colour-coated wares, grey wares and calcite-gritted wares. The colour-coated wares are probably all from the lower Nene valley, and this is probably also true of the bulk of the grey wares; where it seems unlikely that a vessel is in

46

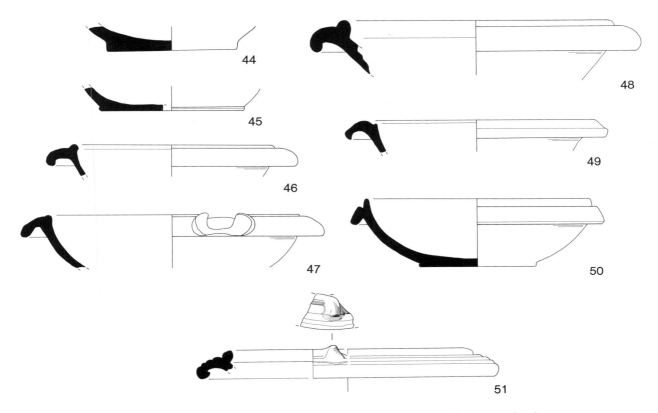

Figure 32 Mortaria, Nos 44–51. Nos 44–50 are missing, and the trituration cannot be shown.
On No. 51, no trituration survived. Scale 1:4

Nene Valley Grey Ware, this has been noted. The other pottery from Site B (Greenfield) (catalogue Nos 108 to 162) is divided into groups by fabric; most of this pottery comes from the area of F8 on Site B West. The abbreviation RPNV refers to pottery types in Howe *et al.* (1980).

Site A
(Figs 33–35)

Colour-coated wares (probably all Nene Valley Colour-Coated Ware)
52. Scroll-decorated beaker. Late second-early third century.
53. Base sherd.
54. Lid. Rouletted decoration. ?RPNV 72. ?Fourth century.
55. ?Beaker. Simple bead rim.
56. Bowl.
57. Dish. ?Fourth century.

Grey wares
58. Jar. ?RPNV 5. ?Second century.
59. Jar.
60. Jar.
61. Jar. ?RPNV 5. ?Second century.
62–66. Jars.
67. Jar (*cf.* Hayes 1984, fig. 126, no. 2). Second century.
68. Jar.
69. Jar. Decorated with oblique burnished lines (*cf.* Potter 1965, fig. 3, C23, C24, C94a; Friendship-Taylor 1979, fig. 38, 89–92). Late second century.
70. Girth beaker. Burnished lattice decoration. Not NVGW. First century.
71. Girth beaker. Not NVGW. First century.

72. Jar.
73. Jar with burnished decoration (*cf.* Hayes 1978, fig. 6, no. 3). Mid-second century.
74. Jar.
75. Jar.
76. Straight-sided bowl, RPNV 18. Second-third century.
77. Bowl.
78. Shallow bowl or dish. Not NVGW. ?First century.
79. Bowl (*cf.* Friendship-Taylor 1979, fig. 42, no. 164). ?First century.
80. Bowl. Probably not NVGW.
81. Bowl. ?NVGW.
82. Bowl. ?NVGW.
83. Shallow bowl or dish. ?RPNV 20.
84. Dish. Perforated.
85. Dish. RPNV 19.
86. Dish. RPNV 19.

Calcite-gritted wares
87–107. A range of calcite-gritted vessels, from small or narrow-mouthed jars (*e.g.* No. 107) through medium-sized forms (*e.g.* Nos 95–100) to larger wide-mouthed examples (*e.g.* Nos 102–107). No. 101 is probably a wide-mouthed bowl. Calcite-gritted wares were common in the area throughout the Roman period, particularly so in the first to mid-second century and in the fourth century. Very few kiln sites producing this ware are known, and dating is virtually impossible; the forms are essentially utilitarian and there seems to be little typological change. There is a tendency for fabrics to be harder and more evenly fired from the second century onwards, but this cannot be used as a reliable indication of date.

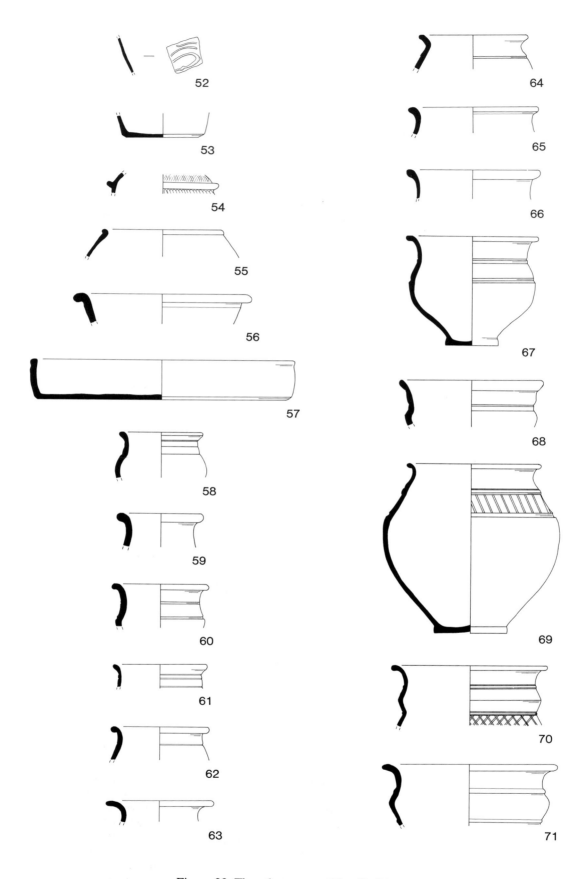

Figure 33 The other pottery, Nos 52–71. Scale 1:4

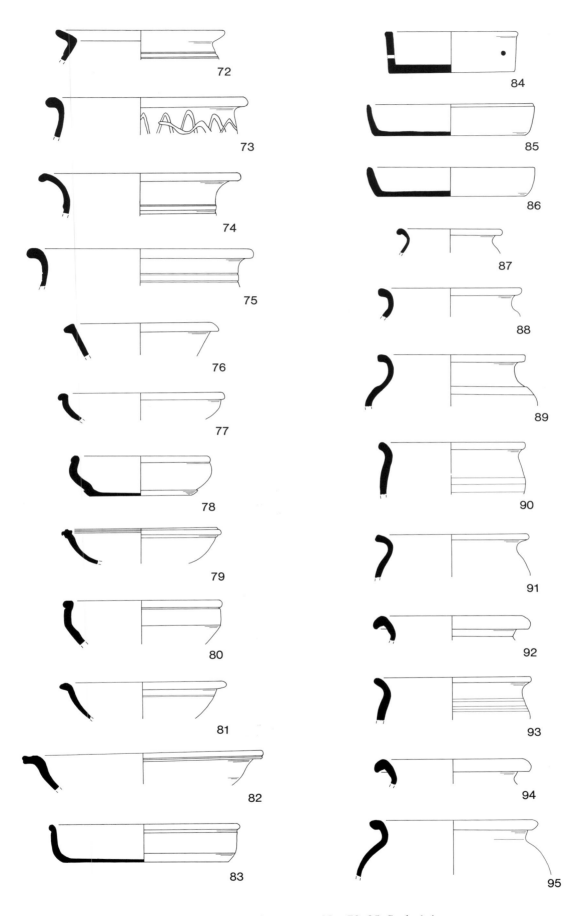

Figure 34 The other pottery, Nos 72–95. Scale 1:4

Site B
(Figs 35–38)

Mica-dusted ware
108. Simple platter. Curving wall and slightly rising base, with a shallow groove at the junction internally. For similar platters see Marsh 1978, figs 6.10, 6.11. Five joining sherds. *XVI, 3 (HO 209 (2)); XVI, 4, F8 (HO 267 (2)); XVI, 4 (HO 313).*

Lead-glazed ware
109. Bowl imitating samian Form 30. The whole vessel is glazed, and on the external surface there is underglaze decoration of near-vertical white barbotine lines. The lead-glazed wares of Roman Britain are comprehensively catalogued by Arthur (1978), and the fabric of this vessel matches that of the South-East English Group, produced in the vicinity of Staines, Surrey, where seconds and wasters have been recorded. The Group includes at least seventeen vessels imitating samian Form 30, and similar decoration occurs on Form 30s and other forms (*cf.* Perrin 1981, 57 and fig. 41, no. 571). This vessel is one of the furthest outliers of the Group, the distribution of which is primarily along the lower Thames valley. Its occurrence in Lincolnshire has not hitherto been recorded (*cf.* Gurney 1984). Late first to early second century. Two sherds. *I, Mossop's spoil heap (HO 330); I, over F31 (HO 331).*

Nene Valley Colour-Coated Ware
110. Angular beaker with everted rim. Orangy fabric with a light red colour-coat. Late second century (OS 46, Form 1). Two joining sherds. *III, 2 (HO 137).*

111. Squat globular beaker with cornice-type rim. Greyish fabric with an orangy-brown colour-coat. Late second century. Two joining sherds. *XVI, 4 (HO 260).*

112. Beaker with simple rounded rim. Greyish fabric with a dark grey colour-coat. Barbotine ?scroll decoration. Late second to early third century. Two sherds. *III, 1 (HO 68).*

113. Roughcast beaker with cornice-type rim. Orangy fabric with a reddish-brown colour-coat. Late second century. Seven joining sherds. *XII, 4 (HO 225); XIII, 4 (HO 232 (5)); XII/XIII, 4 (HO 300).*

114. Lid-seated jar. Off-white fabric with an orangy-brown colour-coat. A form also made in NVGW (*cf.* Hadman and Upex 1975, fig. 7, no. 3). Twelve joining sherds. *XIII (HO 320 (7)); XIII, 5 (HO 322 (2)); XIII, 5 (HO 350 (3)).*

115. Large deep vertical-sided bowl. Off-white fabric with a reddish-brown colour-coat. Rouletted decoration. An unusual form in NVCC, not in RPNV. Similar vessels have been found at Chesterton, one of which came from a context dated to the second half of the second century (R. Perrin pers. comm.). Two joining sherds. *XVI, 4 (HO 270); I, F13 (HO 394).*

116. Bowl with grooved rim. Off-white fabric with a dark grey colour-coat. ?Third century. *VI, F1 (HO 28).*

117. Dish with grooved rim. White fabric with a red colour-coat. ?Third century. Two joining sherds. *XIII, 4 (HO 232); XII, on natural (HO 303).*

Fabric R1
118. Lid. *F32 (HO 382).*
119. Jar, probably of slashed-cordon type (*cf.* Hayes 1984, fig. 130, nos 66–67; Wild 1975, fig. 7, no. 9). Mid-second century. *XVI, 4 (HO 260).*
120. Jar. Vertical burnished lines. Five joining sherds. *XVI, 5 (HO 324).*
121. Bowl, imitating samian Form 30. Stamped decoration including lozenge (*cf.* RPNV 25 and for similar decoration on other imitation samian forms Hayes 1984, fig. 131, no. 76 and fig. 132, no. 87). Mid-second century. *XVI, 3 (HO 208).*
122. Jar. Grooved neck. Mid-second to third century. OS 46, Form 12. Four joining sherds. *XV, 4 (HO 250 (2)); XIII/XVI, 4 (HO 314 (2)).*
123. Jar. Grooved neck. Mid-second to third century. OS 46, Form 12. Sixteen joining sherds. *XVI/XVII, 3 (HO 295); 5 (HO 324 (13)); XVI/XVII, 5 (HO 356 (2)).*

124. Shallow dish with internal burnished decoration. Late first or early second century. Two joining sherds. *VII, 3, F1 (HO 351).*
125. Shallow bowl with footring. Third century. Seven joining sherds. *XVII, 4 (HO 272 (5)); XII, on natural (HO 303); XVI, 4 (HO 313).*
126. Cheese-press lid. Unperforated. *XV, 4, F8 (HO 244).*
127. Cheese-press lid. Perforated. *I, F13 (HO 294).*

Fabric R2
128. Jar. Everted rim. *XVI, 4 (HO 257).*
129. Pinched-neck flagon. ?Third century. *XIII, 4 (HO 242).*
130. Lid. Two joining sherds. *XVI, 4, F8 (HO 267).*
131. Squat jar with grooved neck. Second century. Two joining sherds. *XII/XVII, F17 (HO 307).*
132. Small jar with grooving on the shoulder. *III, 1 (HO 67).*
133. Jar with slashed cordon. Mid-second century. Seven joining sherds. *XII, 4 (HO 225); XIII, 4 (HO 232 (4)); XIII/XVI, 4 (HO 314 (2)).*
134. Jar with grooved neck. Mid-second to third century. OS 46, Form 13. Five joining sherds. *XVII, 4 (HO 278 (2)); XVII, 4 (HO 284); XII/XVII, 4 (HO 298); XII/XVII, F17 (HO 307).*
135. Jar with burnished wavy line decoration on the neck. OS 46, Form 16. Mid- to late-second century. Three joining sherds. *XV, 4, F8 (HO 244).*
136. Jar with burnished wavy line decoration on the neck. Mid- to late-second century. Eighteen joining sherds. *XII, 4 (HO 316 (16)); XVI, 5 (HO 324); XII/XIII (HO 350).*
137. As No. 136. *XVI, 5 (HO 324).*
138. As No. 136. Two joining sherds. *XII/XIII (HO 350).*
139. Globular necked jar with rouletted shoulder. OS 46, Form 6. Second half of the second century. Ten joining sherds. *I, 1 (HO 119).*
140. Globular necked jar, undecorated. OS 46, Form 7. Second half of the second century. Seventeen joining sherds. *XV, 4, F8 (HO 244 (5)); XVI, 4 (HO 252 (3)); XV/XVI, 4 (HO 297 (2)); F8, 4 (HO 349 (3)); XV, 5 (HO 355 (4)).*
141. Dish with plain rounded rim. OS 46, Form 31. Late second to third century. *I, 1 (HO 109).*
142. Dish with plain rounded rim and champhered base. *XVII, 5 (HO 318).*
143. Shallow bowl or dish. Burnished decoration. Five joining sherds. *XV, 4, F8 (HO 250 (4)); Test-hole 87, 3 or 4 (HO 305).*
144. Bowl. Burnished decoration. Two joining sherds. *XII, 4 (HO 219).*
145. Dish. *XV, 4, F8 (HO 244).*
146. Shallow bowl. *IV, 4, F1 (HO 9).*
147. Shallow bowl. Two joining sherds. *XII/XVII, 4 (HO 298).*
148. Flanged bowl (*cf.* Hayes 1984, fig. 132, no. 102). Second century. *XIII/XVI, 4 (HO 314).*
149. Cheese-press lid. Perforated. *V/VII, 4, F1 (HO 357).*

Fabric R3
150. Large jar with grooving on the shoulder. *XVI, 5 (HO 324).*
151. Straight-sided bowl. OS 46, Form 27. Late second to mid-third century. *IV, 4, F1 (HO 8).*
152. Bowl. Two joining sherds. *I, F33 (HO 154).*

Fabric R4
153. Small jar. *XXI, 2 (HO 370).*
154. Narrow-mouthed jar. *I, F31 (HO 169).*
155. Jar with grooving on the body. OS 46, Form 9. Two joining sherds. *XVII, 5 (HO 318).*
156. Jar with grooving on the shoulder. Three joining sherds. *XVI, 5 (HO 324); XVI/XVII, 5 (HO 356); XVI/XVII, 4 (HO 359).*
157. Jar. Four joining sherds. *XVII, 4 (HO 272); XVII, 4 (HO 278 (2)); XVI/XVII, 4 (HO 359).*
158. Jar with horizontal grooving. Two joining sherds. *III, 1 (HO 64); III, 1 (HO 76).*
159. Jar with incised wavy line on the shoulder. ?OS 46, Form 11. *VIII, 4, F1 (HO 6).*
160. Jar with horizontal grooving. Three joining sherds. *XIII, 4 (HO 239).*

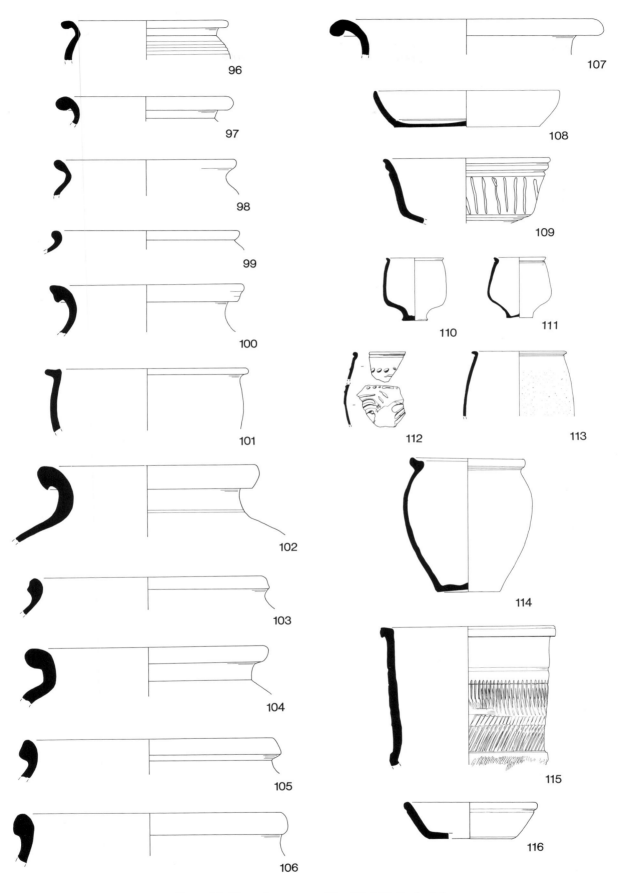

Figure 35 The other pottery, Nos 96–116. Scale 1:4

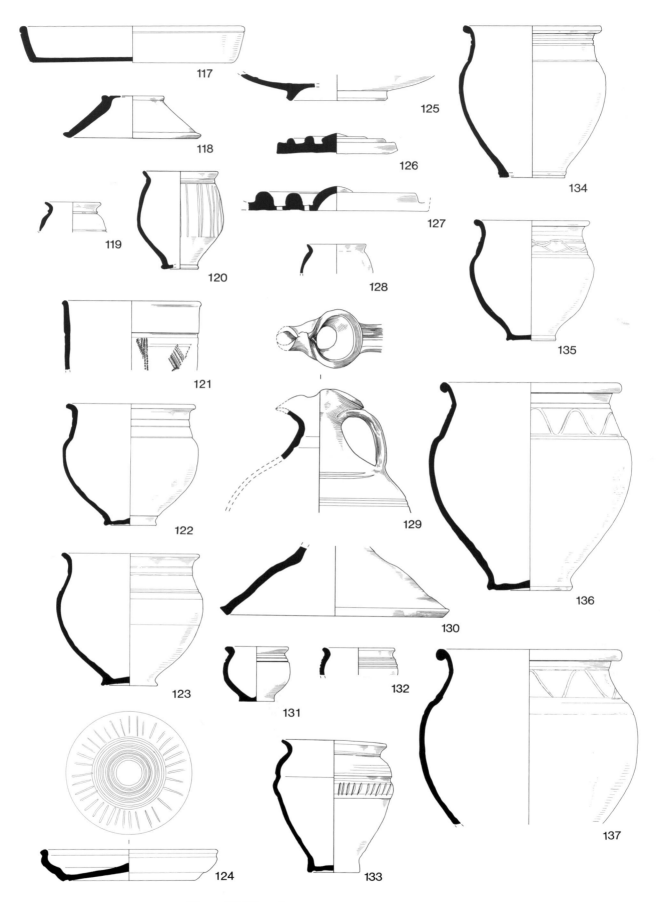

Figure 36 The other pottery, Nos 117–137. Scale 1:4

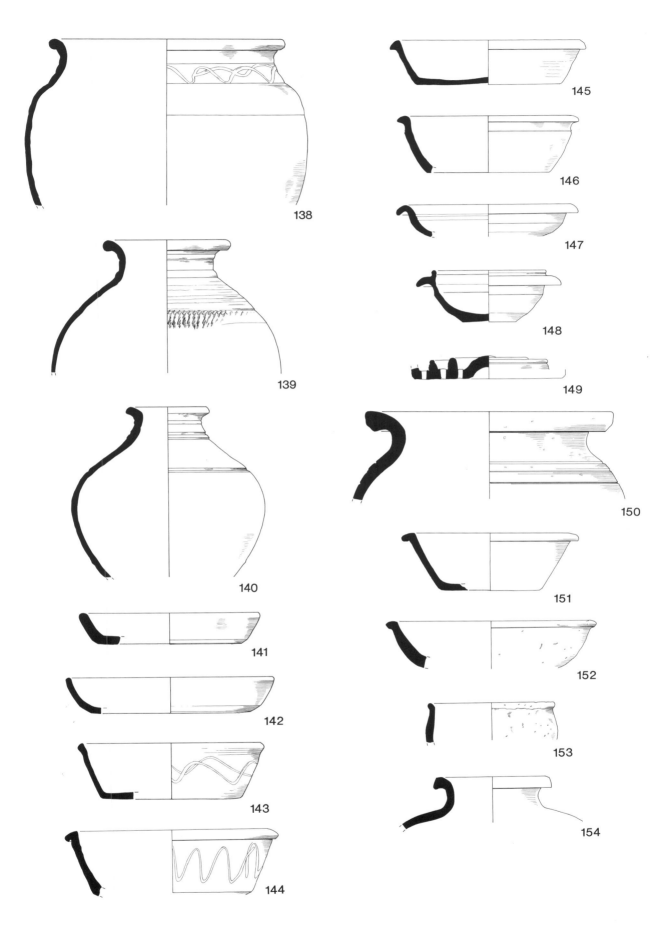

Figure 37 The other pottery, Nos 138–154. Scale 1:4

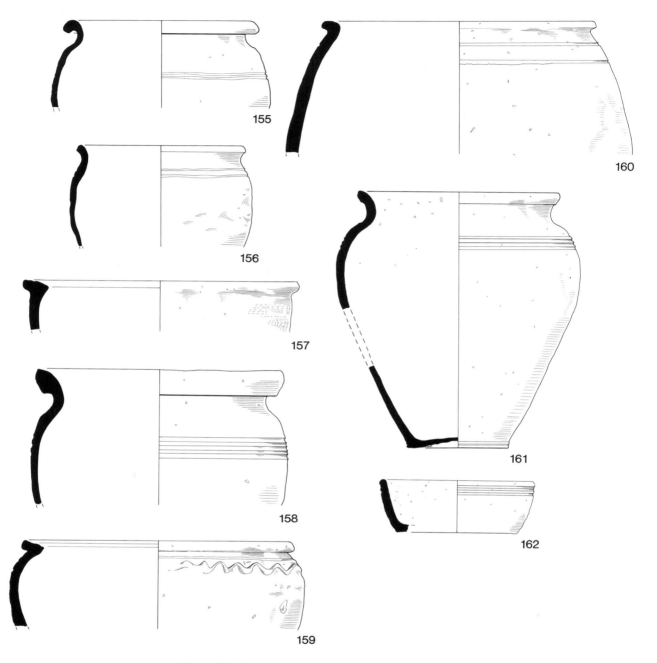

Figure 38 The other pottery, Nos 155–162. Scale 1:4

161. Jar. Horizontal grooving. Three joining sherds. *XVI, 4 (HO 267 (2)); XII, 4 (HO 316).*

162. Shallow bowl. Horizontal grooving below the rim. *III, 2 (HO 84).*

Discussion
(Fig. 39)
As noted previously, the pottery from Site A was not available for study, being known only from drawings. A report on the samian was prepared by Brian Hartley shortly after the excavation, and this has been updated where possible.

The samian sherds from Site A represent some twenty-seven vessels, ten of South Gaulish manufacture, sixteen from the Central Gaulish factories, with a single East Gaulish sherd. The earliest sherd (No. 25) is dated to

c. 55–75. The bulk of the samian from Site A is Central Gaulish, and Antonine in date. The mortaria from Site A probably all came from the factories at Mancetter-Hartshill or in the lower Nene valley. The other pottery, while not available for study, appears to include material from perhaps the late first century through to the fourth, with the bulk of the pottery probably of second century date.

Approximately 44kg of pottery were recovered from Site B, the bulk of this (more than 80 per cent by weight) from the area of *F8* on Site B West (Fig. 39). This points to the presence of domestic occupation, while the other excavated areas on Site B produced evidence of essentially industrial activity, with deposits rich in briquetage, but with little domestic pottery.

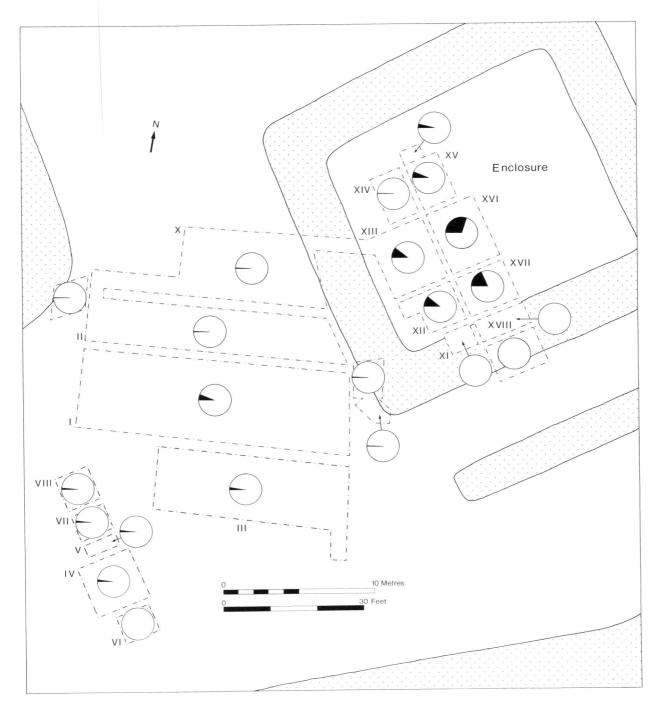

Figure 39 The Romano-British pottery distribution on Site B West. Pie charts show the relative amounts of pottery from each trench as proportions of the total collection by weight. Scale 1:250

The samian sherds from Site B include material from the Trajanic period, although the bulk is of Antonine date. All but one of the sherds came from Lezoux. As on other Fenland sites, the lack of prosperity is reflected in the samian, there being very little decorated ware, and many vessels show evidence of repair. A single mortarium was represented by two sherds, a Nene Valley product probably of third-century date.

The distribution of the samian sherds on Site B West is intriguing when compared to the distribution of the other pottery. The bulk of the other pottery came from the area around *F8* but this area produced only five of the thirty-

three samian sherds recovered. Most of the samian sherds came from Trenches I, III and VI to the west, in the area of *F1*. The samian sherds from these two areas are certainly contemporary, and there are a number of joining sherds between the areas. There is no obvious explanation of this distribution; activity in and around *F1* seems to have been primarily of an industrial nature.

The other pottery from Site B West represents a minimum vessel population of some 259 vessels. The date-range of this assemblage is broadly similar to that of the pottery from OS 46 to the south (Bell, this volume), probably mid-second to early-third century, with little earlier or later material. The pottery is essentially of local production, with perhaps only two exceptions, the mica-dusted platter and the lead-glazed bowl.

Leaving aside these two possible 'imports', the remaining pottery is all of local production, the main source of this being the grey and colour-coated kilns of the lower Nene valley, some 15 miles (24km) to the south-west. The colour-coated wares from this source account for only 5 per cent of the minimum vessel population, and of these, only a single vessel is decorated (barbotine scroll beaker, No. 112). Decorated vessels, like the samian, may have been treasured possessions on this relatively low-status settlement. Grey wares, again mostly from the lower Nene valley make up the bulk of the assemblage (nearly 60 per cent of the vessel population), mostly utilitarian jars and bowls or dishes. Fragments of three cheese-press lids were recovered, and these seem to be common Fenland finds (Hartley and Hartley 1970, 168) although this has never been quantified. If nothing else, their occurrence at least suggests subsistence dairy farming in the area, and the industrial activity of salt-production may have been only one (?seasonal) activity within the broader economy of the settlement. Finally, calcite-gritted wares make up the remaining 33 per cent of the vessel population, again a range of essentially utilitarian forms.

The briquetage
(Figs 40–45; Pl. XXVI)

Introduction
Approximately 3.8kg of briquetage were retained, a collection of the larger and more complete excavated fragments. It is clear that much briquetage was discarded. The fabric is generally soft, with variable amounts of organic inclusions and is usually light red (2.5YR 6/8) in colour throughout. The surfaces are frequently discoloured pale brown or have a purplish tinge.

Classification of the briquetage
The briquetage can be divided on the basis of shape into seven artefact types. Not all of these are represented in the extant collection, but are known to have been present from the site notebooks.

1. *Vessel fragments* (Fig. 40). These seem to come from large, shallow trough-like containers which were perhaps *c.* 60cm long, *c.* 20cm wide and *c.* 7–8cm deep. The wall thickness was probably *c.* 1cm, and the sides of the vessel met the base in a curve, while the ends of the vessel met the base at a right angle (see Swinnerton 1932, 244–6 and fig. 7, and Hallam, S.J. 1960, 38–9). As Swinnerton also notes (1932, 246), 'one curious feature about these dishes is the fact that their rims are usually broken, or have been mended by the addition of fresh clay'. Two of the illustrated vessel rims from Holbeach have been repaired in this way (Fig. 40, Nos 6 and 7). Broken rim fragments are found trapped in the gap between the central stem and projections of bridges (see 3 below), suggesting that bridges were used in close association with the vessels, and that the removal of bridges after use is responsible for the frequent fracture of the vessel rims.

2. *Seats* (Fig. 41, Nos 15–18). These are squat cylindrical objects, with a diameter of *c.* 5–6cm, thick bases, and short thin walls projecting only 2–3cm above the top of the base. A similar object is illustrated by Swinnerton (1932, 248 and fig. 8, no. 3) who suggests that they were used in conjunction with other supports. Similar, but more carefully-shaped objects are illustrated by Riehm from the Saale valley in Central Germany (1962, Abb. 20), where they were supposedly used to support the bases of cylindrical pedestals.

3. *Bridges* (Fig. 41, Nos 19–30). These are small mushroom-shaped pieces of fired clay, which appear to have been squeezed between and over the rims of closely-spaced vessels (see 1 above). Two

Plate XXVI Holbeach St Johns, OS 33; Site B East, briquetage slabs or bricks *in situ*

examples retain such rim fragments in the gap between the central stem and one of the projections. A similar object is illustrated by Swinnerton (1932, 250 and fig. 9, no. 10; 'Accessory 5') and others are noted by Hallam, S. (1960, 40 and pl. III).

4. *Props* (Fig. 42, Nos 31–39; Fig. 43, A, D). This category embraces a wide variety of supports, including very roughly-shaped cylindrical supports and supports which have been more carefully manufactured. Mayes' site notes refer to objects similar to a support illustrated by Swinnerton (1932, fig. 8, no. 2a; 'Accessory 2'). This has been carefully shaped; one end has a concave surface, while the other has a right-angled notch (Fig. 44, A).

5. *Bars* (Fig. 42, Nos 40–41). Hallam notes that 'crossbars', when they occur, are not like the 'square cigar' bars like those from Runcton Holme (Hawkes 1933, fig. 51) or the tapered firebars of the Essex Red Hills (see for example Reader 1908, de Brisay 1975, Rodwell 1979), but are roughly curved cylinders with flattened ends, similar to the 'handles' from Goldhanger, Essex (Reader 1908, 178 and fig. 15, nos 1–3), and an object described by Swinnerton (1932, 249–50; 'Accessory 4').

6. *Flat slabs and bricks* (Fig. 43, Bi–Biv; Pl. XXVI). These are noted by both Greenfield and Mayes, although none are extant. Many are planned by Mayes (see Fig. 26). Greenfield noted that one slab was *c.* 2cm thick, 12.5cm wide and 23cm long. Swinnerton refers to similar slabs ranging between 8cm by 9cm and 19cm by 21cm (1932, 246; 'Accessory 1').

7. *'Truncated pyramidical stilts'* (Fig. 43, Ci–ii) are known only from Greenfield's notes. They appear to be similar to an object illustrated by Swinnerton (1932, fig. 9, no. 7; 'Accessory 3'), which was a tapered block with flat angled sides, flat base and smaller flattened top.

Catalogue
(Figs 40–42)

1.   Vessel rim. Simple rounded rim. External surface has white surface deposit and scorching; the core has a purplish tinge. *XXIII, 3 (HO 376).*

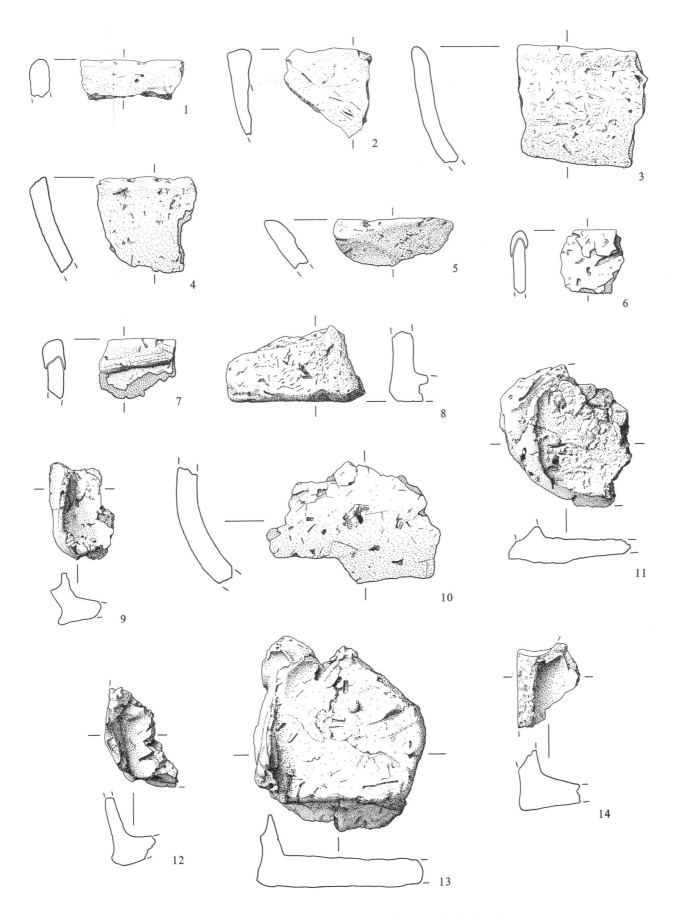

Figure 40 Briquetage vessel fragments, Nos 1–14. Scale 1:2

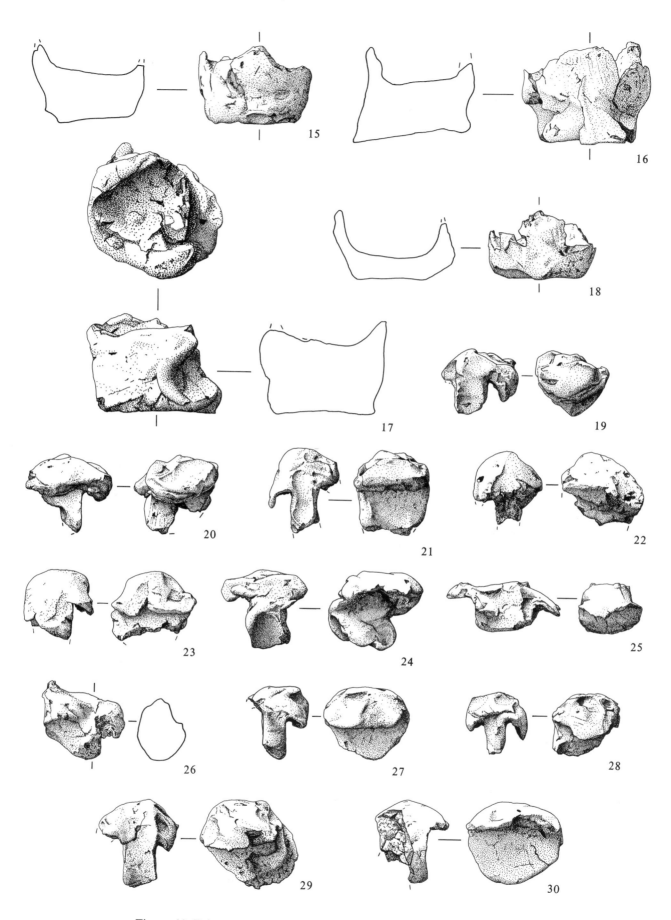

Figure 41 Briquetage seats (Nos 15–18) and bridges (Nos 19–30). Scale 1:2

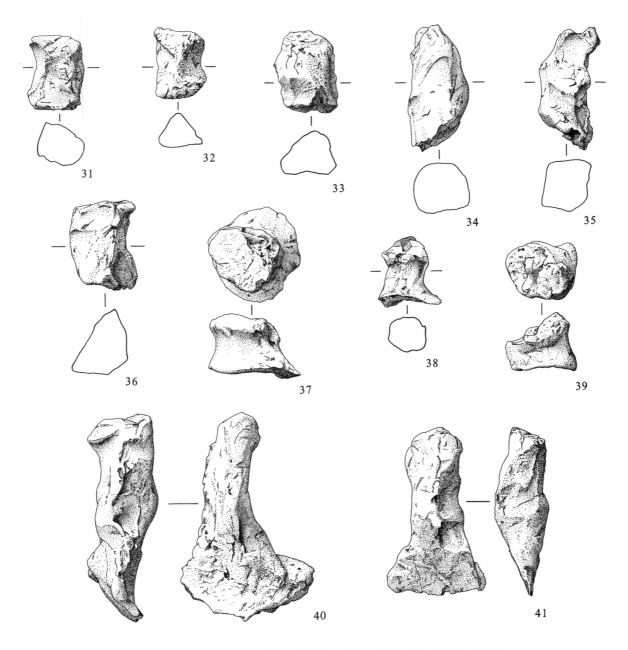

Figure 42 Briquetage props (Nos 31–39 and bars (Nos 40–41). Scale 1:2

2. Vessel rim. Flattish irregular rim. Very pale brown core with reddish-yellow surfaces. Much of the internal surface is missing. *IV, 4, F1 (HO 1–3)*.

3. Vessel rim. Irregular, rounded rim. Reddish-yellow throughout. The lower part of the external surface, below a line *c*. 3cm below the rim is discoloured purple. *VII/VIII, 4 (HO 386)*.

4. Vessel rim. Irregular angled rim. Grey core, reddish-yellow margins and very pale brown surfaces. *V, 4, F1 (HO 37)*.

5. Vessel rim. Irregular rounded rim. Reddish-yellow throughout. *XVI, 4, F8 (HO 252)*.

6. Vessel rim. Repaired by the application of a squeeze of clay over the rim. Grey core, reddish-yellow surfaces. *XX, 2 (HO 373)*.

7. Vessel rim. Repaired by the application of a squeeze of clay over the rim. Purplish throughout. *XX, F55 (HO 158)*.

8. Vessel base angle. Pink throughout. *VII/VIII, 4 (HO 386)*.

9. Vessel base angle. Reddish-yellow, with discoloured white external surfaces. *IV, 4, F1 (HO 1–3)*.

10. Vessel wall fragment. Very pale brown throughout. *VII/VIII, 4 (HO 386)*.

11. Vessel base angle. Reddish-yellow with white discoloration on the external surface of the wall. *VII/VIII, 4 (HO 386)*.

12. Vessel base angle. Purplish. *Unstratified*.

13. Vessel base angle. Reddish-yellow throughout, with white discoloration on the external surface of the wall. *VII, 4, F1 (HO 380)*.

14. Vessel base angle. Reddish-yellow throughout with a slight purplish tinge. *XXIV, F50 (HO 385)*.

15. Seat. The base internally and externally is reddish-yellow with patchy purplish discoloration; the sides are discoloured very pale brown. *VII, 4, F1 (HO 380)*.

16. As No. 15. *VII, 4, F1 (HO 380)*.

17. As No. 15, but the purplish and very pale brown discoloration is less marked. *VII, 4, F1 (HO 380)*.

18. As No. 15. *VII, 4, F1 (HO 380)*.

19. Bridge. Reddish-yellow with a slight purplish tinge. *XX, F55 (HO 387)*.

20. Bridge. Reddish-yellow with patchy pale brown discoloration. *XXIII, F56 (HO 388)*.

21.   Bridge. Reddish-yellow with patchy pale brown and purplish discoloration. *XXIII, 3 (HO 376)*.

22.   Bridge. Reddish-yellow with a purplish tinge. *XX, F55 (HO 387)*.

23.   Bridge. Reddish-yellow with a purplish tinge and patchy pale brown discoloration. *XX, F55 (HO 387)*.

24.   Bridge. Reddish-yellow with pale brown discoloration except on the top. The base of the central stem has a wattle impression. *XXIII, F56 (HO 388)*.

25.   Bridge. Reddish-yellow with pale brown discoloration. *VII/VIII, 4 (HO 386)*.

26.   Bridge. Pale brown. The rim of a vessel survives on one side, trapped between the central stem and one of the projections. *V, 4, F1 (HO 37)*.

27.   Bridge. Reddish-yellow. *XX, F55 (HO 387)*.

28.   Bridge. Reddish-yellow with patchy pale brown discoloration. *XX, 2 (HO 373)*.

29.   Bridge. Reddish-yellow with patchy pale brown and purplish discoloration. *XX, F55 (HO 387)*.

30.   Bridge. Reddish-yellow with a purplish tinge. The rim of a vessel survives on one side, trapped between the central stem and one of the projections. *VII/VIII, 4 (HO 386)*.

31.   Small prop. Pale brown. *V, 4, F1 (HO 37)*.

32.   Small prop. Pale brown. *IV, 4, F1 (HO 1–3)*.

33.   Small prop. Reddish-yellow with pale brown surfaces. *IV, 4, F1 (HO 1–3)*.

34.   Small prop. Reddish-yellow with pale brown surfaces. *IV, 4, F1 (HO 1–3)*.

35.   Small prop. Reddish-yellow with pale brown surfaces. *V, 4, F1 (HO 37)*.

36.   Small prop. Reddish-yellow with pale brown surfaces. *V, 4, F1 (HO 37)*.

37.   Small prop. Reddish-yellow. *XX, F55 (HO 387)*.

38.   Small prop. Reddish-yellow. *V, 4, F1 (HO 37)*.

39.   Small prop. Reddish-yellow. *XX, F55 (HO 387)*.

40.   Tapered bar or 'handle'. Reddish-yellow with patchy pale brown and purplish discoloration. *VII, 4, F1 (HO 380)*.

41.   Tapered bar or 'handle'. Reddish-yellow with pale brown discoloration and scorching. *VII/VIII, 4 (HO 386)*.

Discussion
(Figs 43–45)

In spite of the amount of briquetage recovered, the actual ways in which most of the objects were used remain conjectural. It is probably not generally appreciated that while finds of briquetage from salt-production sites have been recorded in large numbers during field survey (Hallam, S.J. 1960; 1970; Phillips 1970, Gazetteer) we actually know very little about these sites due to lack of excavation. Until further research and excavation on the salt-production on sites of the silt Fens is undertaken, the best we can do is to speculate on the rather scanty and often inadequate data generated by small rescue excavations like that described here. Some comments and parallels for the briquetage artefact types have been included in the Classification of the Briquetage (above), and this discussion will be resumed at this point.

Firstly, it can be safely assumed that the material in question, the briquetage, is associated with the industrial activity of salt-production rather than with any other process. This is clear from the distinctive fabric and surface discoloration of many objects, particularly the 'glaze' noted by Mayes on the objects from Saltern I. There are also numerous parallels with objects from other sites in Lincolnshire which have been identified as being salt-production sites.

Secondly, the problem of whether these objects were being *manufactured* or *used* on the site must be considered. While on-site production of the briquetage can

by no means be discounted, the 'glaze' and surface discoloration suggests that the briquetage was in use, and had been in contact with brine and heated.

Thirdly, the objects of briquetage must themselves be considered. *In situ*, we have only the three supports in Mayes' Saltern I (Fig. 26; Fig. 27, Section 8). These were carefully shaped, and while the objects themselves are not available for study, the notes provide sufficient information for a reconstruction to be attempted (Fig. 43, A). As found, the supports near the edges of Saltern I each had a right-angled notch at the top, this facing towards the centre of the feature, while the bases had concave surfaces, pressed into the blue clay lining of the feature. The shaping of the bases in this instance seems unnecessary, unless these supports were prefabricated and could be used either way up. It seems probable that the ends of these supports were shaped to fit different angles of the object (presumably a large container or trough) to be supported, and that when these supports were positioned, the appropriate end would be selected to fit the container, the other end being temporarily 'redundant'. After use, the support might be removed and re-used in the same position or inverted. A similar support is illustrated by Swinnerton (1932, fig. 8, 2a) with its concave surface uppermost and there is a support with a concave surface from Norwood, March in the central Fenland (Potter 1981, fig. 17, no. 11). Mayes was of the opinion that these shaped supports were placed at the ends of large trough-like containers within Saltern I. Many fragments of containers were recovered from the site, and it would appear that base angles of 90, and base angles with a more rounded profile are represented. If the reconstruction of these containers by Swinnerton is followed (1932, fig. 7), then the ends of the large 'dishes' have a right-angled junction of the wall and base, with a rounded angle along the sides. Mayes' supports at the edges of Saltern I would therefore have supported the ends of a container placed transversely across the feature, with additional support in the centre being provided by the flat-ended support in the centre of the feature. Unburnt patches on the bases of containers where they were supported have been noted by Baker (1960, 27; 1975, 31). A further characteristic of the containers or troughs, noted by Swinnerton (1932, 246) is that their rims are frequently missing. Among the fragments from OS 33, there is not only evidence of such rim fracture and its repair (Fig. 40, Nos 6–7), but also small pieces of clay ('bridges') which seem to have been squeezed between and over the rims of adjacent troughs, in two instances retained fragments of container rims, trapped between the central stem and the projection on one side (Fig. 41, Nos 26 and 30). This suggests that the containers were placed side by side within such features as Saltern I, with these small 'bridges' providing some degree of lateral support.

On the evidence from Saltern I, it may therefore be suggested that large containers or troughs were arranged transversely across the feature, these resting on prefabricated supports. The butt-end of Saltern I was described as a stoke-hole, and the feature can perhaps be interpreted as a semi-sunken hearth, although there was no evidence that fires were set at intervals along the base of the feature. Possible parallels for this type of hearth, with a stoke-hole and semi-sunken feature in which briquetage containers were supported might be the 'flues' of Red Hill VIII, Goldhanger (Essex), Ingoldmells (Lincs) and Funton (Kent) (Rodwell 1979, fig. 10).

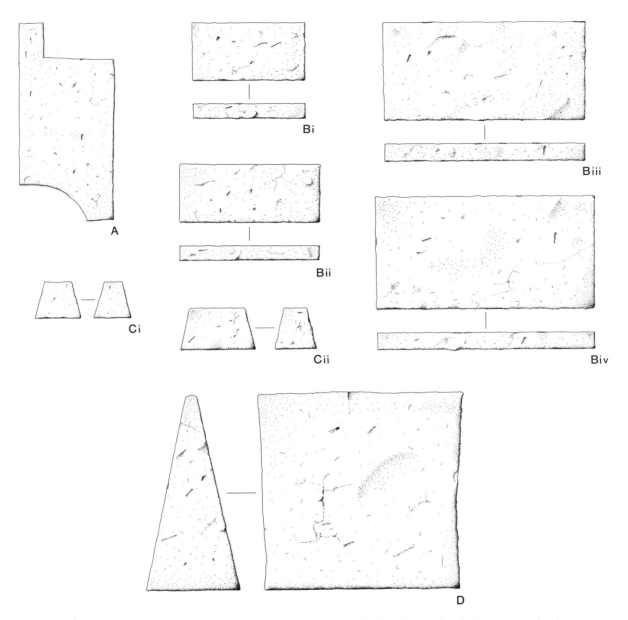

Figure 43 Suggested appearance of briquetage objects described in the site notebooks but not retained.
A. Shaped prop or support (Mayes Saltern I; Fig. 18, Section 8). Scale 1:4
B. Flat slabs or bricks (Greenfield notebook), Bi and Bii from Trench IV,
Biii and Biv from Trench XXIII. Scale 1:8
C. 'Truncated pyramidical stilts' (Greenfield notebook). Scale 1:4
D. Tapered support (Mayes, Salterns I and III). Scale 1:4

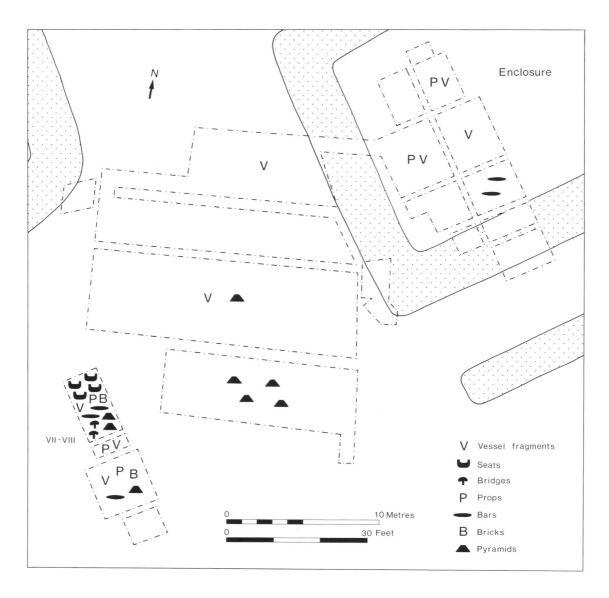

Figure 44 Site B West; distribution of briquetage types. Scale 1:250

Apart from these shaped supports, a wide range of other supports or props was encountered (Fig. 42), these perhaps being small supports (not necessarily prefabricated) which might have been used to level up the containers. The 'seats' (Fig. 41, Nos 15–18) remain enigmatic, there being no obvious explanation of their function. Similar objects have been interpreted as supports for the bases of pedestals (Riehm 1962, Abb. 20), although this seems far from satisfactory; greater stability would certainly have been achieved by lodging the base of a pedestal in the clay lining of a feature than by resting it in a 'seat', which would have made the whole arrangement intrinsically unstable.

Equally enigmatic are the flat slabs or bricks (Fig. 43, B; Pl. XXVI) and the 'truncated pyramidical stilts' (Fig. 43, C), both of which are known only from the site notes and Mayes' plan of Saltern I. The 'stilts' are candidates for a second category of support, although how these were used, assuming that they served a different purpose to that of the other supports, remains unknown. A third, larger type of support is known only from Mayes' notes, Salterns I and III (Fig. 43, D).

The flat slabs or bricks seem to have been present in some quantity, and they clearly belong to some part of the salt-production process. Swinnerton refers to similar objects, rectangular, elongated oval or circular in shape (1932, 246; Accessory 1), although no interpretation of their function is offered. There was no evidence to suggest that they formed raised floors within the features, although their use as such cannot be totally discounted.

Turning now to the features in which significant concentrations of briquetage were apparently either recovered or recorded, it is clear that this industrial evidence came primarily from four features; Mayes' Saltern II and Mayes' Saltern I/Greenfield F55 (same feature) on Site B East, and *F1* and *F8* on Site B West. Distributions of the various briquetage artefact types on Site B West and Site B East are illustrated on Figures 44 and 45.

Three of the features which produced quantities of briquetage, *F1, F8* and *F55*/Saltern I, had numerous stake-holes cut into their bases. Attention has already been drawn to Hallam's statement that 'Mr Greenfield's fire-trenches showed circular settings of stake-holes of the

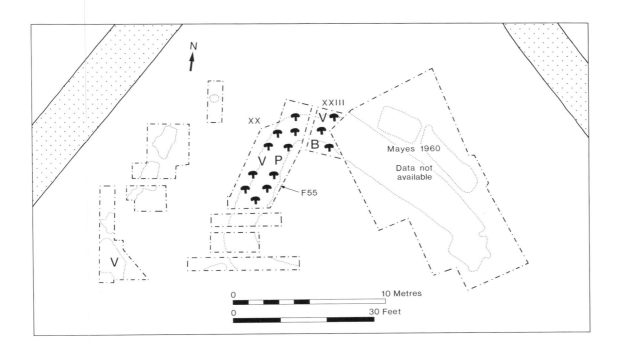

Figure 45 Site B East; distribution of briquetage types. For key see Figure 44. Scale 1:250

right dimensions for supporting such a pot (calcite-gritted 'pancheon') in position'. Additionally, the entry in the Gazetteer in Phillips (1970), states that the stake-hole circles were *c.* 1yd (90cm) in diameter. The 'pancheons' referred to are large circular calcite-gritted pans, with rim diameters up to 1m. They are known from finds at Crowland (Phillips 1970, Site 3012), Moulton (Site 2916), Weston (Site 2716S), Fleet-Gedney (Site 3516S) and Saturday Bridge, Holbeach (Site 3520) (Hallam, S.J. 1970, 86, n. 142). A close examination of the original site plan (drawn at a scale of 1:24) of *F1* and *F8* suggests that this assertion cannot be sustained; there is no apparent pattern to the stake-holes in the bases of these features, and there are no obvious circular stake-hole settings. What then were these stake-holes for? The majority seem to have been quite substantial, *c.* 11cm deep, while a few were *c.* 33cm deep or deeper. Stakes within these would have had sufficient strength to support either large containers or troughs, or equally a raised floor of the flat slabs which were found in abundance in several features. The evidence here is inconclusive, although it is certain that fires cannot have been set within these features, as this would have resulted in an instant collapse of whatever these stakes supported. As suggested previously, any heat source must have been confined to a stoke-hole, with the feature acting as a flue. It is possible that there may have been turf walls on either side of the features, and an area of turves was recorded in the fill of *F8* (Fig. 21). The salt-production process does not require particularly high temperatures, and for the evaporation of thickened brine to crystalline salt or the drying of salt crystals, a warm through-draught, such as might be produced in a semi-sunken flue with a turf wall superstructure and fired from a stoke-hole at one end, would be sufficient.

V. Zoological and Botanical Evidence

The animal bones
(not illustrated)
The animal bone collection was hand-picked, and consisted of 138 identifiable bones. These are now missing, but they were identified in 1970 by Dr Ralph Harcourt (Ancient Monuments Laboratory Report 1561).

The species represented were cattle, sheep/goat, pig, horse, fish and dog. Eighty-eight of the bones came from a dog burial in *F8* (Trench XVI, Fig. 22). The dog skeleton was that of a male, with a shoulder height of *c.* 56cm. One abnormal feature was noted, which was that the tibiae and the fibulae were fused.

Further environmental evidence
(not illustrated)
The following species of marine shells were represented (identified by the author); *Cerastoderma edule* (L.) (cockle), *Ostrea edulis* (L.) (oyster) and *Mytilus edulis* (L.) (mussel).

A wood sample from the 'hut' on Site A was identified as coming from one of the following species (report in archive, author unknown): *P.Canescens* (grey poplar), *P.Tremula* (aspen) or *P.Nigra* (black poplar).

A sample of bark from the 'hut' on Site A was identified by G. Taylor as poplar.

Twenty-one charcoal samples were taken. The following species were represented: (AML Report, unnumbered, author unknown): *Populus* (poplar), *Corylus* (hazel), *Pinus* (pine), *Tilia* (lime), *Fraxinus* (ash), *Acer* (maple), *Quercus* (oak).

The pollen samples
by the late Professor H.Godwin
Two samples of peat were taken for pollen analysis. Peat Sample A was taken from a section across the Enclosure ditch on Site B West (Fig. 23), and Peat Sample B came from the Auger Hole, layer *4*.

Sample A
(Table 3)
The presence of fruits of *Chara* and seeds of *Typha*
indicate the freshwater nature of the peat, but one pollen
grain of *Althaea officinalis*, the marshmallow, suggests
brackish water conditions. The very high proportion of
pollen of herbaceous plants in relation to trees indicates
that the woodland was by no means widespread or
continuous. On the other hand, the number and variety of
weed types suggests considerable arable cultivation.
There are indications also in the pollen of local swamp or
fen development (high *Cyperaceae, Sparganium, Typha*
etc). The presence of a substantial amount of *Calluna* is
interesting, and it might have come from heath somewhere
in the neighbourhood along with the tree pollen.

Sample B
No pollen were recovered, but the presence of abundant
Juncus seeds and *foraminifera* suggest saltmarsh or
brackish conditions.

Sample A	
Travs.	17
Betula (birch)	26
Pinus (pine)	10
Ulmus (elm)	4
Quercus (oak)	29
Tilia (lime)	1
Alnus (alder)	28
Fagus (beech)	2
Corylus (hazel)	80
Salix (willow)	1
Hedera (ivy)	2
Gramineae (grasses)	170
Cyperaceae (sedge)	116
Artemisia (mugwort)	13
Calluna (heather)	10
Caryophyllaceae (campions *etc.*)	1
Chenopodiaceae (fat hen *etc.*)	11
Compositae (daisy *etc.*)	15
Cruciferae (brassicas *etc.*)	6
Plantago lanceolata (plantains)	3
Ranunculaceae (buttercup *etc.*)	14
Rubiaceae (goose grass)	2
Rumex (dock and sorrel)	2
Umbelliferae (wild carrot, cow parsley *etc.*)	10
Centaurea nigra (knapweed)	1
Menyanthes	4
Myriophyllum	4
Sparganium	90
Typha latifolia	7
Filicales	493
Polypodium	1
Pteridium (bracken)	6
Althaea officinalis (marshmallow)	1

also: fruits of *Chara*, seeds of *Typha*, fern
Spoxaufia and insect remains

Table 3 Holbeach St Johns, OS 533; Pollen Analysis of
sample A

VI. Discussion

Introduction
(Fig. 46)
The excavations at Shell Bridge, Holbeach St Johns by
Ernest Greenfield and Philip Mayes have left us with an
intriguing insight into the industrial activity of
salt-production on the silts south of the Wash in the
Romano-British period. This area is well-known and
frequently referred to as an area in which this activity was
widespread (Hallam, S.J. 1960; 1970; Simmons 1980a),
and recent survey has drawn further attention to the subject
(Hall 1978; 1981) (Fig. 46). It is perhaps not generally
appreciated, however, that while survey data provides us
with a distribution map of the industry, this is not
complemented by adequate excavation. Local workers
have engaged in limited excavation, but the results remain
largely unpublished.

The excavation of the site at Shell Bridge cannot be
held up as an example of how these sites should be dealt
with, although this was by no mans the fault of the
excavators. Working under rescue conditions in 1961,
given the excavation and recording methods of the time,
Greenfield made a valiant attempt to excavate and record
the enigmatic features within the excavated areas, and to
understand the function of the briquetage which was
recovered. However, it remained unclear throughout the
excavation precisely what was being excavated, whethre
the briquetage was being manufactured or used on the site,
and if the latter, what it was being used for. The excavation
summary of August 1961 left these problems unanswered.
Consequently, post-excavation work on the site records
has not resolved many problems arising from the
excavations. It is hoped that future research and
excavation will be able to provide answers to some of the
questions asked here.

The excavations: Site A
On Site A, large volumes of pottery (mainly of second and
third century date) had been ploughed up, and there
appeared to be a discrete 'occupation area', coincident
with a dark soil-mark. The excavation exposed two
features, the so-called 'Hut' and a pit, within a triangular
enclosure. On the south side of Site A, there were two
small square enclosures, similar to the enclosure on Site
B West (see below).

There are few details of the excavated features, and
interpretation must necessarily be cautious. The
identification of an oval or subrectangular ash-filled
hollow as a 'hut', implying some kind of dwelling or
structure, seems improbable. The presence of what is
described as a 'hearth', suggests industrial activity of
some kind.

The excavations: Site B West
The period of occupation on Site B West dates, on the
evidence of the pottery, to the mid-second to early third
century. Two large 'hollows', *F8* and *F32* were excavated,
and a number of other linear and non-linear features were
exposed. The bases of one of the hollows, *F8* and one of
the linear features, the ditch *F1*, were cut by large numbers
of stake-holes. *F8*, the ash-filled irregular hollow, was
described by Greenfield as a 'hut', but this interpretation
seems, in retrospect, highly improbable, and its ashy fills
suggest industrial activity in this area of the site. Perhaps

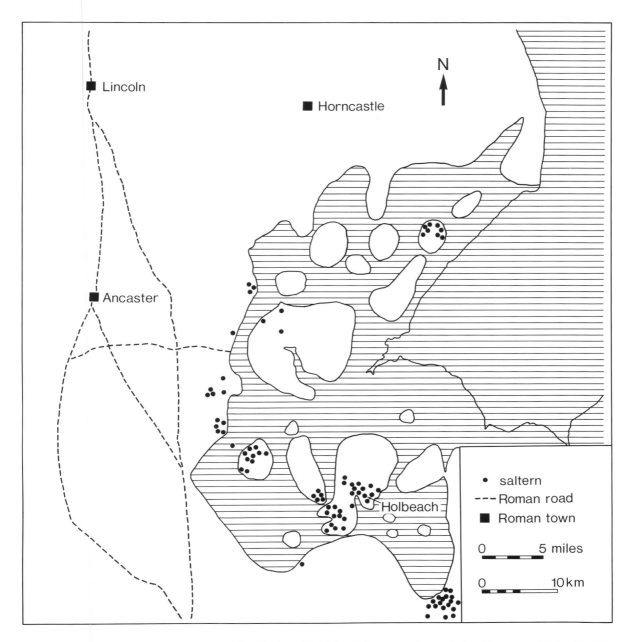

Figure 46 The Roman coastline around the Wash *c*. AD200 and Roman salterns (after Simmons 1980a, fig. 31).
Scale 1:500,000

in a phase of occupation following the period of industrial activity, the disused feature became a dump for household debris. The Enclosure ditch which circumnavigates *F8* may not be contemporary with *F8*, and Greenfield certainly believed that it was later in date. The fills of the Enclosure ditch unfortunately contained no finds which might have dated it.

There were no obvious patterns in the distribution of the stake-holes in the bases of *F1* and *F8*. It might be possible to envisage these features as semi-sunken flues with some kind of temporary superstructure but any conclusive evidence of how these features operated is lacking. If *F8* and the ditch to the west, *F1*, were similarly used (as suggested by the stake-holes in both features), then it is possible that *F1* was an existing linear feature which was utilised for the same activities as those being carried out in the 'hollows'.

F32, between *F1* and *F8* seems not to have had stake-holes in its base, neither was much briquetage apparently recovered from its fills. Perhaps *F32* was, as Greenfield described it, a large 'clay-pit', filled with ash from the working of the hearth-like features nearby.

F13 to the west of *F32* provided more tangible evidence of a possible hearth-like feature. The sides of *F13* were burnt as a result of intense heat, and at one end a small circular hollow may have been a stoke-hole. Within the feature there seems to have been a rectangular hollow or scoop, and this small hearth-like feature is reminiscent of the hearths at Ingoldmells (Baker 1960, fig. 5), Peldon, Essex (de Brisay 1978, fig. 3), Cliffe, Kent (Miles 1975, fig. 13) and Funton Creek, Kent (Detsicas 1984, fig. 1).

In summary the excavation of Site B West exposed a number of enigmatic features, the functions of which are unclear. Ash-filled hollows or linear features with numerous stake-holes and finds of briquetage suggest industrial activity, while the amount of pottery recovered also indicates occupation perhaps of a more domestic character in the vicinity.

The excavations: Site B East

The evidence from Site B East was essentially industrial. Finds from the excavated features consisted almost entirely of briquetage, particularly in Saltern I/*F55*. The virtual absence of domestic occupation debris is in marked contrast to Site B West.

The main feature exposed in this area by Mayes and Greenfield was a U-shaped broad shallow feature, lined with a thick layer of blue clay and filled with briquetage and ash (Saltern I/*F55*. During the excavation of the feature, the question of its function was never resolved. Greenfield initially thought it to be a saltern, and later a corn-drier, although the latter theory was soon abandoned.

Within Saltern I/*F55*, briquetage supports were found *in situ*, and it was suggested that these supported briquetage containers or troughs. A butt-end of the feature was interpreted as a stoke-hole. Information from Greenfield cited in Philips (1970, 309) refers to 'trenches whose clay linings had been baked hard by heat'. stake-holes cutting the base of the feature (like those in *F1* and *F8* on Site B West) were recorded in one area.

Saltern I/*F55* appears to be similar in some respects to the hearth-like features of Site B West, and it seems probable that on both areas of Site B, similar or related activities were taking place. Mayes noted that much of the briquetage was coated with a 'glaze', suggesting that brine-processing may have been that activity. There are also indications that similar 'glazed' patches were found on the clay-lined base of the feature.

Other features on Site B East consist of Salterns I and II excavated by Mayes and a number of other non-linear features recorded by Greenfield. These are all outside the U-shaped Saltern I/*F55*, and they were described as 'clay pits'. Their ashy fills with briquetage may be material cleared from Saltern I/*F55*. There may have been features within the area enclosed by Saltern I/*F55*, but this area was not excavated.

The evidence for salt-production

It is clear from the briquetage recovered that the industrial activity being carried out on the site was that of salt-production. Similar briquetage objects have been recovered from many sites in Lincolnshire, among them Ingoldmells (Swinnerton 1932). There are however few excavated sites which provide information about how the briquetage was used, and in the absence of detailed evidence from excavated salterns, the mechanics of the industry must remain largely conjectural.

We can be reasonably certain that the briquetage was being used on the site, but the on-site manufacture of the briquetage objects can by no means be discounted.

Excavations at Denver (Fig. 47) on the Norfolk Fen-edge by Charles Green in 1960 provided more conclusive evidence of how the briquetage recovered there was used, and it was proved possible to suggest a model for the salt-production process (Gurney 1986, 138–141). The briquetage at Denver was however quite different to that from Shell Bridge, consisting mainly of robust cylindrical supports, large evaporation troughs and smaller circular vessels. The distinctive 'seats' and

'bridges' of Holbeach were not represented, and neither were there the flat slabs or bricks, or the 'truncated pyramidical stilts'. There are certainly important differences between the few excavated briquetage assemblages which demand comparison and explanation, although this will perhaps only be feasible when further material from the various areas of the Fenland is available for study.

The excavated features consisted mainly of linear features and irregular hollows with ashy fills and briquetage. It seems reasonable to assume that these features were utilised for the salt-production process. One linear feature, Saltern I/*F55*, was clay-lined, it had evidence of burning and a possible stoke-hole in a butt, and briquetage supports were found *in situ*. This feature was, however, U-shaped in plan and some 30m long, and it is difficult to see how this might have operated as a semi-sunken hearth along its whole length. On Site B West, *F13*, a shallow hollow *c*. 3m long and *c*. 80cm wide with a stake-hole at one end and extensive burning seems far more convincing as a hearth, and can be more easily paralleled.

Several of the excavated features had large numbers of stake-holes cut into their bases, and these remain enigmatic. Greenfield thought that they supported briquetage containers, but the evidence is not conclusive, and parallels are lacking. It has been suggested to the present writer by Brian Simmons that these stake-holes might have held stakes supporting some kind of flimsy roof structure, the function of which would have been to prevent rain water from diluting reservoirs of salt water. This would have resulted in considerable economies in fuel in the event of rain, and natural evaporation by sun and wind might not have been seriously hampered by such an arrangement; brick and tile makers have protected their pre-fired products from rain damage in similar ways.

Thus, while there are parallels at other salt-production sites for, for example, the briquetage types and the small hearth *F13*, there are equally a number of elements which, to the author's knowledge were not found elsewhere. The most important of these would appear to be the complexes of stake-holes in the bases of features. Questions which might have been answered at the time of the excavation still need to be resolved. We know that several of the features produced evidence of burning but the precise extent of this was not planned, not any record made of its apparent intensity. If some of the features were semi-sunken hearths, evidence of any superstructure might have survived around the edges or in the fills of the features, and careful excavation might have provided an answer. Various categories of briquetage artefact were abundant in the feature fills, notably the flat slabs or bricks, but are not represented in the extant collection, and these would be crucial to any reconstruction of the salt-production process. Similar slabs were found at Ingoldmells by Swinnerton (1932, 246), at Hogsthorpe (Kirkham 1981, 8), at Helpringham (pers. comm. Brian Simmons) and at Cooling, Kent (Miles 1975, 28). Slabs found at Middlewich, Cheshire were thought to have been used in semi-sunken hearths, to seal up gaps around evaporation troughs resting upon cylindrical supports, thereby conserving heat (Bestwick 1975, 69).

One further nettle that has yet to be grasped is how a supply of salt water was brought to the site. The linear features which traverse the area around Shell Bridge may

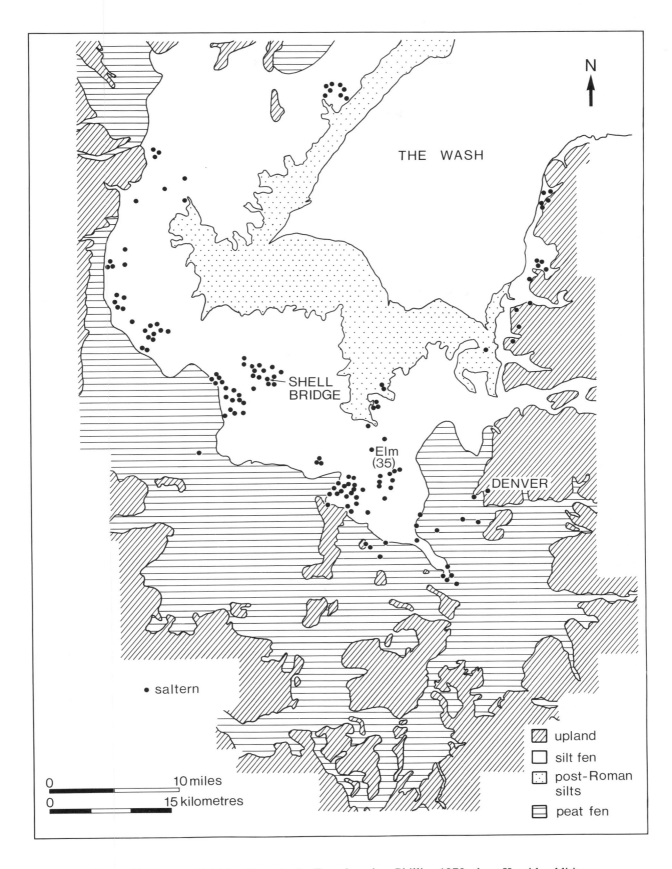

Figure 47 Romano-British salterns in the Fens, based on Phillips 1970, sheet K, with additions

have functioned as site subdivisions, but equally they might have been involved in channelling water to areas of the site where salt extraction was taking place. The droveways which are the most obvious and long-distance features of the Romano-British landscape, if not for livestock management and/or movement could have been canalised roddons (pers. comm. Brian Simmons), in which case the apparent emphasis on livestock on the silts would become far less certain. Unpublished work on the soils from sites in Hacconby Fen (cf. Simmons 1980b, fig. 26) has suggested that the 'droveways' may not have been primarily for livestock (pers. comm. Brian Simmons), but detailed study of the soil types and the funciton of the 'droveways' within the Romano-British landscape are needed before the question can be resolved.

Romano-British settlement in the Holbeach area

In the Iron Age, the coastline ran well to the west and south of Holbeach, the area around Shell Bridge being part of a shallow salt water lagoon with only a single island (Simmons 1980a, fig. 32). Early in the Roman period, following a significant change in the relative levels of the sea and the land, the silts deposited in the Iron Age in what is now South Lincolnshire had emerged to become dry land suitable for settlement, and by c. AD 200, there were a number of large islands. Shell Bridge seems to have been on the southern edge of the largest of these, at the head of a small inlet (Fig. 46). This would have been scrubby country, cut by deep tidal creeks, but attractive for occupation; the area was virgin territory, and free from forests needing clearance. There would also have been considerable assets in such coastal territory, not only teeming with fish and wildfowl, but also an ideal location for salt-production.

Settlement in this area seems to have started in the late first century AD, and the *floruit* of occupation was probably during the second century, when even clay areas as low as 4–5ft OD were ditched (Hallam, S. 1970, 45). Generally, however, the minimum level at which flood-free occupation could be expected was probably c. 7ft OD (Salway 1970, 3). The settlement pattern which developed on the newly-emerged silts is characterised by small farmsteads and villages, and the area apparently lacks evidence of ordered land divisions, substantial buildings or administrative centres. The silts, transversed by a tortuous network of watercourses could hardly have been divided up into regular holdings, and settlement would necessarily have had to be irregular; this led to a wide variety of settlement and field patterns.

Salterns certainly seem to have been active by the Hadrianic period, and like those elsewhere in the Fens (Hall 1978, 26 and fig. 2); Evans and Mostyn 1970, 10 and fig. 6) these were located by the sides of tidal creeks, from which could be obtained an inexhaustible supply of salt water. Figure 47 illustrates the distribution of salterns over the whole Fen area, excluding as yet unpublished results from the Fenland Survey. There are a number of saltern sites on the silts around Holbeach, a group of fifteen (including Shell Bridge) in Whaplode Fen, Holbeach Fen and Fleet Fen, and sixteen a short distance to the west in Weston Fen and Moulton Fen. Another major group lies to the south-east between Elm, where thirty-five saltern sites have been recorded by Hall (1978), and the northern edge of the 'boot'-shaped gravel island of March, Cambridgeshire. To the south and north-east, there are scattered salterns along the Old Croft River to Littleport, sites with briquetage in the peat Fen between the Old Croft River and the upland at Denver, and a number on the skirtland in north-west Norfolk. North-west of Holbeach, sites are scattered along the west side of the silt fen in Pinchbeck South Fen and Pinchbeck North Fen, Horbling Fen, Bicker Fen and Holland Fen, and finally a cluster of eight sites on Wrangle Common.

This distribution makes sense when viewed against Simmon's probable Roman coastline (Fig. 46), the sites either being located on the seaward edge of the silts, or on islands. As Simmons also notes, the salterns seem to cluster on the leeward sides of the islands, probably not only for protection from the harshness of the North Sea, but more importantly, where there are more likely to be tidal ponds which might have acted as natural evaporating basins (1980a, 65).

Turning now to the Romano-British landscape around Shell Bridge, it is clear that the area is covered with a complex system of droveways, fields or large paddocks and small enclosures. These linear features and enclosures remain undated, but Greenfield was clearly of the opinion (and this is to some degree supported by the evidence of the excavations) that the droveways and field systems post-dated the period to which the excavated features belong, that is, the mid-second to early-third century. It is unfortunate that the excavations by Greenfield did not take the opportunity to examine and date at least some of the features which survived as earthworks at the time of the excavation.

Within this complex landscape, areas of 'occupation' can be suggested from concentrations of pottery in the topsoil, usually coincident with areas of dark soil. These are plotted on Figure 16 and apart from small isolated area of 'occupation', the main concentration of these areas lies between Site B and the droveway, within large fields or enclosures bordering the side-drove leading to Site B. At present we have little idea of the structures and dwellings which must have been dotted across the Romano-British landscape. Hallam refers to 'sometimes precisely defined sub-rectangular sites of structures fo perishable materials', presumably mud or turf structures with reed thatch, and also in Weston Fen, a subrectangular area 38ft by 28ft bordered by a narrow V-shaped eaves-drip gully (Hallam, S.J. 1964, 21 and 26). The small square or subrectangular 'curtilage' enclosures, like those on Site A and Site B may well have been for, or adjacent to areas of 'domestic' occupation, although while the interior of the Enclosure on Site B West produced much occupation debris, the evidence points equally to industrial activity in this area of the site.

The close association of domestic and industrial occupation or activity seems to be quite common on the settlements in the area, and Hallam notes that 'groups of small ditched enclosures were found to coincide with groups of concentrations of Romano-British domestic debris (sherds, bones, shells, quern fragments, and areas of soil discoloration), and that scattered among these concentrations of domestic debris were other concentrations of saltern debris, forming part of the same group' (1960, 41). Within individual settlements, the domestic and industrial components were rarely precisely coincident, and on the ground the different areas are visible as patches of dark soil with pottery (domestic occupation) and patches of loose red soil with briquetage (industrial areas) (Hallam, S.J. 1960, 43). Such a situation may well have been the case at Shell Bridge, with domestic occupation within the Enclosure on Site B West, and industrial activity a short distance to the east (Site B East).

As far as the later Roman period is concerned, the extensive settlement of the silt Fens in the first half of the second century does not seem to have been a complete success; many Hadrianic sites were abandoned by the late second century, and there seem to have been increasing problems with drainage (Salway 1970, 14). In the mid-third century, many Fenland sites were subjected to a period of freshwater flooding, perhaps caused by a breakdown or total collapse of existing drainage systems. This particularly affected low-lying sites in the southern and central Fenlands, while on the silts, occupation does not come to an end, but there is certainly a reduction in its intensity (Salway 1970, 15). Whether or not sites on the silts were directly affected, the catastrophe in the southern Fens may have had far-reaching effects on the Fenland as a whole. The later settlements on the silts tend to be larger, more compact nuclei, in contrast to the small clustered settlements of the early Roman occupation. These larger nuclei seem to date from the mid-third century through to the late fourth (Hallam, S.J. 1970, 58).

In this area, salt-production seems to have been an important activity, although it seems unlikely that it was the mainstay of the economy. Sheep- and cattle-rearing may well have formed the economic basis of the farmsteads in the area (three cheese-presses among the pottery point to dairy farming), and if this was the case, then the production of salt, perhaps on a seasonal part-time basis, would have provided an essential commodity for preservation of meat (and other foodstuffs) and for tanning hides. Given the saline conditions which must have prevailed in the area, large-scale arable cultivation seems unlikely, although a number of quern fragments were recovered. Hallam, S.J. (1970, 63) concludes that the 'detailed R.-B. lay-out raised doubts whether cereal cultivation round the Wash can have been at more than subsistence scale'. Her analysis of the field-systems (1970, 64–7) shows great variety, although small enclosures tend to cluster around settlements, with a looser mesh of ditches covering the areas between settlements. Overall, 'the field pattern indicates that pasture was more important than arable' (Hallam, S.J. 1970, 66).

Finally, looking at the silt Fens as a whole, the question of the area as part of an imperial estate must be considered. The arguments for (the absence of villas or administrative centres, the relatively low status of the settlements, the fact that the area was virgin territory which might have been absorbed automatically into the emperor's domain, and the fact that salt-production as an extractive industry may well have been under imperial control; Salway 1970, 10) are attractive, but direct evidence is lacking.

In conclusion, while the excavations at Shell Bridge have done little to elucidate the process of salt-production in the area in the Romano-British period, the questions arising from the excavation suggest possible avenues for future research. The period between 1961 and 1986 has seen little work in the Holbeach area (but see below, Bell/this volume), and there are no sites in the area with which the site described here can be compared. When further excavation does take place, it is possible that the enigmatic features excavated by Greenfield and Mayes may be better understood.

Chapter 3. The Romano-British Salt-making Site at Shell Bridge, Holbeach St Johns: Excavations 1983

by A.C. Bell

I. Summary

Parts of a Romano-British landscape were sampled — one droveway in the northern part of the field and another with two adjacent enclosures to the south.

Of the northern droveway, only the silt trackway and the lower profile of one of the ditches survived. The surviving ditch produced only three small sherds of Romano-British pottery.

The southern droveway, which also followed a rodham for part of its course, was sampled in three segments and the ditches were found to be devoid of finds. Part of the western ditch and the interior of an enclosure on the north side of this droveway were excavated, without any signs of occupation. The droveway also cut an enclosure on its southern side. A dog-leg ditch was excavated in this enclosure, and yielded a large group of pottery dated to the late second to early third centuries AD.

The drove ditches in the southern part of the field had been recut but truncated by subsequent ploughing. The droveway had also been cut by an obliquely angled ditch with an atypical marine mollusc content contained within its fill, presumably accruing during a different depositional environment.

II. Introduction

(Fig. 48)

In September 1983 the Central Excavation Unit (CEU) undertook a plough damage evaluation of field OS 46, part of the Romano-British fenland drove and enclosure system at Holbeach St Johns, Grid Ref TF 339159 (Fig. 48). Part of this system lies within field 46, which is located on the southern bank of the South Holland Main Drain, some 8 miles south-east of Spalding and, which with neighbouring field 45 to the east, forms SAM site Lincolnshire No. 168. Previous excavations by P. Mayes, E. Greenfield and J.C. Mossop have been conducted on the drove system in fields OS 45 and 33 (OS 33 this volume. See also Hallam S.J. 1970, 102 sites 3416N Holbeach, Shell Bridge N and 3416S Holbeach, Somerset House).

As no earthworks survive in this field, the excavation research design was based upon available aerial photographs (St Joseph NZ 21, NZ 22, NZ 25; NMR TF 3415/2/235, TF 3415/3/299, TF 3415/4/310). It was apparent from the cropmarks showing on these photographs that the field systems of this settlement extended not only between fields OS 45 and 46 but for several miles in all directions. The droveways and the associated enclosures were sampled by excavation as these constitute the major features of the landscape and

offered the best possibility of determining any occupational or functional evidence for the part of the settlement within field OS 46.

Parts of two droveways were excavated: Droveway 31 in the north-eastern and Droveway 58 in the south-eastern corner of the field (site sub-divisions 1 and 2–3 respectively), the latter drove having been sectioned previously by Mossop and Mayes in field OS 33 on the northern side of the South Holland Main Drain (this volume).Two enclosures associated with Droveway 58 were also excavated (one in site sub-division 6, the other in site sub-divisions 3, 4 and 5). Both are of the sub-rectangular shape common in the Fens.

III. The Excavations

Droveway 31. Site Sub-division 1
(Figs 49, 50, 55)

Droveway 31 was found to be sited upon the raised bed of a rodham (an extinct watercourse left upstanding by shrinkage of the surrounding peats: Salway 1970, 2; Fowler 1950, 7; Godwin 1938). The use of rodham beds for droves is common in the Fens (see Simmons 1980a, 59 for Hacconby). Usually such a droveway has a ditch on either side, but only part of the western ditch (*16*) survived. This ditch had been cut by a post-medieval ditch (*7*) which followed its line, and only half of the profile remained, suggesting an original U shape. Only three sherds of Nene Valley grey ware were recovered from this ditch, and it is impossible to offer a precise date for this feature.

The assumed eastern drove-ditch had been completely removed by the insertion of a post-medieval ditch (*9*) which also followed the line of the droveway. It seems that the Roman ditches survived to this period and were reused.

The post-medieval ditches *7* and *9* appear to have been for drainage purposes, with ditch *4* being added on an east/west axis to increase the catchment area. This would suggest that the droveway had ceased to be used by this period. Ditches *7* and *4* filled contemporaneously, with sherds from individual pottery vessels occurring in both. However, whilst ditch *7* was only 0.6m deep, ditch *9* was 1.46m in depth, considerably wider, and similar in proportions to the modern dykes.

Both ditch *7* and ditch *9* had steep-sided flat-bottomed profiles, whilst ditch *4*, designed to collect the maximum amount of water possible, had been dug in a perfect U shape. The pottery and commemorative medallion from these ditches suggest a *terminus post quem* of the late sixteenth to early seventeenth centuries for all three (Fig. 55).

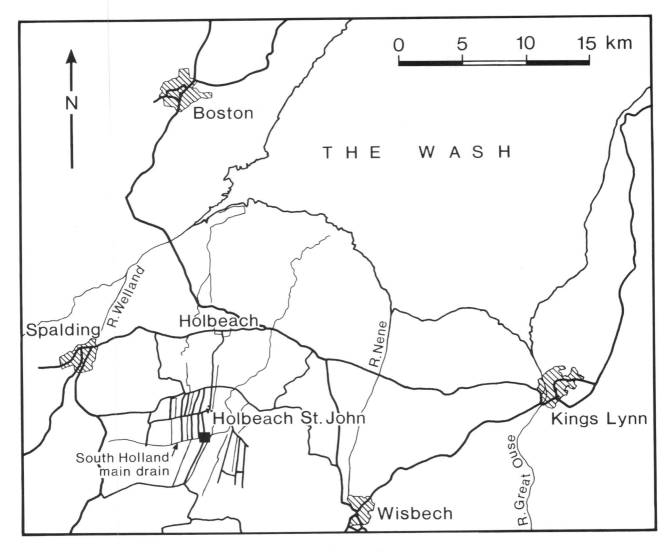

Figure 48 1983: location map

The ploughing in this area had cut the top of the rodham, whose silts formed a distinct lens in the top fills of the ditches, suggesting that these also have been truncated.

Droveway 58 and Associated Enclosures. Site Sub-divisions 2 to 7
(Figs 49, 51)

Two enclosures and the southerly droveway were investigated in these site sub-divisions.

The earliest feature proved to be the enclosure on the southern side of the droveway. Site sub-division 6 was sited in this enclosure and revealed a dog-leg shaped ditch (*81*). This ditch had a flat-bottomed, steep-sided profile which was apparent only to a height of some 0.4m before the edges became indistinguishable. The surviving ditch profile was 1.6m wide and between 0.7m to 0.8m in depth.

A group of Romano-British pottery was found in this ditch, mainly in the lower gleyed silt fill, but also to a lesser extent in the upper peaty fill. No other evidence of occupation was found in this site sub-division but the ceramic assemblage suggests that a domestic focus was nearby. Fieldwalking evidence indicates that this is located in the neighbouring field immediately to the south of the

modern field boundary dyke. The pottery dates to the late second early third century AD (Figs 52–54). A radiocarbon sample from the peaty top fill of this ditch, which would have formed over a period, gave a date of 397–562 cal AD (HAR-6364; 1580 ± 80 BP).

This enclosure seems not to have been respected by the droveway, as the southern drove ditch *59* appeared to cut ditch *81*, although the possibility of the drove ditch having been recut at a later date cannot be ruled out. Both this drove ditch and the smaller northern one (*52*) had, flat-bottomed shallow to near steep sided profiles in their lower portions, filled by mottled silts which varied only slightly from segment to segment. Both showed evidence of more rounded, recut profiles with a peaty fill near their tops. These recut profiles were severely truncated by ploughing, but probably represent the redigging of the drove ditches which would have been necessary after the seasonal flooding, an event that was prevented until drainage schemes of the later eighteenth century. No artefacts were recovered from the drove ditches, but a radiocarbon sample from the peaty top fill of ditch *59* gave a *terminus ante quem* of 459–648 cal AD (HAR-6362; 1480 ± 80 BP).

71

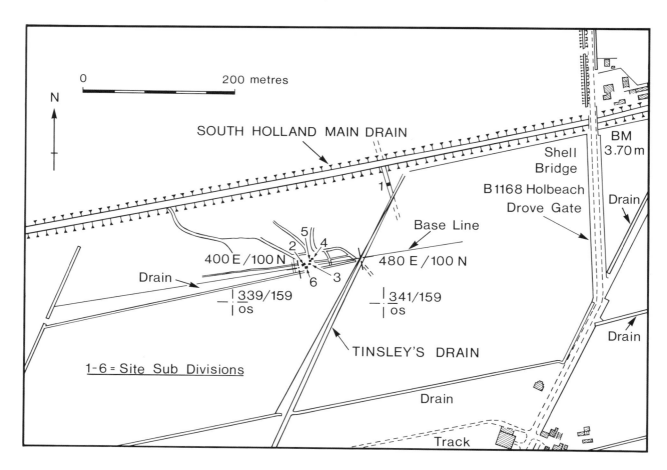

Figure 49 1983: location of the site showing the cropmarks

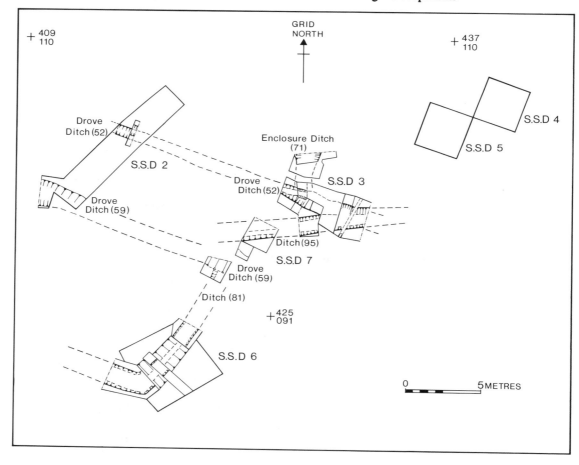

Figure 51 1983: site sub-divisions 2 to 7

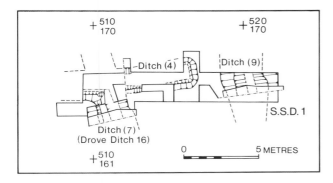

Figure 50 1983: site sub-division 1

Drove ditch *59* was between 1.7m and 1.8m wide, drove ditch *52* between 1m and 1.2m. Both survive to a depth 0.6m in depth. These dimensions are similar to those recorded by Mossop and Mayes for their section of this droveway in field OS 33 (this volume).

Contemporary with the northern drove ditch *52* was ditch *71*. This formed the western ditch to an enclosure situated on a raised rodham on the northern side of the droveway. Ditch *71* had the usual shallow sided, flat bottomed profile, a silty primary fill and a peaty secondary fill. The silt fill produced one sherd of unabraded samian of Antonine date. Ditch *71* varied between 1.6m and 1.7m in width, but survived only to a depth of 0.4m. The interior of the enclosure bounded by this ditch was excavated to the rodham silt natural in site sub-divisions 4 and 5 and was found to be devoid of occupation material.

Despite being the major landscape feature, the droveway was not respected by the latest ditch (*95*). This obliquely cut drove-ditch *52* in site sub-division 3. In common with the other ditches, ditch *95* was flat bottomed, but was characterised by its near vertical sides and a thin layer of land molluscs. This had formed on its bottom before much silting had taken place. The intersection of these ditches had been removed by the insertion of a post World War II field drain.

A few fragments of iron were the only artefacts recovered from ditch *95*.

IV. The Artefacts

Introduction

In addition to the material described below a small number of iron, glass, stone, brick and tile objects were recorded. These have not been published as all were either modern or unstratified.

The Commemorative Medallion

(Not illustrated)

Most probably a commemorative medallion issued to mark the coronation of William III and Mary II in 1689. The obverse has lost all trace of the busts but part of the legend is visible (GULIELMUS ET MARIA REX ET REGINA). The possible initials L.G.L.(?) also remain and are presumably the makers initials.

The reverse shows a version of the Garter Arms and has a legend (HONI SOIT QUI MALY PENSE). (Layer *22*, above fill *23*, ditch *9*, segment *10*)

The Romano-British Pottery
(Figs 52–54)

The following drawn vessels all came from Ditch *81* (SSD 6). The ditch fill numbers where sherds were located are given for individual forms. Vessel forms and fabrics are briefly described. The code given refers to the full fabric description, which forms part of the archive. All the illustrated forms are products of the Nene Valley.

Fabrics

Summaries of the main fabric types are as follows:

R1   Hard reduced fabric with a soapy or rough feel. Tempered with moderate quantities of fine to medium sized quartz grains and containing sparse quantities of medium sized magnetite. Usually light grey in colour throughout. Nene Valley grey ware.

R2   Hard to very hard and dense reduced fabric with a smooth feel. Tempered with sparse to moderate quantities of fine to medium sized quartz grains and containing sparse quantities of medium sized magnetite. Usually light grey with dark grey surfaces often burnished to a metalic lustre. Nene Valley grey ware.

R3   Hard reduced fabric with a soapy or smooth feel depending upon the condition of the surviving sherd. Inclusions as for R2. Usually light grey in colour with dark grey surfaces which seem to have been caused by the application of a slip using a linear, possibly wet hand technique. Nene Valley grey ware.

R4   Hard reduced fabric with a rough feel. Tempered with abundant quantities of coarse to very coarse crushed shell fragments, but also containing moderate quantities of medium sized quartz grains. Invariably black in colour throughout and usually burnished where the form allows access.

O1   Hard oxidised fabric with a slightly rough feel. Tempered with moderate quantities of medium sized quartz grains. Buff in colour with red brown colour coated surfaces. Nene Valley?

O2   Soft oxidised fabric with a soapy feel. Containing moderate quantities of quartz and haematite of coarse size. Possibly represents briquetage rather than pottery.

O3   Similar to fabric 02. Nene Valley?

O4   Hard oxidised fabric with a powdery feel due to poor ties fine sized quartz grains and containing sparse to moderate quantities of fine to medium sized haematite. Nene Valley?

F1   Typical Nene Valley colour coated fine ware fabric. White in colour with moderate quantities of fine quartz temper and containing sparse quantities of medium sized haematite.

M1   Hard oxidised mortarium fabric with a smooth feel. Tempered with moderate quantities of fine sized quartz grains and containing sparse quantities of medium sized haematite. Nene Valley.

Forms
(Figs 52–54)

Figures 52–54 illustrate each of the 33 forms as listed below.

Form 1   (Fill *87*) Angular beaker with everted rim. Colour coated Nene Valley fabric (Fabric F1).
Gillam 86; York, Bishophill 351–2 (Late second century AD); Fengate 4, fig. 130, 64, fig. 131, 79 (Antonine); Chesterton 130 (late second century AD, probably. Unpublished). OS 33, fig. 26, 110.

Form 2   (Fill *86*) Tall fairly globular beaker with everted rim. Colour coated Nene Valley fabric (Fabric F1).
Gillam 90; York, Bishophill 326 (second half of the second century AD); Ver. 1045 (barbotined *c.* 160–175 AD); Southwark 1690 (early third century AD); Maxey, Gurney 1985, fig. 85, no. 104 (residual in a third century context).

Form 3   (Fill *86*) Small globular beaker with upright rim. Reduced light grey fabric with patchy dark grey surfaces (Fabric R3). A Nene Valley product.

Form 4   (Fills *86, 87*) Large indented beaker. Colour coated Nene Valley fabric (Fabric F1).
Similar to two vessels from Chesterton, 158–159 (second half second to early third centuries AD).

Form 5   (Fills *85, 102*) Corrugated jar with upright rim; oxidised buff fabric with patchy red brown colour coated surfaces (Fabric 01). Form with decorated cordon more common. Chesterton 26–8 are undecorated (second half of second century AD). Also in pit groups in Normangate Field, Castor (*c.* 130–150 AD); OHF 1667, 2587 (mid to late second century AD). Probably first to second-century type which survives.

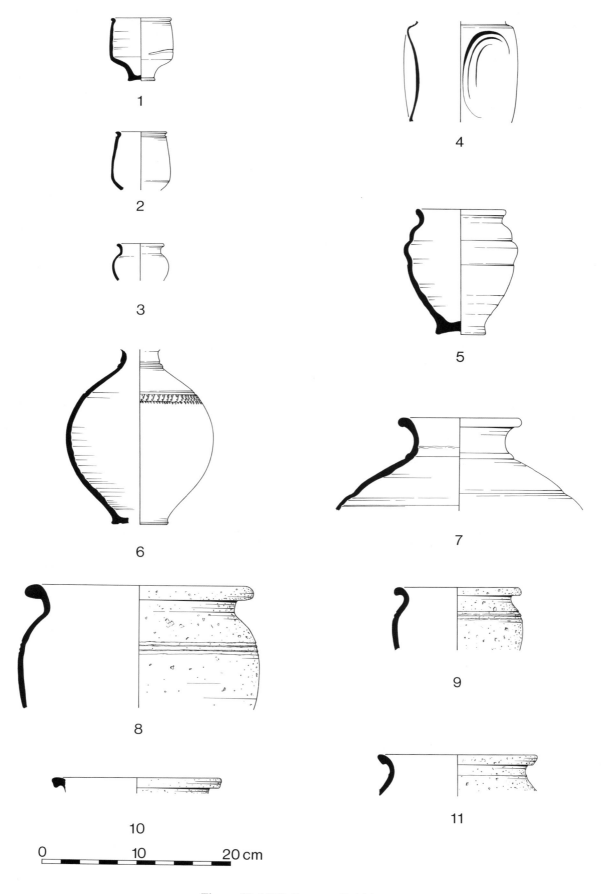

Figure 52 1983: Romano-British pottery

Form 6 (Fills *85, 87, 101*) Globular necked jar with rouletted shoulder. Hard reduced fabric, gun metal grey throughout and with a burnished exterior surface (Fabric R2). Not easy to parallel. Monument 97 (599, 727) has them in mid second century levels, also OHF 2667, 2669, 2756, 2704, all second half of the second century. None are decorated. Fengate 4 (Hayes 1984) fig. 127 11, 130, 57, 131, 71 (all Antonine) are narrow mouthed jars of various sorts.

Form 7 (Fills *86, 87*) Necked jar with cordoned neck, grooved shoulder and upright rim. Reduced light grey fabric with gun metal grey surfaces burnished on the exterior (Fabric R3). A Nene Valley product. Parallels as for Form 6.

Form 8 (Fills *86, 87*) Wide mouthed jar with heavy rim and grooved shoulder. Reduced heavily calcitic fabric, black throughout and with burnished exterior surface (Fabric R4). A Nene Valley product. Similar vessels occur in mid to late second century deposits at Monument 97 (677, 726, 727); Chesterton 434, 438 (Form 8 *cf.* 446, third century); Fengate 4 (Hayes 1984) fig. 126, 9; OHF 2584, 2767, 1672, 1707, 1755 *etc*. The form is found on all sites in the Fens and the Nene Valley.

Form 9 (Fills *85, 86, 88*) Small wide mouthed jar, similar in form to 8 above. Fabric as Form 8 (Fabric R4). Parallels as for Form 8. OS 33, fig. 26, 155.

Form 10 (Fill *87*) Rim probably of wide mouthed bowl. Fabric as Form 8 (Fabric R4). Parallels as for Form 8.

Form 11 (Layer *70*, above ditch *81*) Possible wide mouthed jar with angular rim. Fabric as Form 8 (Fabric R4). Parallels as for Form 8.

Form 12 (Fills *86, 87*) Wide mouthed bowl with upright rim and cordoned neck. Hard-high fired reduced fabric with oxidised-red brown margins. Core and surfaces gun metal grey highly burnished surfaces with a metalic sheen (Fabric R2). A Nene Valley product. Very common form. Both decorated and undecorated at Monument 97 (677, 726 mid second century AD); OHF 2207, 2347, 2209, 2669, 2702, 2704, 2756; Chesterton 33–41; Fengate 4 (Hayes 1984) fig. 136, 3–6, 27–28, fig. 129, 43–4, 51; Howe, Perrin and Mackreth 1980, no. 4. The type is basically mid second to third century AD. Decorated versions may not outlast the second century.

Form 13 (Layer *70*, Fills *83, 86, 87, 88*). Wide mouthed bowl similar to form 12. Reduced light grey fabric with patchy dark surfaces (Fabric R3). Parallels as for Form 12.

Form 14 (Fills *86, 87*) Small bowl with S shaped profile. Reduced light grey fabric with patchy dark surfaces, probably slipped (Fabric R3). Parallels as for Form 12.

Form 15 (Fill *85*) Probably a wide mouthed bowl similar to Form 12. Reduced light grey fabric with dark slipped surfaces burnished on the exterior to a near metallic lustre (Fabric R3). Parallels as for Form 12.

Form 16 (Fill *86*) Wide mouthed bowl with upright rim and burnished wavy line decoration on the grooved and cordoned neck. Reduced light grey fabric with dark, slightly patchy surfaces burnished externally (Fabric R3). Parallels as for Form 12.

Form 17 (Fill *87*) Bowl similar to Form 16. Reduced light grey fabric with gun metal grey surfaces, highly burnished externally (Fabric R2). Parallels as for Form 12.

Form 18 (Fill *86*) Bowl similar to Form 16. Fabric as for Form 17 above (Fabric R2). Parallels as for Form 12.

Form 19 (Fill *86*) Large bowl similar to Form 16. Reduced light grey fabric with patchy dark surfaces burnished externally (Fabric R3). Parallels as for Form 12.

Form 20 (Fills *86, 87*) Globular bowl with gravel and cordoned shoulder and angular rim. Reduced light grey fabric with very patchy dark surfaces (Fabric R3). Uncommon in being plain. Chesterton 44–45 (probably third century); OHF 2347 (third century); Maxey, Gurney 1985, fig. 90, no. 198 (later third century).

Form 21 (Fills *86, 87, 88*) Globular jar with rouletted shoulder and angular rim. Reduced light grey fabric with very patchy dark surfaces (Fabric R3). Similar to Form 20. Again uncommon being a rouletted jar, Howe, Perrin and Mackreth 1980, no. 9 is the more usual.

Form 22 (Fill *86*) Small carinated bowl with incised decoration on the carination. Reduced light grey fabric with patchy dark surfaces (Fabric R3).

Form 23 (Fill *84*) Flat rimmed bowl. Reduced calcitic fabric, black throughout with burnished surfaces (Fabric R4). Chesterton 486, 491–493 are similar (probably third century). At OHF such vessels are fourth century *e.g.* 87, 120, 472.

Form 24 (Fill *86*) Segmental bowl with reeded, near hammerhead rim. Badly preserved oxidised cream fabric (Fabric O4). Nene Valley product, probably Antonine or slightly later.

Form 25 (Fills *85, 87*) Strainer bowl with slight cordon at the carination. Reduced light grey fabric with dark surfaces burnished overall (Fabric R3). A vessel at Chesterton in a smooth grey ware, 416, was undated.

Form 26 (Fill *86*) Wide bowl or platter with grooved rim and foot ring. Reduced light grey fabric with dark surfaces. Lightly burnished overall (Fabric R3). The form occurs in Nene Valley Grey Ware, grey colour coat and other colour coated wares. OHF examples in NVGW or grey colour coat include 798, 552, 2347. Chesterton 96 (NVGW) was from an undated layer; the OHF examples are third century AD. Most of the grey colour coated examples ('Indixivicus', Dannell 1973), *e.g.* Wakerley 87, 170, 171 are third century.

Form 27 (Fill *88*) Flat rimmed bowl or dish with chamfer. Reduced light grey fabric with dark surfaces slightly burnished overall (Fabric R3). Very common form, occurring in both colour coated and Nene Valley Grey wares. OHF examples include 2512, 2359, 2561, 2684, all late second to mid third century. Chesterton 72, 76–80 (NVGW) and 219–221 (colour coated) are also late second to mid third century AD. OS 33, fig. 28, 151.

Form 28 (Fill *88*) Flat and grooved rim dish with chamfer. Reduced light grey fabric with patchy dark surfaces possibly burnished overall (Fabric R3). A similar rim occurred on a jar from Chesterton (17) of probable second century date. Not easily paralled.

Form 29 (Fills *86, 88*) Bowl or dish with simple rim and slight chamfer. Reduced light grey fabric with dark surfaces (Fabric R3). No exact parallel can be found but it is probably to be grouped with Forms 30 and 31.

Form 30 (Fill *86*) Dish with simple rim and slight chamfer. Reduced light grey fabric with patchy dark to mid grey surfaces possibly burnished overall (Fabric R3). A very common form. OHF examples include 361, 822, 2209, all late second to third century. Chesterton 88, 90, late second, Howe, Perrin and Mackreth 1980, no. 19 is the larger, mainly third century version. The form also occurs in colour coated fabric. Not all the colour coats need be late third to fourth century.

Form 31 (Fill *88*) Dish with simple rim and slight chamfer. Reduced light grey fabric with dark surfaces (Fabric R3). OS 33, fig. 28, 141. Late second to early third century.

Form 32 (Fills *86, 87*) Similar to Form 31. Reduced light grey fabric with dark surfaces slightly burnished overall (Fabric R3).

Form 33 (not illustrated) (Fill *86*) Mortarium flange. Oxidised cream or off-white fabric with fine quartz tempering. (Fabric M1) Possibly burnished overall.
Mrs Kay Hartley writes: 'Almost certainly made in the lower Nene Valley perhaps in the period AD 140–200 although a later date cannot be entirely ruled out'.

Discussion

A total of 103.04kg of coarse pottery was recovered, mostly as fairly complete vessels, representing a minimum vessel count of 35.

The date range of the assemblage is from the mid second to early third century, similar to that of the field OS 33, Site B West group (this volume).

The pottery is all of local manufacture, consisting mainly of grey and colour-coated vessels from the lower Nene Valley the centre of which industry was located some 15 miles (24km) to the south-west. The colour-coated wares account for only 5.8% of the minimum vessel count, and none are decorated. The grey wares total 70.5% and the calcite-gritted vessels a further 14.7%. Both the latter wares consist of utilitarian jars, bowls and dishes, which, coupled with the lack of colour-coated or samian vessels, suggest a domestic assemblage of low status similar to that recovered from field OS 33 (this volume).

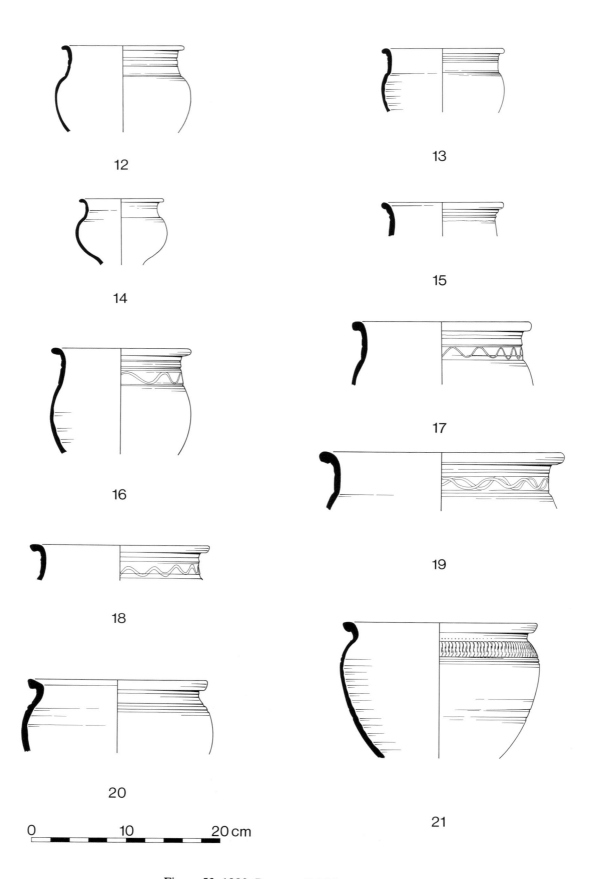

12

13

14

15

16

17

18

19

20

21

0   10   20 cm

Figure 53 1983: Romano-British pottery

76

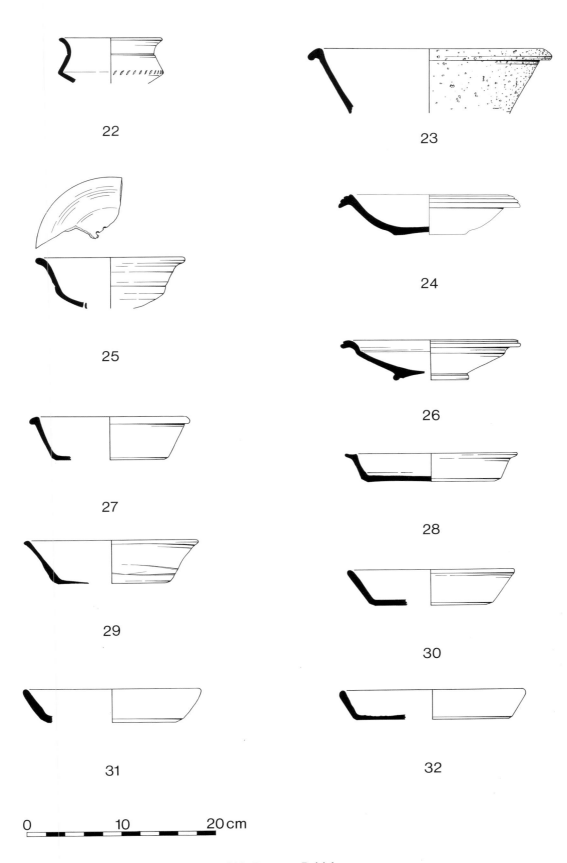

22

23

25

24

26

27

28

29

30

31

32

0   10   20 cm

Figure 54 1983: Romano-British pottery

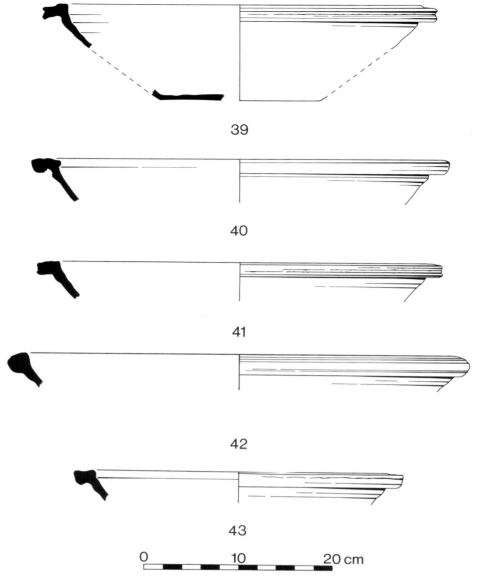

39

40

41

42

43

0   10   20 cm

Figure 55 1983: post-medieval pottery

The Samian
by Brenda M. Dickinson
(not illustrated)
Form 34 (Layer *80*, associated with Ditch *81*) Dish or bowl, Central
Gaulish. Late Hadrianic or Antonine.
Form 35 (Fill *83*) Flake of a bowl Drag 31 or 31R, Central Gaulish,
Antonine.
Form 36 (Fills *85, 88*) Drag 33, East Gaulish. Late second or early third
century AD.
Form 37 (Fill *84*) Two sherds perhaps from the same vessel (Drag 33?)
Central Gaulish, Probably Antonine. Eroded.
Samian From Enclosure Ditch *71* (Site Sub-Division 3)
Form 38 (Fill *76*). Drag 30 or 37, Central Gaulish. Antonine.

The post-medieval pottery
(Fig. 55)
The vessels are all from site sub-division 1, ditches *4, 7*
and *9*. These ditches appear to have been dug as part of the
same drainage scheme, and some vessel types are common
to all of them. Full fabric descriptions form part of the
archive. The author is grateful to Varian Denham for the
provenancing and dating of the post-medieval pottery.

Iron glazed coarsewares

Oxidised red-orange fabric with red-brown slipped surfaces and iron
glazed interior. The fabric and form occurs over the whole of the
Midlands and Lincolnshire. The fabric suggests the vessels are seventeenth century rather than eighteenth (Fabric PM1). The following drawn
vessels are all bowls with flanged rims (Pancheons).
39. Ditches *4* and *7*; fills *5* and *12* and fill *13* respectively.
40. Ditches *4* and *7*; fills *12* and *13* respectively.
41. Ditch *9* fill *23* and layer *2* containing pottery derived from
ditches *7* and *9*.
42. Layer *22* above Ditch *9* fill *23*.
43. Layer *2* containing pottery derived from ditches *7* and *9*.

Discussion
Other findings include two sherds of late medieval/early
post-medieval oxidised ware, two sherds of Staffordshire
slipware, one sherd of Staffordshire manganese glazed
ware, and two sherds of English stoneware. The range of
vessels is very similar for ditches *4, 7* and *9* in which the
most prevalent types are the iron glazed coarsewares. The
date range for the group, including those from layers *2* and
22, which need not be derived from the ditches, spans the
seventeenth to eighteenth centuries. Vessels known to
come from the ditches date to *c.* AD 1650–1750.

The Briquetage

Five sherds of coarse shell and quartz tempered ceramic material (Fabric O3) were recovered. Four sherds came from fills *83* and *86* of ditch *81* (Site Sub-division 6), one sherd from layer *108* (Site Sub-division 7). No form is determinable but the sherds obviously come from large vessels with curved sides. The sherds may represent large storage jars but are very similar in both fabric and curvature to the large pan-like vessels used for evaporation of water to obtain salt. Such vessels seem to have been used throughout the Romano-British period in the Fens. Similar briquetage has been recovered from the neighbouring field to the north of the South Holland Main Drain.

V. Zoological and Botanical Evidence

Animal Bones
by Mark Beech

A total of 408 fragments of animal bone were recovered from the site of which approximately 75% were identified to species. By far the greatest percentage of these were from a single skeleton of an immature horse. Sheep/goat, cow, pig and domestic fowl were also present (listed in order of abundance) but were only represented by a few bone fragments each. With such sparse data little can be said about the nature of the fauna. Measurements (according to Jones *et al.* 1978), butchery and ageing data were recorded and details are kept with the site archive.

The horse skeleton

The major part of a skeleton of a young foal was found articulated within fill *85* of ditch *81*, although some of the right hand side fore limb and left hand side hind limb were missing. Part of the former was scattered within the fill (distal epiphysis of humerus, radius and ulna), there was no trace of the left hind limb in any adjacent contexts. A few other bones of a mature horse were also recovered.

The bones were generally in quite a good state of preservation although a few showed signs of minor erosion and very slight mineralised concretions to the bone surface.

Details of the anatomical elements present, their degree of fragmentation, fusion data, and measurements *etc.* are included in the archive. Although it is not usual to measure immature bones, *i.e.* unfused specimens, in this case it seemed of relevance considering the completeness of skeleton. Measurements were taken to give a general indication of the size of the animal and to facilitate comparison with other immature specimens should the need arise.

The majority of the bones in the skeleton were unfused and immature. Two of the earliest fusing bones in the horse (not already fused at birth) are the scapula (super glenoid tuberosity fuses at 1 year, Silver 1963) and the proximal 2nd phalange (fuses at 9–12 months (Silver 1963). Both of these are unfused in this horse skeleton, suggesting that it had died in its first year.

The tooth eruption and wear also indicates that the animal died sometime during its first year. It had deciduous teeth and its 3rd incisors had not yet erupted. According to Silver (1963) the deciduous 3rd incisors erupt at *5 1969* months after birth. The teeth were not very worn (the deciduous 2nd incisors are only just worn) so the horse probably died before it was six months old.

It is not possible to ascertain the immediate cause of death. There was no evidence of any pathological conditions, as indicated by surface bone alteration, but not all diseases necessarily leave traces on bone (*e.g.* various types of blood borne diseases).

The pollen analysis of peat levels within the Romano-British ditches
by N.D. Balaam

Two ditch sections containing substantial deposits of peat were examined and sampled for pollen anaylsis. Radiocarbon assay of the peat from one of these (context *45*, HAR-6362) yielded a date of AD 530 ± 80. A similar peat horizon from elsewhere on the site produced a date of AD 370 ± 80 (context *84*, HAR-6364). It is assumed that the pollen spectra are both of approximately the same age.

A total of five samples were examined in detail, of these, two were from context *45* and three from context *30*. Pollen preparation was by standard techniques (Moore and Webb 1978) and identification and terminology is based on published keys of Moore and Webb (1978) and Faegri and Iversen (1964). Reference was also made to specimen collections at the Ancient Monuments Laboratory and the University of London Institute of Archaeology.

Although there are a number of minor differences in the taxa represented in the different samples and different contexts they are sufficiently similar for them to be considered as one group.

It is important to note that the peat and its associated pollen may date to a period significantly later than that of the creation of the ditched enclosures. The environment and agricultural regime suggested by the pollen analysis may, therefore, not be linked with any certainty to the setting out and first use of the field systems.

Discussion

The most readily apparent character of the spectra represented (Fig. 56) is the very low numbers of pollen grains of trees and shrubs. This is indicative of a very open landscape and there can have been very little woodland or scrub for some distance around the site at the time of formation of the peats.

The dominant feature of the herb pollen spectra is the high proportion of grasses (around 80% of the total land pollen). In most samples the grass pollen includes isolated grains of cereal type pollen, these grains are few in number and probably do not indicate any significant arable activity in the neighbourhood. The other herbaceous taxa presenty also seem more indicative of a pastoral landscape.

The pollen diagrams presented here compare well with the data derived from the analyses undertaken by Miss Andrew on samples from earlier excavations (1961) in the area. It is notable that Andrew's analyses reveal slightly higher proportions of tree pollen than are present in the analyses of the CEU material and this may indicate local variation in the landscape. The presence of higher proportions of tree pollen together with a signifcant amount of *Calluna* (ling) pollen might, however, be due to the greater representation of a long distance transport element in Andrew's samples.

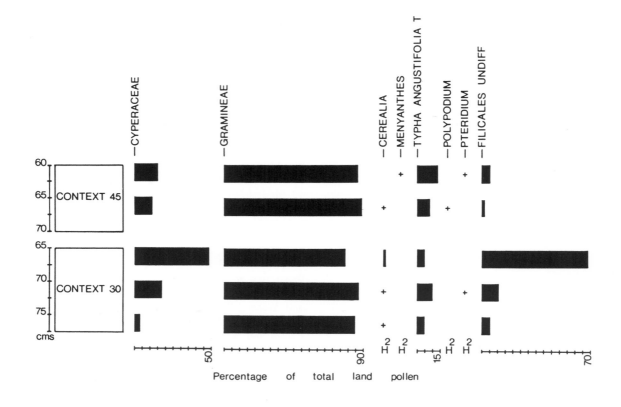

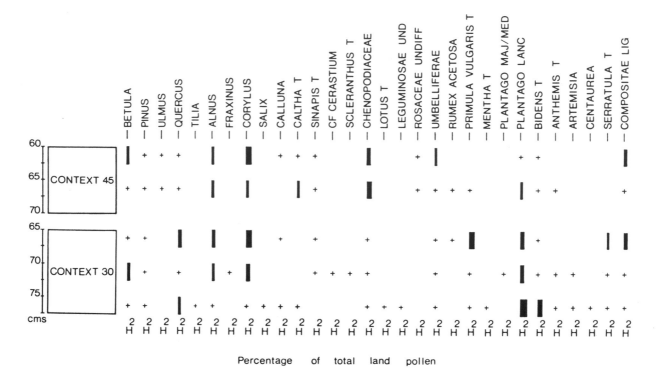

Figure 56 1983: pollen analysis

VI. Discussion

Only the enclosure cut by the southern droveway yielded a dateable ceramic assemblage (Figs 52–54). This offers a probable *terminus ante quem* for the droveway, although this cut may represent a recutting of the droveway.

Although this assemblage only provides a date for activity within the earliest enclosure, the date of late second to early third centuries AD is Hallams' proposed period of maximum Romano-British occupation of the Fens (Hallam S.J., 1961a, 152–5). The aerial photographs and previous archaeological evidence suggest that the drove system sampled during this excavation supported small settlement foci of Hallams' 'open' type, typical of the late second and early third centuries (Hallam S.J., 1961a, 152–5; 1970, 60 sites 3416N and 3416S). Neither enclosure produced any signs of occupation. Both field walking and the horizontal distribution of the finds from the excavation suggest that the settlement focus is located to the south, immediately beyond the modern field boundary. The results of J. Mossop's 1930s excavations in Field OS 45 and other excavations (see Simmons 1980a, 59 for Hacconby) make it clear that pottery finds of this sort are very local to such foci.

Simmons' conclusions about the Lincolnshire coastline during the Romano-British period places the excavated area on an island in the Silt Fens (Simmons 1980a, 70, fig. 73). Such an island would have been prone to seasonal floodings, although less of a problem at this time than in later the medieval period (Phillips 1934, 123–4).

The lack of ceramic or other evidence beyond the early third century may be explained by the hypothesised flooding of the Fens in that period, and the resultant 'third century gap' in occupation over the silt Fen as a whole (Salway 1970, 14–15). Such extensive flooding, riverine or marine, would help to explain the gleyed horizon found across the entire site at the level of the lowest ditch fills. The secondary peaty fills such as those which gave the radiocarbon dates, may have formed subsequently.

As no evidence of occupation was found the function of the site remains uncertain. Given the droves and enclosures, and the presence of mollusca in at least one ditch fill, Simmons' proposed economic basis of cattle rearing, combined with tidal oyster, wildfowl and salt exploitation is not unreasonable (Simmons 1980, 69), and is supported by the pollen analysis which additionally suggests limited cereal growing (Fig. 56).

The pollen analyses of the peats confirm the pastoral nature of the Romano-British activity in this area. The vegetation was most probably predominantly drained meadowland with very little woodland or scrub.

81

Chapter 4. A Medieval Salt-making Site in Bicker Haven, Lincolnshire

by Hilary Healey

I. Summary

In 1968–9 part of a salt-making site was excavated in Bicker Haven in the parish of Quadring, Lincolnshire, on the west side of the Wash. Principal discoveries were a pair of hearths associated with a small domestic building. An adjacent pit may have been contemporary, but was filled with a later soil deposit which also overlay the whole site. Similar features were seen below the main complex. Finds of local pottery and a token suggest that the main period of activity was towards the end of the first quarter of the fourteenth century.

II. Introduction

General

In 1960, during casual fieldwalking in the Quadring/Gosberton part of Bicker Haven, the writer noted patches of ploughed out ash and red burnt soil as well as a light scatter of medieval pottery. Eight years later, in September 1968, when two mounds (the fields formerly known as First and Far Hill) were being levelled on behalf of Quadring Eaudyke farmer Mr R. Bratley, the remains of a fired clay structure was exposed below some 1.83m of overburden, at grid reference TF 253 334.

Geography, geology and topography

The Lincolnshire fenland sediments consist of alluvium with marine clay and silt deposits. Surface peat occurs in the extreme south-west of the area, near Bourne, and is part of a band which, as recently as 100 years ago, extended along much more of the fen edge than it does at present (Skertchly 1877, 125 and 135). This was a relatively thin layer and much has since been removed through cultivation, drainage and erosion.

Bordering the limestone uplands are the fen edge gravels (Hayes and Lane, 1983, 9) to the east of which extends up to 5km of low ground, much of it only 2.5m above sea-level. This was fresh water fen from at least the thirteenth century, with parts of it remaining unenclosed until the early 1800s. Seaward the ground rises in a silt ridge between 2km and 5km wide, known to historical geographers as the Townlands (Molyneux and Wright 1974, 2; Grigg 1966, 21), which rarely rises above 5m OD. This is where the medieval villages are situated and between here and the coast is yet higher land again, the accumulation of former marsh deposits interspersed with the lines of sea banks which show the sequence of coastal reclamation. The earliest banks were probably in existence before 1086 (Hallam, H.E. 1958) and the continuing process of enclosure can be seen in places today.

Prehistoric occupation of the fen edge is well attested and a possible Iron Age coastline has been postulated from the distribution of sites and finds, including contemporary salt-making areas (Simmons 1980a, 63 and fig. 29). There is also evidence of extensive occupation of the fens in the Romano-British period (Hallam, S.J. 1970). Information in the past from both archaeological and pedological studies had suggested that the Townlands were largely post-Roman in origin since all Roman finds then recorded came from below depths of silt deposit varying from 1m to 20m (Hallam, S.J. 1970). More recently, both the results of the Fenland Survey and chance discoveries have shown that not all Roman sites are quite so deeply buried.

H.E. Hallam (1954, 4) pictured the original Townlands as a 'series of spurs or fingers of mineral alluvium, with deep tidal creeks running between them'. For many years, despite considerable coverage from local fieldwork, there were no Saxon finds recorded earlier than the ninth century. Archaeological evidence for post-Roman re-settlement came first from discoveries of seventh-century Ipswich ware on a number of sites, all of them close to the centre of medieval villages, that is, not far from the church (where there was one), or at least the supposed centre of the settlement (Healey 1979). The Fenland Survey has shown not only Middle but also Early Saxon occupation to be much more widespread than was previously believed, and not necessarily in places occupied by later settlers (Hayes 1985, 53–4).

Bicker Haven
(Figs 57, 58, Pl. XXVII)

The area formerly Bicker Haven lies in the south-east corner of the Lincolnshire fenland (Fig. 57). On both the first edition one inch to one mile Ordnance Survey map (Fig. 58) and its modern successor the recent 1:50,000 scale sheet (No. 131) one can find the words Bicker Haven spread almost diagonally across an area between Spalding and Boston. The limits of this feature are not precisely defined. Today the area is entirely dry land but on the ground the position of the former estuary can be charted from the surviving medieval sea banks. Despite always being referred to locally as 'Roman' banks there is as yet no evidence to show them to be of that date, and the idea seems to have been based on the assumptions of antiquaries such as William Stukeley. The work of H.E. Hallam, however, did establish a medieval origin for many of the sea and fen banks (Hallam, H.E. 1965).

The Haven is believed to have been at one time the outfall for a southerly arm of the River Witham, taking a course from a point near the junction of the River Slea and the Kyme Eau and then south through the present Heckington and Swineshead fens.

Each parish around the Wash had its area of Townland together with a portion of both marsh and fen. In Lincolnshire there is a clear distinction between marsh, which is subject to salt water flooding, and fen which is affected by fresh water. Constant deposition and accretion outside the sea bank causes the marsh gradually to become literally high and dry, and between the eleventh and the

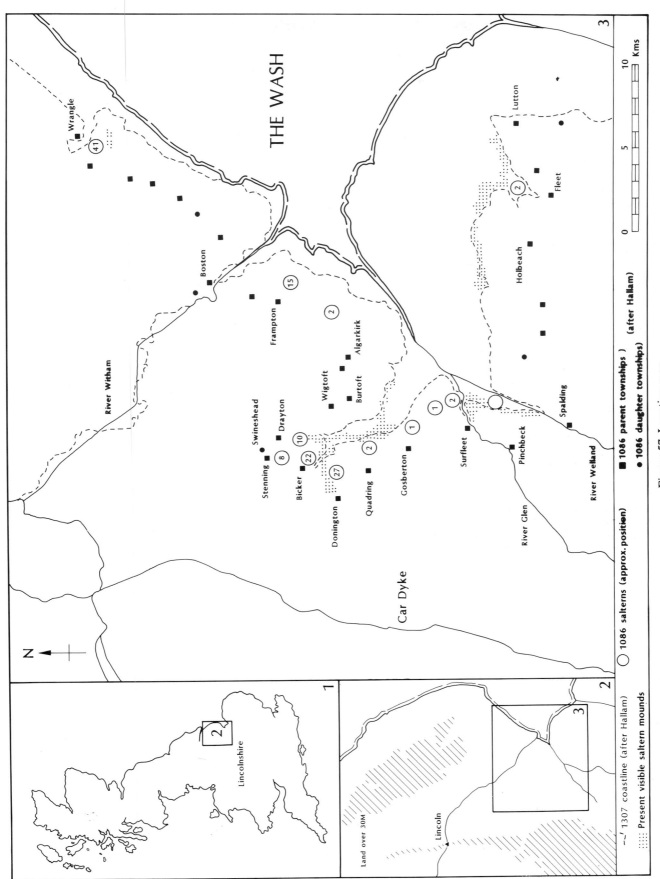

Figure 57 Location map

THE WASH

N

River Witham

Wrangle

Boston

Frampton

Car Dyke

Swineshead

Stenning

Drayton

Bicker

Donington

Quadring

Gosberton

Wigtoft

Burtoft

Algarkirk

Surfleet

Pinchbeck

River Glen

Spalding

River Welland

Holbeach

Lutton

Fleet

41

15

2

8

22

10

27

2

1

2

1

2

■ 1086 parent townships)
● 1086 daughter townships)   (after Hallam)

◯ 1086 salterns (approx. position)

—ᷧ 1307 coastline (after Hallam)

⣿ Present visible saltern mounds

0   5   10
Kms

Lincolnshire

2

Land over 30M

Lincoln

2

3

1

2

3

83

Plate XXVII Aerial view, centre of Bicker Haven, showing distinctive soil marks of the medieval saltern sites. North is at top of picture, arrow indicates site

seventeenth century this happened not only to Bicker Haven but also to other havens along the Lincolnshire coast, from Wainfleet in the north to Fleet in the south. In these former havens and in several places along the medieval or 'Roman' bank, can be seen groups of low mounds up to 4m in height which have traditionally been associated with the process of salt-making, and are always referred to by local historians as 'salterns'. Those in Bicker Haven were drawn as small hills on the first edition one inch Ordnance Survey map (Harley *et al.* 1987, 38) although they do not come out well in the reproduction here, and it is interesting to see that they are recorded on the latest metric scale 1:25,000 map (sheet 23/33). From the air they exhibit a distinctive pattern of light and dark soils (Pl. XXVII).

III. The excavation
(Pls XXVIII–XXXVI)

Introduction
In 1968 permission was initially given for a fairly rapid examination and recording of the site. Subsequently, when a wet winter began to set in, the mound levelling was suspended and the investigation developed into approximately a year's excavation lasting until September 1969. Although a grant for expenses and equipment was provided by the Ministry of Public Building and Works, the work was carried out entirely by part-time volunteers at weekends, evenings and holidays.

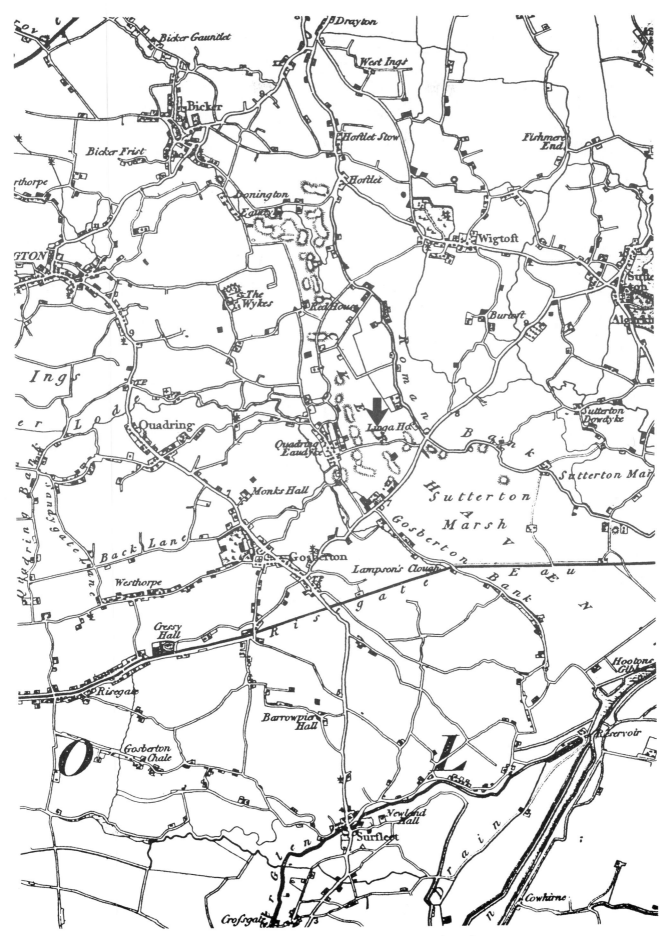

Figure 58 1825 1 inch to 1 mile OS map (enlarged)

Plate XXVIII Oblique aerial view of excavation from the south-east, 1969

Method

An area 12 × 23 metres was selected to include the fired clay feature first identified as well as a large spread of burnt material on its east side. Initially the smeared soil left by the graders was trowelled clean, and all features subsequently exposed were planned on a single main plan at a scale of 1:12, using imperial measurements (Fig. 59). Hollow features were sectioned, and some of these were later emptied. After a period of exceptionally heavy rain at an early stage of the excavation it became necessary to dig an emergency trench straight across the site from A to A[1] in order to remove surface water; this trench was cleaned up and the section used to provide information on the stratification of deposits (Fig. 60). At the close of the excavation parts of the recorded features were dug away quickly in order to examine those underlying, but it was not possible to attempt to dig through to any old ground surface that might pre-date the formation of the mound. At all stages of the excavation photographic recording was carried out on colour slide and on black and white film. Samples were taken of all the deposits and substances encountered.

The Features

The principal discoveries consisted of a small group of structures apparently linked by a common occupation level. The first features to be uncovered were two kilns or hearths, F1 and F2 (Fig. 59), which lay approximately at the centre of the mound. They were arranged as a pair, parallel to each other and linked by a wall (F21) of an earth mixture 61cm thick. Against the north side of the main complex were the remains of a small structure, F13, with a pit F11, on the southern side. The hearths were aligned approximately east-west with deep stoke-holes at their eastern ends (Pl. XXIX). A large spread of ashy material, F8, lay to the immediate east, and there were other less distinct features, some of earlier date, uncovered as the excavation progressed.

The hearths

Internally each hearth was 1.37m in length, 38.1cm wide and 47cm deep. The hearth construction was of a substance resembling soft brick when fired. It was identified as fine silt rather than clay. For the inner lining this silt had been mixed with what appeared to be grass or hay, the length of fibres up to 3cm, which seems to be too long to have been derived from dung. Its internal face had been subjected to high temperatures. In places a slag or glaze had formed, the result of the fusion between ash and clay. The inner wall, which was of a more clay-like character, had been hard fired to a depth of only 2.5cm though burnt red for an additional 7.5cm. The substance of which the outer linking wall (F21) was made was a mixture not only of silt, grass or dung, but also contained ash and fragments of a calcareous deposit; together these had formed a relatively firm fabric. When originally made up this was probably a 'mud' mixture similar to the traditional 'mud and stud' of Lincolnshire buildings, which is often found to incorporate a variety of ingredients in addition to the basic clay and water.

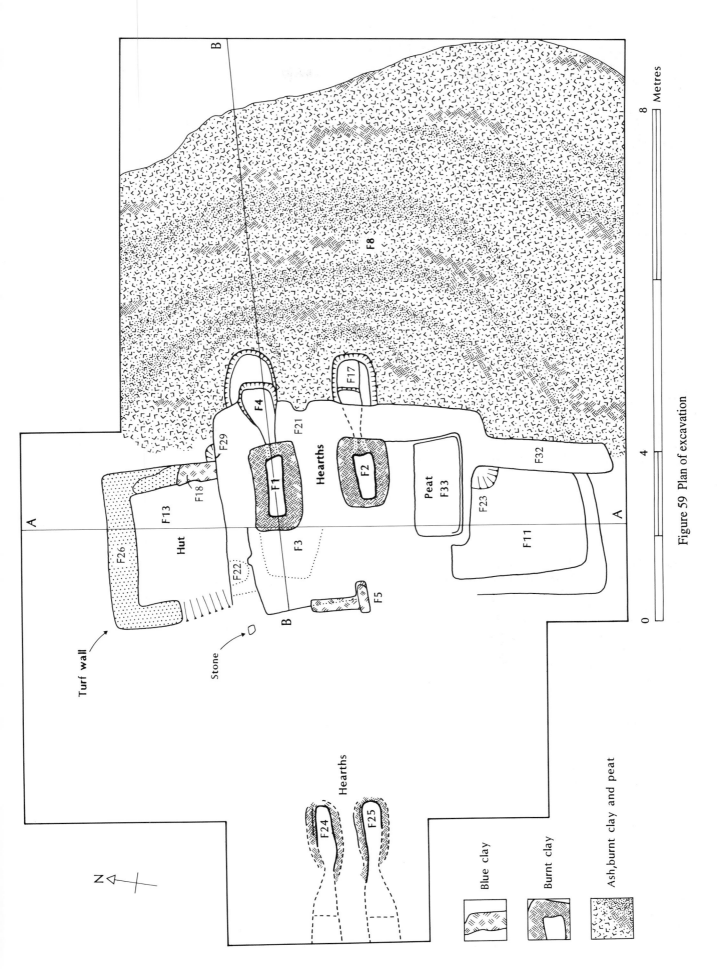

Figure 59 Plan of excavation

87

Plate XXIX General view of site from the east looking towards stoke-hole *F4* and hearth *F1*

Plate XXX Flue arch *F2*

The interiors of the hearths were full to a 15cm depth with a burnt red and black crumbly material identified as peat ash. From the east end of each hearth a furnace throat or 'flue' led downwards to connect with the stoke-hole. The arch for this 'flue' survived in both instances, each measuring 18cm in both height and width and just over 31cm in length between hearth and stoke-hole (Pl. XXX). There were no indications as to the nature or size of the superstructure. The hearths had been constructed in trenches dug into other features, such as pits, and layers of assorted ash and clay debris.

The wall *F21*, linking the hearths, extended southwards beyond the second hearth *F2* and here formed the east side of a rectangular depression *F33* containing a layer up to 5cm thick of a blackish deposit. Another less regular shaped depression *F3*, also with a darkened surface, lay to the west of hearth *F1* (Fig. 59). The blackish deposit referred to was identified as peat.

At 6.71m west of the main hearths another pair was discovered. These, *F24* and *F25*, had been cut into clean silt and sealed by the occupation layer. For convenience these are not indicated at a lower level on the plan (Fig. 59). Compared with the first pair these hearths had survived in relatively poor condition (Pl. XXXIII). They appeared to have been of less substantial construction and had also suffered much more animal damage. A striking characteristic of the site was that the various soils and substances encountered were noticeably lacking in organic matter. At this depth from the modern ground surface there was a complete absence of activity by either earthworms or rodents, with the result that both in plan and section all the edges of features were as clear as when they were first made. The only animal disturbance seen was to the west of the main complex, closer to recent plough levels. Hearths *F24* and *F25* had been cut into silt rather than into older features, and there was little indication that they had been in use for any length of time. Another difference from *F1* and *F2* was that although similarly on an east-west alignment the stoke-holes of *F24* and *F25* were at the west end rather than at the east end of the hearths.

A further hearth, *F22*, aligned north-south, was seen below features *F3* and *F13*; time did not permit more than its rapid removal in the final days of the excavation and its pair was not seen. The evidence of the orientation of the hearths may suggest that the saltmakers were not interested in taking advantage of the prevailing west wind. Another view could be that the short life of *F24* and *F25* demonstrates that a hearth built without reference to wind direction was not successful, but this leaves no satisfactory explanation for the alignment of *F22*. In the final stages of the excavation part

Plate XXXI Section of *F8* east of hearth *F1* showing tip lines in underlying pit

Plate XXXIV Harrow marks below *F8*

Plate XXXII Hut *F13* from the north-west (foreground) with hearth complex beyond

Plate XXXV Spade marks below *F22*

Plate XXXIII Hearths *F24* and *F25*

Plate XXXVI Stoke-hole of another hearth on the westerly mound First Hill

of the structure of *F2* was dug away revealing another hearth beneath it on a similar east-west alignment but slightly further south. This was not fully examined.

The waste heap

The spread of multicoloured ashy debris, *F8*, extended eastwards from hearths *F1* and *F2* to a maximum distance of 10.7m (Fig. 59). It consisted of alternating colourful layers of burnt or clean silt and red or black peat ash, sometimes mixed with slag and calcareous lumps. There was the occasional other find such as a piece of lead or bone, pottery or sea shells. The position of *F8* suggested that those engaged in stoking the fires had raked out the ash after or during the firing and shovelled it behind them, probably initially in a heap. The east-west section through *F8* illustrates a possible sequence of events (Fig. 61). Beneath the thin layers were deeper deposits of pale silt into which various pits had been dug. Assorted debris, ranging from ash to clean silt, had been tipped into these pits, and periodically all this waste appeared to have been levelled off, thus forming the horizontal layers (Pl. XXXI).

The upper part of the mound was seen to have been entirely man-made, for the two excavated sections (Figs 60–61) showed that the main features of the site had all been cut into earlier features in which the typical waste materials, including some very clean-looking silt, had been deposited. Around the edge of the stoke-hole for *F1* a possible path had been laid consisting of flat pieces of a hard calcareous substance identified by L. Biek as lime-mud. It was impressed with grass marks. There were many examples of this lime-mud which is derived from a deposit occurring in standing water such as in settling ponds or storage tanks. The fine soil of the salterns is very unstable in wet weather, as the excavators more than once observed, and with no natural stone or gravel to hand, any piece of relatively solid material such as this, or fired clay and slag, would have been fully utilised to consolidate the ground surface.

The structure

To the north of *F1* were the remains of a small structure, *F13*, abutting on the outer hearth wall. It measured 2.74m by 2.13m internally, being more or less rectangular with an entrance taking up about half its west side (Fig. 59). At this entrance there was a slope down from the external ground level of some 46cm. The base of the wall, which had an average thickness of 17cm and height of 30cm was of turves but on the north and east sides were fragmentary remains of mud walls resting on the sods. Lumps of this mud lying on the hut floor have been interpreted as collapsed walls (Pl. XXXII).

Evidence for timber construction was a possible post-hole, *F29*, 38cm by 23cm against the outer east wall of the hut at its junction with the north wall of the hearth, but it is not clear whether it would have been part of a covering over the hearths or of the hut. If there had been timbers resting on or embedded in a turf sill there was no indication of this. If padstones had been used there were none *in situ*, although three pieces of granite, measuring from 13 to 31cm across, found outside the hut entrance, may originally have served this purpose. There is no natural stone locally and any such material around would readily have been utilised. Unfortunately only one of these stones was recorded in position, but none were found inside the building.

The pits

South of *F13* was a large pit *F11* filled with the same brown soil which overlaid the entire site (Fig. 60); this soil had a very even colour and consistency. The pit was approximately 2.44m × 2.44m in plan with a slight overhang from the north wall as if the side had started to fall inwards. It was 61cm deep with almost vertical sides. This suggested either that it had not been open very long or that the sides had been lined with wood or wicker which was still present when the fill was thrown in. No samples were taken from the sides. A thin black layer at the bottom of the pit, about 3mm thick, was sealed by a whitish lime mud deposit consistent with sediment settling.

Post-hole F23

In one angle adjacent to *F11* was a hole of more or less triangular shape, *F23*, which appeared to be another post-hole (Fig. 59). It was 53cm across its widest part and had been cut into *F32* close to the edge of *F11*. It is unlikely that either this hole or the similar one *F29* on the opposite side of the site could have been caused by burrowing animals, and they have tentatively been interpreted as the remains of post-holes.

Immediately west of the main hearths were traces of other features and levels. However, it was later discovered that some of these had actually been artificially created by the weight of the grading machine compressing layers into those below. This is the reason that some features shown in the plan published in 1974 (Healey 1974), numbered *F12*, *F27* and *F34*, have now to be disregarded. The clay wall fragment *F5*, however, did appear to be the remains of a structure, perhaps connected with *F3* (Fig. 59).

The section A-A[1] (Fig. 60) yielded useful information even though it was not precisely aligned at right angles to the layout of the main features (Fig. 59). The second cross section B-B[1] (Fig. 61) cut through hearth *F1*, its stoke-hole (*F4*) and part of *F8* (Fig. 61). These two sections not only demonstrate the extreme clarity of definition referred to above, but also emphasise the artificial nature of the mound. The central industrial complex was built directly over a number of earlier hearths and pits.

In two places the contrasting colours and textures of these different deposits produced unexpected information. In the first case, where a short section east of *F13* was dug in order to establish the limits of *F8*, it cut through clear furrows made by a large rake or harrow (Pl. XXXIV). In the second instance the equally sharp edges of spade cuts outline the initial marking out in apparent preparation for the semi-circular shaped end of *F22* (Pl. XXXV). The marks showed a spade blade of 17cm width. During levelling of the mound to the west, traces of other pairs of hearths were seen. Once again the precise shape of the stoke-hole of one of these, cut into relatively clean silt, was perfectly preserved. However, it was evidently not intended to be used exactly as first cut, presumably because the silt would collapse if pressure were put on it. It had been immediately packed with small hard loose crumbs of slag and clay by way of an attempt to provide a firmer foundation (Pl. XXXVI).

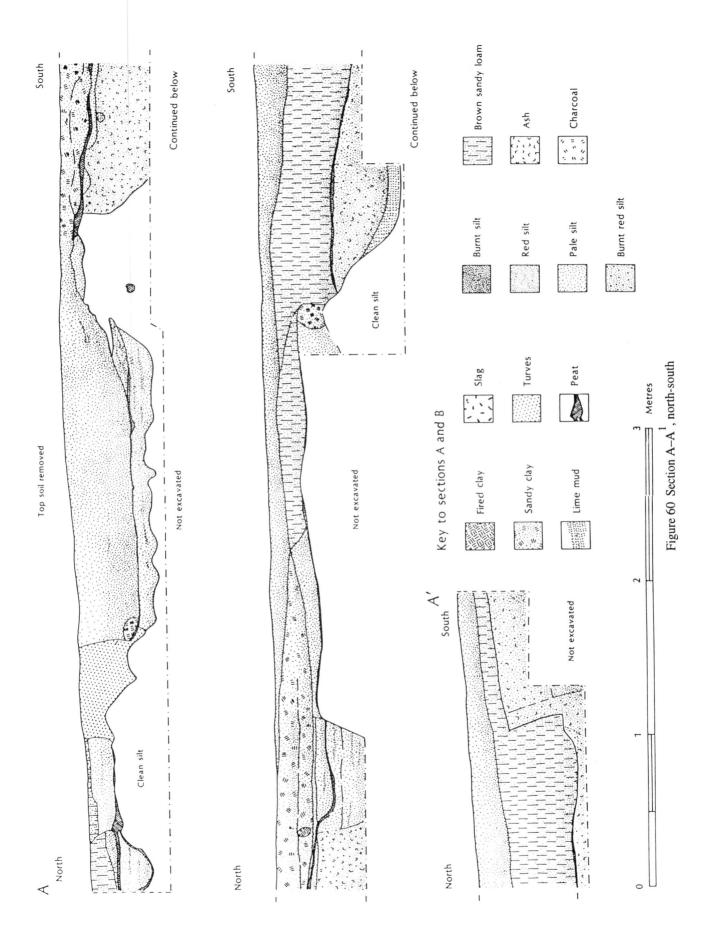

Key to sections A and B

Brown sandy loam

Ash

Charcoal

Burnt silt

Red silt

Pale silt

Burnt red silt

Slag

Turves

Peat

Fired clay

Sandy clay

Lime mud

Figure 60 Section A–A^1, north-south

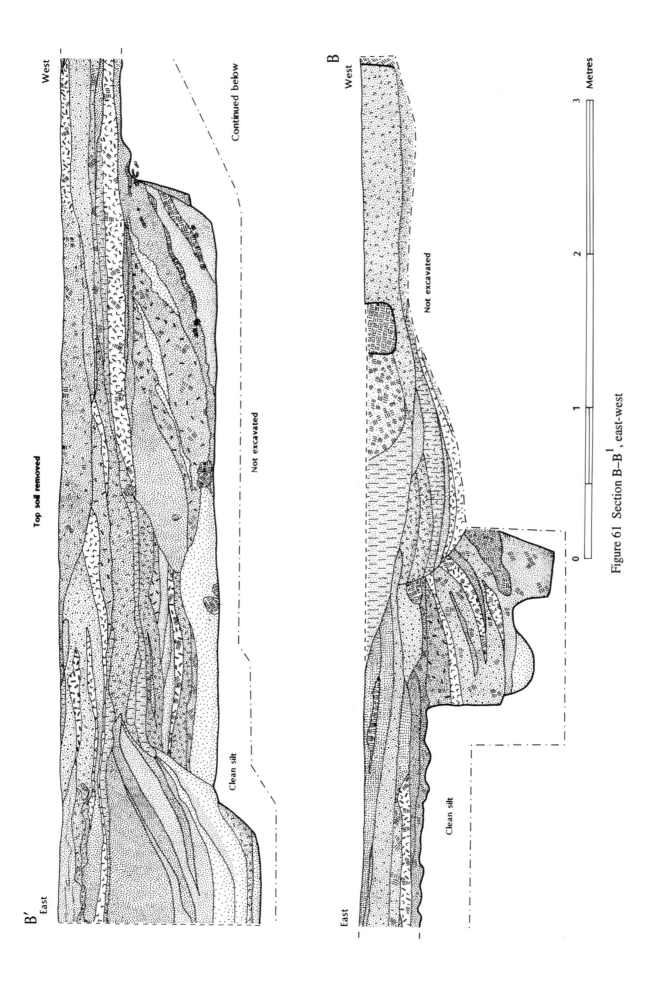

Figure 61 Section B–B^1, east-west

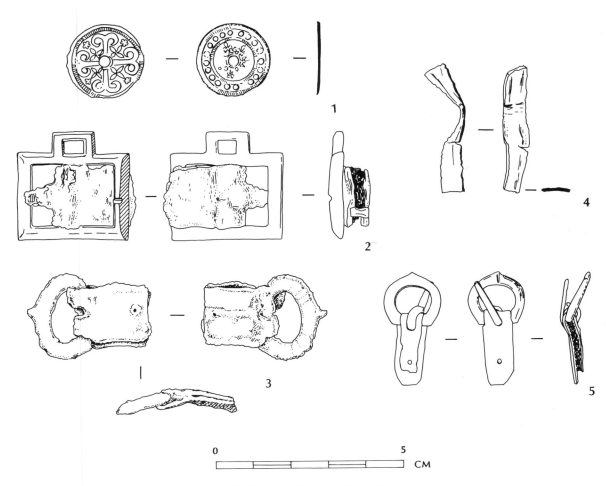

Figure 62 Objects of copper alloy. Scale 1:1

IV. The Artefacts

Introduction

The layer of dark occupation soil which appeared to be the contemporary ground surface produced chiefly potsherds, lead fragments, bones and seashells.

More potsherds, including those of a complete medieval Toynton jug, as well as fish bones, animal bones and shellfish, had been trodden into the floor of *F13* which was firm and well compacted. The fish bones were chiefly those of larger fish, in particular of skate (thornback). Although samples of the compacted layer were taken no smaller bones were recorded, and it is possible that soil conditions were in some ways unsuited to their survival. A number of iron nails were found on the ground in and around the structure, suggesting that there had been timber in the superstructure. Although the lower part of the wall on the north and west sides was made of sods, the clay base of the east wall and the lumps of clay lying on the floor suggest that the main building had been of this material; a tradition of building known as 'mud and stud', using mud, timber and vertical wooden slats, persisted in Lincolnshire until the present century. The use of nailed timber and clay or mud '*pisé*' for walls tallies with a description of saltcote buildings noted by H. Hallam in an account of saltern expenses during the first decade of the fifteenth century (Hallam, H.E. 1960, 98). A fourteenth-century copper alloy jetton was found in the occupation level south of the hut entrance.

It has been established from the ash that peat was the fuel in use on the site. The traces of peat found in *F3* suggest that there had been a peat stack close to the fires; it would have been convenient to have kept a small quantity near at hand where it would be dry, even if there were larger stacks elsewhere.

The fill of pit *F11* included some large animal bones and an iron sickle, copper alloy buckles, a piece of limestone quern and potsherds. No organic matter was found in the samples taken other than one small piece of reed (*Arundo australis*) in one of the layers of *F8*.

Catalogue of illustrated finds

Objects of Copper Alloy

(Fig. 62)

1.	Token
2.	Half buckle, with leather adhering
3.	Buckle with strap attachment and remains leather
4.	Copper alloy strip
5.	Buckle with strap attachment and remains leather

Objects of Iron

(Fig. 63)

6.	Sickle
7.	Knife blade
8–13.	Knife fragments
14–16.	Miscellaneous fragments
17.	S-hook
18.	Key
19–21.	Parts of 3 horseshoes
22–28.	Nails

93

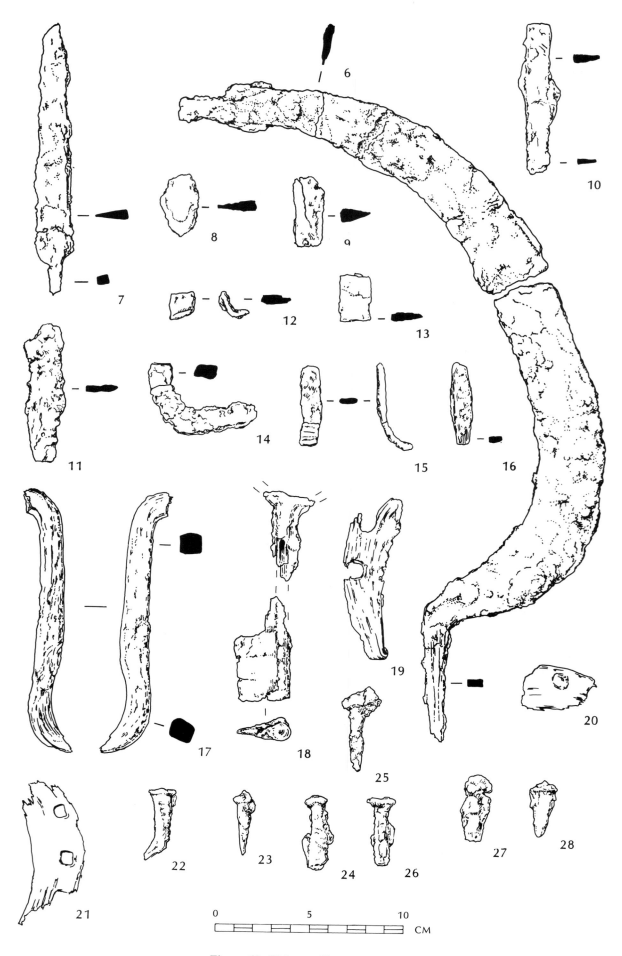

Figure 63 Objects of iron. Scale 1:2

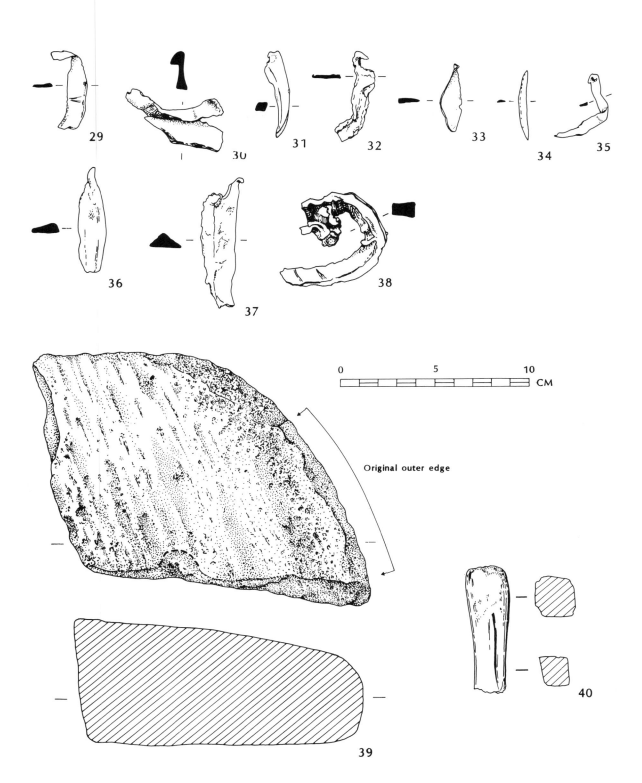

Figure 64 Objects of lead and stone. Scale 1:2

Objects of Lead
(Fig. 64)
29–38. Pieces of lead

Objects of Stone
(Fig. 64)
39. Mica-schist whetstone
40. Worked limestone fragment

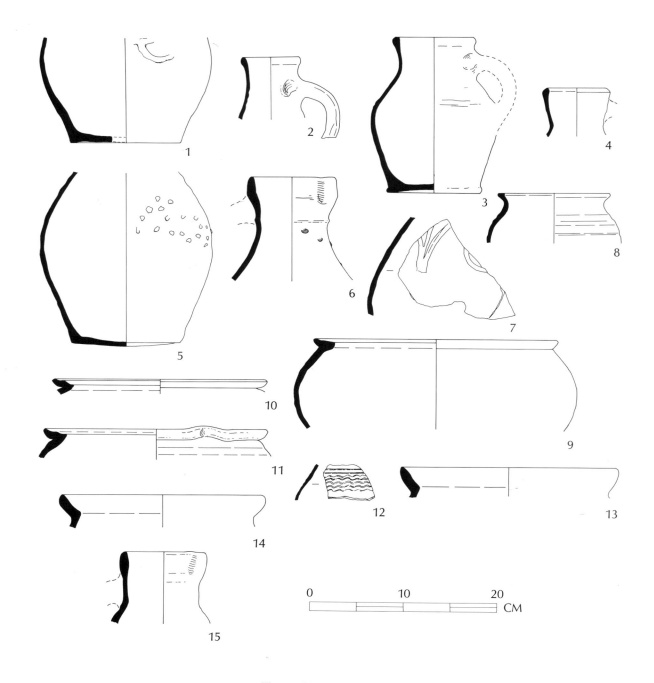

Figure 65 Pottery. Scale 1:4

Pottery
(Fig. 65)

Toynton ware
1.   Jug, applied decoration. Base diam. 12cm.
2.   Drinking jug. Rim diam. 6.5cm.
3.   Jug, complete profile. Ht. 17cm., rim diam. 9cm., base diam. 10cm.
4.   Drinking jug, rim diam. 7cm.
5.   Jug, decoration of applied spots. Base diam. 12cm.
6.   Jug, decoration of applied spots. Rim diam. 9.5cm.
7.   Jug, body sherd with applied *fleur de lys* decoration.

Bourne ware
8.   Pipkin. Rim diam. 26cm.
10.   Cooking pot. Rim diam. 22.5cm.
11.   Cooking pot, thumbed indentation. Rim diam. 23.5cm.
12.   Jug, body sherd, combed wavy line decoration.

Potter Hanworth
13.   Cooking pot. Rim diam. 23cm.
14.   Cooking pot. Rim diam. 23cm.

Lincoln ware
15.   Jug rim. Copper green glaze. Diam. 9cm.

V. Zoological and Botanical Evidence

Animal bones
(identified by Helen Gandy)

The chief result of the examination of the animal bones was identification of species present. Few bones had been affected by butchering, although a small number exhibited the results of contact with burning or teeth marks from gnawing. The total quantity of bones from well stratified contexts is insufficient to allow any statistical information. No articulated skeletons were recovered.

The main species represented were sheep (seventy-three bones) and cattle (thirty-three bones). A small quantity of bird bones was present, including a few of domestic fowl, but most of these were too small to be attributable to a particular species. An unidentified songbird bone came from the context *BHAR* (soil overlying feature *F11*), which post-dated the salt-making phase on the site. Half the lower jaw of a horse approximately two years old was also found in *BHAR*, indicating continued activity after the site went out of use. The only evidence for smaller domestic animals was part of a cat jaw amongst the many bones, largely from food species, found in the fill of pit *F11* (*BHAS*) and a possible dog phalange from *BHBZ*, also a context overlying the industrial phase. The only evidence for pig products was a single tooth in *BHC*, the silt fill of hearth *F3*. The predominant sheep bones included pieces of skull, jaws, scapula, ribs, vertebrae, pelvis and legs, including bones of juveniles. Cattle were not as numerous; bones recorded included parts of skull, teeth, vertebra, pelvis and legs with a single butchered rib in *BHCC* (the silt filling of stoke-hole *F4*) after it had gone out of use. The lack of butchered bone is noted; it may be that some of the bone remains are the result of accidental death, for example through drowning after exceptional tides.

Fish bones
by Andrew Jones

A small number of bones were collected by hand during the course of the excavation. Laboratory sieving three small soil samples failed to produce further fish material. The bones were identified using comparative material prepared by the Environmental Archaeology Unit, York and the Faunal Studies Project, Southampton.

The fish bones recovered from this site represent four species of marine fish, thornback ray, cod, plaice and turbot. All are abundant in the North Sea off the Lincolnshire coast and all can be caught using simple fishing equipment from small boats. The most likely tackle would be long lines carrying several baited hooks.

The presence of cod and plaice head bones as well as axial skeletal remains suggests that the fish were brought onto the site as whole fresh fish and it would seem most probable that the people working the salterns would be able to turn their hands to fishing.

While many of the bones found at Bicker Haven are very small and demonstrate the great care with which the site was excavated, it is almost certain that some species of fish bones were present on the site and have not been recovered. Eel and herring bones are amongst the commonest fish remains recovered from many early medieval sites and their absence from this assemblage does not necessarily mean that they were not present in the excavated deposits; representative samples of fish and other small bones can only be obtained when large amounts of soil are sieved.

Mollusca
by John Redshaw

Fragments of *Cepaea nemoralis* and *Helix aspersa* were identified. These species are typical of hedgerows or of coarse grass with a few bushes. One would not expect to find them here without traces of former brushwood or scrub but the remains are not calcified, so they were not necessarily brought in with fuel for brine evaporation fires.

Soils
(identified by J.D. Robson)

Almost all the soil samples examined were calcareous and consistent with the coastal location, although with some variations. They range from samples of the fine sandy silt loams typical of toftland and middle salt marsh, which were present over the entire site and samples S4 and S7, the middle-lower salt marsh. The laminated silty clay in *F5* possibly had an upper marsh source. Soils of these types were previously recorded by Robson in another medieval salt-making area, the Wrangle/Friskney toftlands (Robson 1984, 53–58). The most calcareous soil is the loamy very fine sand of the lower marsh or substratum of mid-lower marsh as found in S8. Another very calcareous sample was S14 (filling of hearth *F22*), which was also ashy. Organic flecks occurred in the silt loam of S23 (fill of *F35*, described from its appearance as a 'peaty hollow') and in another depression *F3*. This feature had also appeared to be peaty, but in fact the black material was humose silt loam including carbon. The only non-calcareous sample was S16, a fine sandy silt loam from the largest 'peaty depression', *F33*. Apart from peat lumps from deposit *F8*, separately identified by other individuals, only S18, from *F4* (the upper part of the stoke-hole filling of hearth 1), actually contained incompletely burnt peat.

VI. Discussion

The date of salt production at Bicker Haven
Dating information comes largely from the pottery. Sherds from the occupation layer and all the main features of the site are predominantly from three Lincolnshire sources; Bourne, Potter Hanworth and Toynton All Saints. The market town of Bourne lies 40km to the south-west where kilns operated from at least the late thirteenth to the seventeenth century (Healey 1969, 109); the fabric found on the site was all Bourne B ware (not A ware as stated in the 1969 note), which is thought to be slightly later than A ware, dating to the first half of the fourteenth century. The Potter Hanworth sherds were all from broad rimmed cooking pots (Healey 1974) again of fourteenth-century type. The Toynton sherds found are all from jugs, including those small ones thought to be drinking mugs. Some sherds from the larger vessels are from the types decorated with the characteristic brown slip trailing of the late thirteenth/early fourteenth century (Healey 1984, 75). Two of the three centres of pottery manufacture might have distributed their wares through Boston market; Potter Hanworth is 36km up the River Witham towards Lincoln and Toynton only 30km north of the town. The Bourne

wares are more likely to have been sent up the River Glen to Spalding.

The only other dating evidence comes from a copper alloy jetton found on the ground surface near the hut entrance. The British Museum collection has no exact parallel, but does include one with the reverse of the Quadring piece 'paired with an obverse using the punches of the penny of type XV, struck at the end of the reign'. This is placed in the period of Edward I, *c.* 1320–1325, possibly even a year or two later, 'for, it is really not certain when the types attributed to Edward II were superseded by the larger, generally more elaborate, types given to Edward III' (Berry 1974). The remainder of the metalwork does not include closely dateable pieces.

The soil which covered the site and also constituted the filling of pit *F11* included sherds of Bourne D ware, a late or post-medieval fabric which ought to follow directly from Bourne B ware, though as yet dates for it earlier than the sixteenth century are lacking (Healey 1969).

Salt manufacture in the Bicker Haven area

A great deal is recorded about the preparation of salt from sea-water in the British Isles in a variety of accounts dating from the sixteenth to the nineteenth century. As Sturman has observed, 'The accounts point to considerable local variation in technique, but it is none the less possible to summarise the main elements in manufacture. Three stages were involved: the gathering of salt-impregnated sand from the beach in the summer months; the washing out of the salt; and the boiling of the resultant solution. This was the method employed in Lincolnshire' (Sturman 1984, 50). The article by Sturman, with its detailed illustrations from an eighteenth-century account of Normandy salt-making, is a significant contribution to studies of the industry and illuminates much of the better known and frequently quoted accounts by William Brownrigg (1748).

The locations most favoured for salt-making in south Lincolnshire seem to have been the estuaries or havens, the relatively sheltered parts of the coast. The presence of a broad expanse of sand or silt which would be exposed at low tide was desirable, as this salt-impregnated mud was the essential raw material of the industry. It was also its chief waste product, the discarded heaps forming the basis of the saltern mounds.

Fresh water, which was necessary for the washing or filtering, was available from streams that flowed through every parish from the high ground of the Kesteven hinterland into the Wash. Rudkin and Owen have shown that a watercourse was frequently mentioned in documents as part of a saltern (Rudkin and Owen 1960, 81).

The manufacture of salt took place between April and September. Rudkin and Owen (1960, 81) noted instances where rent was paid in salt for half the year only, at June and Michaelmas, and there is similar information from an early seventeenth-century court roll for the manor of Monks Hall, Gosberton. This relates to the same part of Bicker Haven with which this paper is concerned. It is evident from inventories of the sixteenth and seventeenth centuries that salt-making was combined with other occupations of a of a less seasonal kind, such as the keeping of livestock (Rudkin and Owen, 1960, 81 and Sturman 1984). The evidence of the hearths suggests that the saltmakers were not interested in taking advantage of the prevailing west wind. Another view could be that the

short life of *F24* and *F25* demonstrates that a hearth built without reference to wind direction was not successful, but this leaves no satisfactory explanation for the alignment of *F22*.

The salterns may initially have been set up directly on or close to the sea bank. Soil from both the high and middle marsh has been identified in the mound debris by D. Robson (archive). The dumps of waste material would rapidly have formed into mounds, and once these were raised above high water mark they would be suitable for the establishment of saltcotes. The great size of some of the mounds in Bicker Haven implies an accumulation over several centuries. The date range of the scattered pottery finds reinforces this view; whilst Far Hill was being levelled late Saxon unglazed Stamford ware, some 2–300 years earlier than the pottery on the excavated site, was found. Continuity of the industry would be more likely to occur within the Haven for as long as a tidal river remained active, than out on the more exposed coast. Caution must be observed in deducing too much about the length of use or number of salterns from the present visible mounds, since there are documentary references to, and a continuing local custom of, carting away of soil from such places (Marrat 1814, 84).

Following the regular overflow of the marsh during the fortnightly high or 'spring' tides, the mud or silt would have a comparatively high salt content. There are many variables affecting soil salinity, especially where fresh water is regularly present to act as a flushing agent. However, the hollows which are the natural saltpans on the middle and upper marsh (Long and Mason 1983, 24–26) would be able to counteract this by achieving high natural evaporation in warm and hot weather. At the time of writing there had been little recent work on soil salinity. The average for sea water is 33:1,000 in the Wash, rising to thirty-four or thirty-five parts. Near a river mouth, as in Bicker Haven it might be down to eighteen or twenty parts, as has been recorded at the mouth of the River Nene. In the early 1960s, the following data on sodium chloride was obtained from samples at Freiston Shore, north of Boston (Seppings *c.* 1961):

Sea Water: *c.* 32gm per kilo of water
Silt after flooding by tide: 12.8gm per kilo of wet soil (but may be as low as 8gms)
Fresh water: 2gm per kilo of water
Estuarine water: 12–15gm per kilo of water
Estuarine mud: 0.05 to 6gm per kilo of wet soil

Seppings concluded: 'On the salt pans at the head of the marshes immediately after a high tide, under conditions of high evaporation, *i.e.* during a dry spell in the summer, it would be possible to scrape up a salt/silt mixture containing 50–75% salt'.

Details of the washing or filtering process were probably much as described in 1748 (Brownrigg 1748, 56), but there are differing opinions as to whether salt or fresh water is necessary to this operation. Brownrigg specifies sea water, but P. Gouletquer, in a letter to B.B. Simmons (Gouletquer *c.* 1973), states that fresh water is required to dissolve some of the bitter salts present. Bridbury explains that at least two of the other salts, calcium carbonate and calcium sulphate, crystallise in the early stages of boiling, and these would be the ones that were removed as scale (Bridbury 1956, 8–9). In addition to the lime mud other calcareous fragments, including calcium sulphate were found amongst the site debris, especially on the old ground surface. No obvious evidence of filtration equipment was found in the Bicker Haven site and it has been supposed that this part of the process was carried out at a slight distance from the boiling. Evidence from the excavations at Wainfleet reinforces this supposition (McAvoy 1994).

The brine was evaporated in shallow lead trays (Rudkin and Owen 1960, 81; Lloyd 1967, 3) and the final product drained off into various types of container, for example, wicker baskets, which could also be used in transport. The word 'tray' has been used here deliberately instead of 'pan' which in discussion can lead to confusion with the word 'saltpan', often used by past authors to refer to the actual salt-making sites or *salinae*.

No wood ash was recorded in any of the samples taken. The only fuel found at the Quadring excavation was peat, the characteristic red residue of which (Skertchly 1877, 139) constituted much of the fill of the main hearths and the dump *F8*. Peat is the ideal fuel for maintaining a steady temperature during firing. There are numerous documentary references to the association of turbary rights with salt-making (Hallam, H.E. 1960, 103) including, for example, one in Pinchbeck Fen in 1327 (Hallam, H.E. 1957, 478). This would have been one of the nearest contemporary sources of peat, being only 9.6km to the south-west. Waste fragments of lead were everywhere on the site; most of them in the form of slivers or small lumps of lead up to 3mm across. Only one piece, a clipping from a sheet 2mm thick might be interpreted as part of a boiling tray (Fig. 64 No. 38). During final levelling of the mounds before reinstatement one or two small piles of lead pieces were retrieved.

Development of Bicker Haven

Roman salt-making sites have been found along the projected route of the watercourse where it may originally have entered the Haven from the north-west. Some of these lie between 1km and 5km north-west of the approximate position of the head of the eleventh-century Haven. This pattern is what might be expected if one assumes a progressive silting up of the estuary. Evidence of salt-making in the Saxon period prior to the *Domesday* record remains elusive but it is unlikely that the knowledge and practice of such a vital industry would have ceased completely between the fourth and the eleventh century.

In 1086 the concentration of 'saltpans' (*salinae*) was at the then head of the Haven with twenty-seven recorded in Donington, twenty-three in Bicker and eighteen in Stenning and Drayton combined (these last two are lost settlements, now both in Swineshead parish) (Fig. 57). Even at this date one saltpan in Bicker was described as 'waste'; this seems to be the earliest reference to silting up in the Haven (Foster and Longley 1924).

The constant deposition of silt referred to above combined with the relatively slow movement of outgoing water in the flat fenlands, gradually blocked Bicker Haven. Since it was essential for the salt boilers or salt wellers to work close to their chief raw material, as the sea receded they had to move also. This move can be followed through the documentary references. For example, whereas in 1086 the villages of Gosberton and Quadring (which lie between Bicker and the sea) had only two and three saltpans respectively, they became the focus of much more activity in the twelfth and thirteenth centuries, when

the *Domesday* sites further inland had quite ceased to function (Hallam, H.E. 1960, 99–100).

Nevertheless, as long as a tidal river flowed there was always some salt-making being carried out in the central part of the Haven, especially on the marshes of Gosberton and Quadring. It had, however, ceased here by the early years of the seventeenth century, not least because of the large scale importation of 'white salt' from the continent into Boston (Hinton 1956). The large saltern mounds are witness to the extent of the industry, as it is these mounds which immediately strike the observer in the flat fen landscape where a rise of even half a metre is described as a 'hill'. The observer from the air will see the characteristic saltern colouring, an almost floriform effect occasioned by the patches of different coloured waste material, silt, ash, fired clay and peat, of which the mounds are composed (Pls XVI, XXVII).

There is a variety of evidence to confirm the salt-making connection. The irregular outline of some of the older enclosures, first recorded in an eighteenth-century estate plan (LAO BRA 1384) has altered little in the last two centuries (Fig. 66). Such field shapes are typical of those formed around saltern mounds as first recorded on Haiward's sixteenth-century plan of Marshchapel on the north-east Lincolnshire coast (Rudkin and Owen 1960, 80–83; Beresford and S. Joseph 1979, fig. III A). This remarkable document shows the gradual assimilation of mounds into an enclosed field system, the sequence being summed up in the cartouche:

> The rounde groundes at the east end of Marsh Chapel are called Maures and are first framed by laying together of great quantities of moulde for the making of salte. When the maures growe greate the saltmakers remove more este and come nearer the sea and then the former maures become in some fewe yeares goode pastur groundes. Those that have the cottages upon them are at this present in use for salt (Walshaw 1935, 196–206).

The mound on which the excavation took place is the one named Far Hill in the eighteenth-century estate plan (Fig. 66), more recently field OS 384. Bicker Creek or Bicker River is the direct descendant of the full river and forms a boundary for several parishes. The excavation site lies in what today is a narrow east-west strip of Quadring parish sandwiched between Wigtoft on the north and Gosberton on the south. The hamlet of Quadring Eaudyke (formerly spelt Eadyke — the 'Eau' spelling is post eighteenth century) lies on the western side of the Haven, between what is probably the 1307 bank (Hallam, H.E. 1958, 41) and an apparent earlier bank represented by a parallel road, now part of Watergate. A chapel in existence by 1300 (Owen, D.M. 1975, 20) was situated in Quadring Eaudyke between these two banks, and the adjacent lane retained the name 'Chapel Lane' until the eighteenth century.

To the south below Quadring where the Haven widens rapidly from from 1.3km to 2km the channel would have been more exposed and subject to the stronger scouring action of the tide. Between this point and the sea there is less evidence of the industry, although a few saltern mounds survive near the northern, Sutterton bank. Written evidence of the state of the Haven continues to appear; between 1359 and 1413 regular efforts were made to maintain a 24 foot (7.3m) wide channel up to Bicker itself

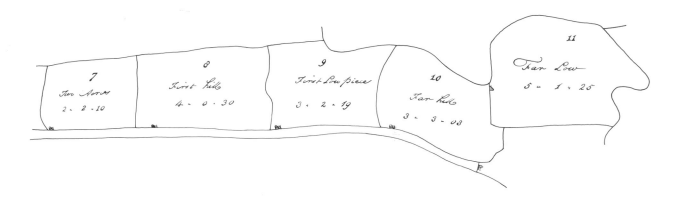

Figure 66 Copy of an eighteenth-century estate plan (Lincolnshire Archives Office).
Warren Road crosses from left to right. North at top

(Dugdale 1772, 199 and 238). By this date much of the ground between the two banks must already have become dry land, although several large streams or drains such as the Mar Lode still entered the main channel from the west. There was clearly sufficient tidal flow for the salt industry to continue into the early seventeenth century, for the saltcotes were still landmarks in 1627 (see below).

Slightly earlier, in 1565, the road between Gosberton and Sutterton, Boston Gate, was described as having a bridge by Quadring 'at the Saltcottes at the end of an old ryver wher the salt water cometh in' (Kirkus 1959, 54). Ten years later the Commissioners of Sewers, inspecting the north side of the Haven, noted that 'the sea bankes of Swineshead and Wigtoft beginneth at the furthest decayed salte cote' (Owen, A.E.B. 1977, 27). The description in 1596 of a road across 'the salt marshes or hills to Sutterton and Boston', (apparently the Boston Gate referred to above) seems to correspond with the the partly sunken way, itself a rarity in the fens, the green lane now known as Warren Road.

The latest references to salt-making in Quadring and Gosberton occur in early seventeenth-century records of the manor of Monks Hall, Gosberton, which owned most of the land in this part of the Haven (CLRO RCE Rentals 6.4). In 1627 several copyholders are listed as paying half their annual rent in measures of salt, a practice referred to earlier. In addition there is an interesting comment inserted in a rental of 1622. The fields on the former saltern sites bear names such as le Sheeptoft, le Lower Marsh, le Salte Marsh, le Sponge, le Saltcotes Hills and le Floores pasture, Angott hills and Salte Flowers. The complaint reads:

> The aforesaid 80 acr land formerly beene of goode vallew when they were used for the makeinge of Salt but now yt is lefte of and the howses decaied and gone, and it is but of little vallew beinge the hills are very Barrene and the Floors or bottoms are very weitt and yieldeth no profitt, and are hardly halfe the rent yt it paies (CLRO RCE-114c).

The acres referred to lie directly south of Warren Road and the mound on which the excavation took place, and are centred on grid reference TF 255334. The word 'floors' appears to refer to settling or collecting ponds, probably artificial ponds developed out of the natural saltpan formation. This low opinion of the state of ex-saltern land is confirmed in a late sixteenth or early seventeenth-century plan of the manor of Burtoft north of the Haven,

where the 'Boston Gate' would have run. Here the land immediately outside the Haven bank is described as 'salcott hills good grounds' and the part beyond that, nearest the river, as 'salcott hills bad grounds' (PRO SC 12/30/32). Subsequently the land must have become tolerable pasture much as Haiward described at Marshchapel. The type of snail shell found in the overburden immediately below modern plough levels shows that the mounds later became scrub and coarse pasture.

The name 'floors' or 'flowers' survived in the place-name Saltgate Floors (a slight corruption of 'saltcote floors') into the present century, in a field south-east of the excavated area. Here is a series of shallow ponds that may be remnants of the industry. Their present plan, which has not changed since it was recorded on a map of 1776, shows them to be of a very peculiar angular form, perhaps created by later activity such as digging for silt. Until the 1960s these pits dried up in summer, a factor which may have helped preserve their unusual interest in supporting a number of plants normally found near the sea or associated with saltmarsh, in particular sea milkwort (*Glauxa maritima*). The occasion of this memorable discovery by the Lincolnshire Naturalists' Union in 1955 was recorded as '...undoubtedly the most exciting meeting of the year botanically' (Gibbons 1956). The site now lies 5km from the River Welland and 9km from the nearest coastal marsh.

In the past significance has been attached to Blaeu's 1648 map of the Wash where Bicker Haven appears as one of the areas of land specifically depicted and described as 'liable to flooding' (the *regiones inundataes*), and therefore thought not to have been enclosed from the sea until about the 1650s (Wheeler 1894, Appendix I, 4). The statements in the Monks Hall documents of the 1620s quoted, suggest that the centre of the Haven near Gosberton was more or less dry by 1600 and unlikely to have been as vulnerable to flooding in the 1640s as his map shows. It is known that there were earlier maps of the Wash area on which Blaeu may have based some of his information, such as that of Hondius of 1610, and it seems that he must either have been relying on these existing sources or that a number of years had passed between his collecting information and the actual completion of the map (Petty and Fairclough 1978). Occurring at a critical time when there was no longer either sufficient flow of water for the salt-making nor sufficient demand for salt, either circumstance could explain why the map was well out of date by the time it was finally published.

Recent discoveries in Lincolnshire

Since the Bicker Haven excavation of 1968–9 there have been further discoveries relating to medieval salt manufacture in Lincolnshire. The Boston and District Archaeological Society carried out a small excavation on a saltern site in Wrangle in 1982 (Bannister 1983) and a year later a much larger operation was undertaken by the Central Excavation Unit on part of Scheduled Ancient Monument no. 320 at Wainfleet (McAvoy 1984). On both sites the remains of the various containers and channels which constitute filtration units were found, those at Wainfleet being linked to an elaborate arrangement of storage and collection pits. On neither site were hearths found, and it may be supposed that to some extent, at least, the two parts of the activity were kept separate. The Wrangle site could not be closely dated, since only a few sherds of medieval pottery were present; the Wainfleet site has recently been published (McAvoy 1994). Filtration structures and hearths have also been noted in association with late Saxon pottery in the upper part of Bicker Haven between Bicker and Donington on a road improvement known as Bicker Bends (Healey 1988). There had not appeared to be any evidence of filtration and storage structures in the vicinity of the Bicker Haven hearths at the time of excavation, but in the light of knowledge gained from these other sites it may be possible to interpret the pit *F11* as having been part of this other side of the process, although not necessarily in contemporary use with the hearths. Not only had there had been water standing in this pit for some time, but the curious inward leaning shape of the pit's upper edge (Fig. 60) might indicate the shape of an original wooden lining.

VII. Conclusion

At the time of its excavation the salt boiling hearth complex in Bicker Haven was the first such medieval site to be excavated and fully recorded in Britain. Although the destruction of some saltern mounds had been observed in Kent in the 1950s (Thompson 1956) no actual hearths were revealed, despite considerable evidence of fires. The Lincolnshire site remains the only coastal example of the remains of this part of the salt-making process, and is well complemented by the subsequent discovery of a filtration complex at Wainfleet (McAvoy 1994). The remarkably well preserved features at Quadring confirm some of the documentary information on the industry, including evidence of a building, and the domestic pottery and animal bone both within and outside this structure suggest at least seasonal human occupation of the site. The presence of numerous lead fragments may be seen as supporting the documentary references for the use of lead vessels for boiling brine. The comparative lack of identifiable organic material on the site was disappointing, since every effort had been made during the excavation to collect adequate samples. However, the information obtained provides useful knowledge of the types of structure and material likely to be encountered in the future on sites in this category. It is hoped that the excavation of a complete coastal salt-making complex may at some time be undertaken, not least in order to establish the relationship of the various industrial features with one another.

Appendix: Radiocarbon Dating

Summary of radiocarbon dating from Low Level Measurements Laboratory, Harwell:

Sample No.	Context	Harwell Ref.	Type	DC13 (0/00)	Age BP	calibrated date
Helpringham						
(AML 775151)	Mound C	HAR-2280	Timbers	-25.7	2180 ± 80	379–116 cal BC
(AML 790489)	Mound A	HAR-3102	Charcoal	-26.9	2330 ± 90	487–370 cal BC
Holbeach St Johns						
45 (AML 8316527)	Fill *39*	HAR-6362	Peat	-29.2	1480 ± 80	459–648 cal AD
84 (AML 8316528)	Fill *84*	HAR-6364	Peat	-28.6	1580 ± 80	397–562 cal AD

Bibliography

Applebaum, S., 1966 — 'Peasant Settlement and Types of Agriculture' in *Rural Settlement in Roman Britain*, Counc. Brit. Archaeol. Res. Rep. 7

Arthur, P., 1978 — 'The lead glazed wares of Roman Britain' in Arthur, P. and Marsh, G. (eds), *Early Fine Wares in Roman Britain*, Brit. Archaeol. Rep. 57, (Oxford), 293-355

Atkinson, D., 1942 — *Report on Excavations at Wroxeter (the Roman City of Viroconium) in the County of Salop 1923–1927*, (Oxford)

Baker, F.T., 1960 — 'The Iron Age salt industry in Lincolnshire', *Lincolnshire Architect. Archaeol. Soc. Rep. Pap.* 8, 26–34

Baker, F.T., 1975 — 'Salt making sites on the Lincolnshire coast before the Romans' in de Brisay, K.W. and Evans, K.A. (eds), *Salt: The Study of an Ancient Industry*, (Colchester), 31–32

Bannister, R.T., 1983 — 'Wrangle Toft' in White, A.J., 'Archaeology in Lincolnshire and South Humberside, 1982', *Lincolnshire Hist. Archaeol.* 18, 164–5

Beresford, M. W. and Joseph, S., 1979 — *Medieval England: An Aerial Survey*, 262–265, (Cambridge University Press) (2nd ed.)

Berry, G., 1974 — *English Medieval Jettons*, (London)

Bestwick, J.D., 1975 — 'Romano-British inland salting at Middlewich (Salinae), Cheshire' in de Brisay, K.W. and Evans, K.A. (eds), *Salt: The Study of an Ancient Industry*, (Colchester), 66–70

Bloch, M.R., 1963 — 'The Social Influence of Salt' in *Sci. American* 209 (1), 88–96, 98

Bond, D., 1988 — *Excavations at the North Ring, Mucking, Essex: A Late Bronze Age Enclosure*, E. Anglian Archaeol. 43

Bridbury, A.R., 1956 — *England and the Salt Trade in the Later Middle Ages*, (Cambridge)

Brown, I.W., 1980 — *Salt and the Eastern North American Indian. An Archaeological Study*, (Lower Mississippi Survey, Harvard)

Brownrigg, W., 1748 — *The Art of Making Common Salt*

Buckley, D.G. and Major, H., 1983 — 'Quernstones' in Crummy, N., *The Roman Small Finds from Excavations in Colchester 1971–9*, Colchester Archaeol. Rep. 2, 73–76

Charlesworth, D., 1972 — 'The glass' in Frere, S., *Verulamium Excavations, Vol.1*, Rep. Res. Comm. Soc. Antiq. London 28, (Oxford), 196–215

Chowne, P., 1978 — 'Billingborough Bronze Age Settlement: an Interim Note', *Lincolnshire Hist. Archaeol.* 13, 15–21

Chowne, P., 1979 — 'Excavations at Billingborough, Lincs.', *Current Archaeol.* 67, 246–8

Chowne, P., 1980 — 'Bronze Age Settlement in South Lincolnshire' in Barrett, J. and Bradley, R., *Settlement and Society in the British Later Bronze Age*, Brit. Archaeol. Rep. British Series 83, (Oxford)

Chowne, P., Cleal, R.M.J. and Fitzpatrick, A.P., forthcoming — *Excavations at Billingborough, Lincolnshire, 1975–8*, E. Anglian Archaeol.

Columella — *De Re Rustica*

Conway, V.M., 1942 — 'Biological Flora of the British Isles: Cladium', *J. Ecol.* 30, 211–216

Crawford, O.G.S. and Röder, J., 1955 — 'The quern-quarries of Mayen in the Eifel', *Antiquity* 29, 68–76

Cunliffe, B., 1974 — *Iron Age Communities in Britain. An Account of England, Scotland and Wales from the seventh century BC until the Roman Conquest*

Dannell, G.B. 1973 — 'The Potter Indixivicus' in Detsicas, A.P., *Current research in Romano-British Coarse Pottery*, Counc. Brit. Archaeol. Rep. 10, 139–42

Darby, H.C., 1952 — *The Domesday Geography of Eastern England*, (Cambridge)

Darby, H.C., 1974 — *The Medieval Fenland*, (Cambridge University Press) (2nd ed)

de Brisay, K., 1975 — 'The red hills of Essex' in de Brisay, K.W. and Evans, K.A. (eds), *Salt: The Study of an Ancient Industry*, (Colchester), 5–11

de Brisay, K., 1978 — 'The excavation of a Red Hill at Peldon, Essex, with notes on some other sites', *Antiq. J.* 58, 31–60

de Brisay, K. and Evans, K.A. (eds), 1975 — *Salt: the Study of an Ancient Industry*, (Colchester)

Detsicas, A.P., 1984 — 'A salt-panning site at Funton Creek', *Archaeol. Cantiana* 101, 165–8

Dugdale, W., 1772 — *Imbanking and Drayning*, (Williams Cole's edition, London)

Ellis, A.E., 1969 — *British Snails*

Elsdon, S.M., 1975 — *Stamp and Roulette Decorated Pottery of the La Tene period in Eastern England: A Study in Geometric Design*, Brit. Archaeol. Rep. British Series 10

Evans, J.G., 1972 — *Land Snails in Archaeology*

Evans, R. and Mostyn, E.J., 1979 — *Stratigraphy and Soils of a Fenland Gas Pipeline*, (Ministry of Agriculture, Fisheries and Food ADAS Land Service)

Faegri, K. and Iverson, J., 1964 — *Textbook of Pollen Analysis*, (Munksgaard)

Farrar, R.A.U., 1975 — 'Prehistoric and Roman Saltworks in Dorset' in de Brisay, K.W. and Evans, K.A. (eds), *Salt: the Study of an Ancient Industry'*, (Colchester), 14–20

Foster, C.W. and Longley, T., 1924 — 'Lincolnshire Domesday and the Lindsey Survey', *Lincolnshire Rec. Soc.* 19

Fowler, G., 1950 — 'A Romano-British Village near Littleport, Cambs., with some observations on the distribution of early occupation, and on the drainage of the fens', *Proc. Cambridge Antiq. Soc.* 43, 7–20

Frere, S.S. and St Joseph, J.K.S., 1983 — *Roman Britain from the air*, (Cambridge)

Friendship-Taylor, R.M., 1979 — 'The excavation of the Belgic and Romano-British settlement at Quinton, Northamptonshire: Site "B" (1973–7)', *J. Northampton Mus.* 13, 3–176

Gibbons, E.J., 1956 — 'Sectional Officers' Report for 1955: Botany', *Lincolnshire Naturalists Union Trans* 14, 35–8

Godwin, H., 1938 — 'The Origin of Roddens', *Geog. J.* 91, 241–50

Godwin, H., 1978 — *Fenland: its ancient past and uncertain future*, (Cambridge)

Gouletquer, P.L., 1975 — 'Niger, Country of Salt' in de Brisay, K.W. and Evans, K.A. (eds), *Salt: The Study of an Ancient Industry*, (Colchester), 45–52

Grigg, D., 1966 — *The Agricultural Revolution in South Lincolnshire*

Guido, M., 1978 — *The Glass Beads of the Prehistoric and Roman Periods in Britain and Ireland*, Rep. Res. Comm. Soc. Antiqs. London 35, (London)

Gurney, D., 1980 — 'Evidence of Bronze Age Salt-Production at Northey, Peterborough' in *Northamptonshire Archaeol.* 15, 1–11

Gurney, D., 1982 — 'Romano-British Salt Production on the Western Fen-Edge: a Reassessment', *Proc. Cambridge Antiq. Soc.* 71 (1981), 81–88

Gurney, D., 1984 — 'A sherd of Romano-British lead-glazed ware from Holbeach St Johns', *Lincolnshire Hist. Archaeol.* 19, 107

Gurney, D., 1985 — 'The Roman Pottery' in Pryor, F.M.M. and French, C.A.I., *Archaeology and Environment in the Lower Welland Valley*, E. Anglian Archaeol. 27, 129–155

Gurney, D., 1986 — 'A salt-production site at Denver; excavations by Charles Green, 1960' in Gurney, D., *Settlement, Religion and Industry on the Fen-Edge: Three Romano-British Sites in Norfolk*', E. Anglian Archaeol. 31

Hadman, J. and Upex, S., 1975 — 'A Roman pottery kiln at Sulehay near Yarwell', *Durobrivae* 3, 16–18

Hall, D., 1978 — 'Elm: a field survey', *Proc. Cambridge Antiq. Soc.* 68, 21–42

Hall, D., 1981 — 'The changing landscape of the Cambridgeshire silt fens', *Landscape Hist.* 3, 37–47

Hallam, H.E., 1954 — *The New Lands of Elloe*, (Leicester)

Hallam, H.E., 1957 — *The Lincolnshire Fenland in the Early Middle Ages*, (Unpublished thesis, University of Nottingham)

Hallam, H.E., 1958 — *Settlement and Society, a Study of the Early Agrarian History of South Lincolnshire*, (Cambridge)

Hallam, H.E., 1960 — 'Salting-making in the Lincolnshire Fenland during the Middle Ages', *Lincolnshire Architect. Archaeol. Soc. Rep. Pap.* 8, 85–112

Hallam, H.E., 1965 — *Settlement and Society: a Study in the Early Agrarian History of South Lincolnshire*, (Cambridge)

Hallam, S.J., 1960 — 'The Romano-British salt industry in south Lincolnshire', *Lincolnshire Architect. Archaeol. Soc. Rep. Pap.* 8, 35–75

Hallam, S.J., 1961a — 'Wash Coast-line Levels Since Roman Times', *Antiquity* 35, 152–5

Hallam, S.J., 1961b — 'Addendum to the Romano-British Salt Industry', *Lincolnshire Architect. Archaeol. Soc. Rep. Pap.* 9, 88

Hallam, S.J., 1964 — 'Villages in Roman Britain: some evidence', *Antiq. J.* 44, 19–32

Hallam, S.J., 1970 — 'Settlement round the Wash' in Phillips, C.W. (ed.), *The Fenland in Roman Times*, Royal Geogr. Soc. Res. Ser. 5, (London), 22–113

Hardon, P., 1973 — 'Rippingale — two Saltern sites, one producing IA domestic pottery' in Majoram, J. (ed.), 'Arch. Notes 1972', *Lincolnshire Hist. Archaeol.* 8, 38

Harley, J.B., Manterfield, J.B. and Manterfield, B.A.D., 1987 — *The Old Series Ordnance Survey Maps of England and Wales* V

Hartley, K.F. and Hartley, B.R., 1970 — 'Pottery in the Romano-British Fenland' in Phillips, C.W. (ed), *The Fenland in Roman Times*, Royal Geogr. Soc. Res. Ser. 5, (London), 165–169

Hawkes, C., 1933 — 'Runcton Holme. Part II. The second occupation: a peasant settlement of the Iceni', *Proc. Prehist. Soc. E. Anglia* 7(2), 231–262

Hayes, J.W., 1978 — 'A group of Roman pottery from Fengate', *Durobrivae* 6, 12–13

Hayes, J.W., 1984 — 'The Roman pottery from the Cat's Water subsite, Fengate' in Pryor, F.M.M., *Excavation at Fengate, Peterborough, England: The Fourth Report*, Northamptonshire Archaeol. Soc. Monograph 2; Royal Ontario Museum Archaeol. Monograph 7, 179–195

Hayes, P.P., 1985 — 'Lincolnshire: the Western Fens I' in *Fenland Res.* 2, 49–53

Hayes, P.P. and Lane, T.W., 1983 — in Lincolnshire Fenland Project Annual Report 1982–83 (unpublished), 9–15

Hayes, P.P. and Lane, T.W., 1992 — *Lincolnshire Survey: The South-West Fens*', E. Anglian Archaeol. 55

Healey, R.H., 1960 — *East Midlands Archaeol. Bull.* 3, 8 [incorrectly described as Bicker parish]

Healey, R.H., 1969 — 'Bourne Ware' in Whitwell, J.B. and Wilson, C.M., 'Archaeological Notes 1968', *Lincolnshire Hist. Archaeol.* 4, 109–9

Healey, R.H., 1975 — 'A Medieval Salt Making Site in Bicker Haven, Lincolnshire' in de Brisay, K. and Evans, K.A. (eds), *Salt: the Study of an Ancient Industry'*, (Colchester), 36

Healey, R.H., 1979 — 'Recent Saxon Finds from South-east Lincolnshire', *Lincolnshire Hist. Archaeol.* 14, 80–81

Healey, R.H., 1984 — 'Toynton All Saints: Decorated Jugs from the Roses Kiln' in Field, N. and White, A. (eds), *A Prospect of Lincolnshire*, 73–8

Healey, R.H., 1988 — 'Bicker Bends', *Fenland Res.* 5, 44

Hermet, F., 1934 — *La Graufesenque (Condatomago)*, (Paris)

Hinton, R.W.K. (ed), 1956 — 'The Port Books of Boston 1601–1648', *Lincolnshire Rec. Soc.* 50

Hodge, C.A.H., Burton, R.G.O., Corbett, W.M., Evans, R. and Seale, R.S., 1984 — 'Soils and their Use in Eastern England', *Soil Survey England Wales Bull.* 13, (Harpenden)

Hörter, F., Michels, F. and Röder, J., 1951 'Die geschichte der basalt lava industrie von Mayen und Niedermendig', *Jahrbuch für Geschichte und Kultur des Mittelrheins und seiner Nachbargebeite* 2–3, 1–32

Howe, M.D., Perrin, J.R. and Mackreth, D.F., 1980 *Roman Pottery from the Nene Valley: A Guide*, Peterborough City Museum Occ. Pap. 2

Isings, C., 1957 *Roman Glass from Dated Finds*, (Groningen)

Jackson, D.A., 1977 'Further Excavations at Aldwinckle, Northamptonshire, 1969–71, *Northamptonshire Archaeol.* 12, 9–54

Jodlowski, A., 1975 'Salt Production in Poland in Prehistoric Times' in de Brisay, K.W. and Evans, K.A. (eds), *Salt: The Study of an Ancient Industry*, (Colchester), 85–87

Jones, R.T., Wall, S.M., Locker, A.M., Coy, J. and Maltby, M., 1978 'Ancient Monuments Laboratory Computer Based Osteometry Data Capture User Manual', AML Report No. 3342

Karnitsch, P., 1959 *Die Reliefsigillata von Ovilava*, (Linz)

Kenyon, K.M., 1950 'Excavations at Breedon on the Hill, Leicester, 1946', *Trans. Leicestershire Archaeol. Soc. 26*, 17–82

Kirkham, B., 1975 'Salt Making Sites found in North-East Lincolnshire since 1960' in de Brisay, K.W. and Evans, K.A. (eds), *Salt: The Study of an Ancient Industry'*, (Colchester), 41–42

Kirkham, B., 1981 'The Excavation of a Prehistoric Saltern at Hogsthorpe, Lincolnshire', *Lincolnshire Hist. Archaeol.* 16, 5–10

Kirkham, B., 1985 'Textile Impressions on Briquetage from Lincolnshire', *Lincolnshire Hist. Archaeol.* 20, 73–4

Kirkus, M., 1959 'The Records of the Commissioners of Sewers in the Parts of Holland I', *Lincolnshire Rec. Soc.* 54

Knorr, R., 1952 *Terra-Sigillata-Gefässe des ersten Jahrhunderts mit Töpfernamen*, (Stuttgart)

Lane, T., 1986 'The Western Fens III', *Fenland Res. 3*, 7–12

Long, S.P. and Mason, C.F., 1983 *Saltmarsh Ecology*

Lloyd, A.T., 1967 'The Salterns of the Lymington Area', *Proc. Hampshire Field Club Archaeol. 24*, 1–17

McAvoy, F., 1984 'The Marine Salt Extraction Industry in the Late Medieval Period at Wainfleet, Lincolnshire', *Fenland Res. 1*, 37–39

McAvoy, F., 1994 'Marine Salt Extraction: the Excavations of Salterns at Wainfleet St Mary, Lincolnshire', *Med. Archaeol.* 38, 134–163

Macan, T.T., 1969 *A Key to British Fresh- and Brackish-Water Gastropods*

Mackreth, D.F., 1982 'Two brooches from Stonea, Cambs. and Bicester, Oxon. and the origin of the Aesica Brooch', *Britannia* 13, 310–315

Marrat, W., 1814 *The History of Lincolnshire 2*, (Boston)

Marsh, G., 1978 'Early second century fine wares in the London area' in Arthur, P. and Marsh, G. (eds), *Early Fine Wares in Roman Britain*, Brit. Archaeol. Rep. 57, (Oxford), 119–224

Maudson Grant, S., 1890 'Ancient Pottery Kilns', *Lincolnshire Notes Queries* 8 (62), 32–38, (Lincoln)

May, J., 1970 'Dragonby: An Interim Report on Excavations on an Iron Age and Romano-British Site near Scunthorpe, Lincolnshire, 1964–9', *Antiq. J.* 50

May, J., 1976 *Prehistoric Lincolnshire*, History of Lincolnshire 1, (Lincoln)

May, J., 1984 'Major Settlements of the Later Iron Age in Lincolnshire' in Field, N. and White, A. (eds), *A Prospect of Lincolnshire*, 18–22, (Lincoln)

Miles, A., 1975 'Salt-panning in Romano-British Kent' in de Brisay, K.W. and Evans, K.A. (eds), *Salt: The Study of an Ancient Industry*, (Colchester), 26–31

Miller, S.H. and Skertchly, S.B.J., 1878 *The Fenland Past and Present*, (Wisbech and London)

Molyneaux, F.W. and Wright, N.R., 1974 *An Atlas of Boston*, History of Boston Series 10, (Boston)

Moore, P.D. and Webb, J.A., 1978 *An Illustrated Guide to Pollen Analysis*, (London)

Nenquin, J., 1961 'Salt: A Study of Economic Prehistory', *Dissertationes Archaeological Gandenses*, Vol. VI, (Brugge)

O.E.D., 1971 *Oxford English Dictionary*, (The Compact Edition, Oxford Univ. Press)

Owen, A.E.B., 1968 'The Records of the Commissioners of Sewers in the Parts of Holland II', *Lincolnshire Rec. Soc.* 63

Owen, A.E.B., 1977 'The Records of the Commissioners of Sewers in the Parts of Holland III', *Lincolnshire Rec. Soc.* 71

Owen, D.M., 1971 *Church and Society in Medieval Lincolnshire*, History of Lincolnshire 5, (Lincoln)

Owen, D.M. 1975 'Medieval Chapels in Lincolnshire', *Lincolnshire Hist. Archaeol.* 10, 15–22

Perrin, J.R., 1981 *Roman Pottery from the Colonia: Skeldergate and Bishophill*, The Archaeology of York 16/2

Petty, M.J. and Fairclough, R., 1978 *J. Blaeu — Regiones Inundatae, 1648*, Cambridgeshire Maps 2

Phillips, C.W., 1934 *The Present State of Archaeology in Lincolnshire*

Phillips, C.W. (ed.), 1970 *The Fenland in Roman Times*, Royal Geogr. Soc. Res. Ser. 5, (London)

Pliny the Elder *Natural History*

Potter, T.W., 1965 'The Roman pottery from Coldham Clamp and its affinities', *Proc. Cambridge Antiq. Soc.* 58, 12–37

Potter, T.W., 1981 'The Roman Occupation of the Central Fenland', *Britannia* 12, 79–134

Price, J., 1980 'The Roman Glass' in Lambrick, G., 'Excavations at Park St., Towcester', *Northamptonshire Archaeol.* 15, 63–69

Pryor, F., 1974 *Excavations at Fengate, Peterborough, England: The First Report*, Northamptonshire Archaeol. Soc. Monograph 2; Royal Ontario Museum Archaeol. Monograph 7

Pryor, F., 1984 *Excavations at Fengate, Peterborough, England: The Fourth Report*, Northamptonshire

Archaeol.Soc. Monograph 2; Royal Ontario Museum Archaeol. Monograph 2

Reader, F.W., 1908   'Report of the Red Hills Exploration Committee, 1906–7', *Proc. Soc. Antiq. London* (ser. 2) 22, 164–90

Reader, F.W., 1910   'Report to Red Hill Exploration Committee. Further details on Goldhanger and Canewdon', *Proc. Soc. Antiq. London* 23, 66–88

Riehm, K., 1961   'Prehistoric Salt Boiling', *Antiquity* 35, 181–91

Riehm, K., 1962   'Werkanlagen und arbeitsgeräute urgeschichtlicher salzsieder', *Germania* 40, 360–400

Robson, J.D., 1985   Soil Survey Record No.88 Sheet TF 45 (Friskney)

Röder, J., 1972   'Die militilsteinbrucke von Mayen', *Bonner Universitatsblüatter*, 35–46

Rodwell, W., 1979   'Iron Age and Roman salt-winning on the Essex coast' in Burnham, B.C. and Johnson, H.B. (eds), *Invasion and Response; The Case of Roman Britain*, Brit. Archaeol. Rep. 73, 133–175

Rodwell, W., 1982   'The production and distribution of pottery and tiles in the territory of the Trinovantes', *Trans. Essex Archaeol. Soc.* 14, 15–76

Rogers, G.B., 1974   'Poteries sigillées de la Gaule centrale', *Gallia* Supplement 28

Rudkin, E.H. and Owen, D.M., 1960   'The Medieval Salt Industry in the Lindsey Marshland', *Lincolnshire Architect. Archaeol. Soc. Rep. Pap.* 8, 76–84

Rudkin, E.H., 1975   'Medieval Salt-making in Lincolnshire' in de Brisay, K. and Evans, K.A. (eds), *Salt: The Study of an Ancient Industry*, (Colchester), 37–41

Salway, P., 1966   'The Roman Fenland' in *Rural Settlement in Roman Britain*, Counc. Brit. Archaeol. Res. Rep. 7, 26–7

Salway, P., 1970   'The Roman Fenland' in Phillips, C.W. (ed), *The Fenland in Roman Times'*, Royal Geogr. Soc. Res. Ser. 5, (London), 1–21

Silver, I.A., 1963   'The aging of Domestic Animals' in Brothwell, D. and Higgs, E. (eds) *Science in Archaeology*

Simmons, B.B., 1975a   *The Lincolnshire Car Dyke*

Simmons, B.B., 1975b   *The Lincolnshire Fens and Fen Edge*, (University of Leicester MA Dissertation)

Simmons, B.B., 1975c   'Salt Making Sites in the Silt Fens of Lincolnshire in the Iron Age and Roman Periods' in de Brisay, K.W. and Evans, K.A. (eds), *Salt: The Study of an Ancient Industry*, 33–36

Simmons, B.B., 1979   'The Lincolnshire Car Dyke: Navigation or Drainage?', *Britannia* X, 183–96

Simmons, B.B., 1980a   'Iron Age and Roman coasts around the Wash' in Thompson, F.H. (ed.), *Archaeology and Coastal Change*, Soc. Antiq. London Occ. Pap. (new series) 1, 56–73

Simmons, B.B., 1980b   'The Lincolnshire fens' in Hinchliffe, J. and Schadla-Hall, R.T. (eds), *The Past Under the Plough*, Directorate of Ancient Monuments and Historic Buildings Occ. Pap. 3, (London), 82–89

Simpson, G., 1966   'Romano-British Settlement on the Welland Gravels' in *Rural Settlement in Roman Britain*, Counc. Brit. Archaeol. Res. Rep. 7

Skertchly, S.B.J., 1877   *The Geology of the Fenland*, Memoirs of the Geological Survey, England and Wales, (Wisbech and London)

Smith, A.G., 1970   'The stratigraphy of the northern Fenland' in Phillips, C.W. (ed), *The Fenland in Roman Times*, Royal Geogr. Soc. Res. Ser. 5, (London), 147–164

Sturman, C.J., 1984   'Salt-making in the Lindsey Marshland in the 16th and early 17th Centuries' in Field, N. and White, A. (eds), *A Prospect of Lincolnshire*

Swinnerton, H.H., 1932   'The prehistoric pottery sites of the Lincolnshire coast', *Antiq. J.* 12, 239–253

Thirsk, J., 1957   *English Peasant Farming*, (Routledge and Kegan Paul, London)

Thompson, F.H. (ed.), 1980   *Archaeology and Coastal Change*, Soc. Antiq. London Occ. Pap. (new series) 1

Thompson, M.W., 1956   'A Group of Mounds on Seasalter Level, near Whitstable, and the Medieval Imbanking in this Area', *Archaeol. Cantiana* 70, 44–67

Thompson, P., 1856   *The History and Antiquities of Boston*, (Boston)

von den Driesch, A., 1976   'A Guide to the Measurement of Animal Bones from Archaeological Sites', *Peabody Museum Bulletin* 1, (Harvard University)

Wacher, J., 1976   'Excavations at Breedon on the Hill', *Trans. Leicestershire Archaeol. Soc.* 52

Walshaw, G.R., 1935   'An Ancient Landscape Map', *Lincolnshire Mag.* 2, 196–206

Wheeler, W.H., 1894   *A History of the Fens of South Lincolnshire*, (Boston and London)

Whitwell, J.B. (ed.), 1963   'Archaeological Notes for 1962', *Lincolnshire Architect. Archaeol. Soc. Rep. Pap.* 10, 1

Whitwell, J.B., 1970   *Roman Lincolnshire*, History of Lincolnshire 2, (Lincoln)

Wild, J.P., 1974   'Roman Settlement in the Lower Nene Valley', *Archaeol. J.* 131, 140–70

Wild, J.P., 1975   'The pottery' in Hadman, J. and Upex, S., 'A Roman pottery kiln at Sulehay near Yarwell', *Durobrivae* 3, 16–18

Wilson, D.R., 1982   *Air Photo Interpretation for Archaeologists*, (London)

Primary Sources

John Thorpe's Survey of Various Manors in the parts of Holland and in Huntingdonshire and Bedfordshire 1622. Corporation of London Records Office RCE–114c

Rental of copyholders of the manor of Monks Hall, Gosberton 1628. Corporation of London Records Office RCE Rentals 6.4

John Cragg's notebooks. Lincolnshire Archives Office, Cragg 1/12/8 Microfilm can 46A

Letter (undated) from P. Gouletquer to B.B. Simmons, early 1970s. Heritage Trust of Lincolnshire records

Seppings, E.R., *c.* 1961 Soil Salinities. Notes prepared for Nottingham University Extra-Mural Class (unpublished)

A Survey of an estate beloning to heirs of Rosseter Lenton (map). Lincolnshire Archives Office BRA 1384

Plan of the manor of Burtoft, Lincs. PRO SC 12/30/32

Index